Positive Psychological Approaches to Disaster

Stefan E. Schulenberg
Editor

Positive Psychological Approaches to Disaster

Meaning, Resilience, and Posttraumatic Growth

Springer

Editor
Stefan E. Schulenberg
Department of Psychology
Clinical-Disaster Research Center
University of Mississippi
Oxford, MS, USA

ISBN 978-3-030-32006-5 ISBN 978-3-030-32007-2 (eBook)
https://doi.org/10.1007/978-3-030-32007-2

This Springer imprint is published by the registered company Springer Nature Switzerland AG
The registered company address is: Gewerbestrasse 11, 6330 Cham, Switzerland

"Being human always points, and is directed, to something or someone, other than oneself – be it a meaning to fulfill or another human being to encounter."

– Viktor E. Frankl

"He who has a why to live for can bear almost any how."

– Friedrich Nietzsche

For Ezra,
For Laura,
Whys to the How

Foreword

> Fundamentally, therefore, any man can, even under such circumstances, decide what shall become of him - mentally and spiritually... It is this spiritual freedom - which cannot be taken away - that makes life meaningful and purposeful.
>
> Viktor E. Frankl, *Man's Search for Meaning*

I am delighted to offer opening comments on this collection of new contributions to the study of disaster mental health and positive psychology, *Positive Psychological Approaches to Disaster: Meaning, Resilience, and Posttraumatic Growth.* As the above quote conveys, humans hold the unique capacity to self-transcend even the most tragic of circumstances and to showcase the triumph of the human spirit in the face of adversity, trauma, and suffering. The unique book you are holding celebrates this spirit with an inspiring voice of hope that speaks throughout the pages. It constitutes an important and timely contribution to scholarly research and practice, but even more, it offers valuable insights into the understanding of human existence as a whole and in particular into human experience in potentially destructive conditions.

Disasters, as an inevitable part of human life, present pressing challenges and far-reaching consequences for individuals and societies. They can shake us to the core, by posing a potent threat to our everyday sense of stability, safety, and predicted order of the world. While the study of the wide range of negative consequences of disaster is naturally essential and important to identifying mental health symptomology and to the development of coping strategies, it does not reveal the full spectrum of human potentiality. Less is known about its complementary aspects of human flourishing in the face of trauma and disasters. Indeed, although disasters and trauma are generally viewed as unwanted, they also hold a constitutive and transformative force that brings us in connection with ourselves and our hidden capacities and strengths. As disasters essentially expose our human vulnerabilities and remind us of our limitations, they may also enable greater awareness of the fragility of our being and surface deeper questions about meaning in our lives.

In a way, the art of living an authentic life in the face of transient existence engages the full range and aspects of the beauty and gravity of being human. Human life is not as neatly organized as theoretical conceptualizations presume it to be; it is a blend, a mixture of colors. New colors emerge from that mixture, richer and more intense than those that just reside next to each other in a painter's palette. At the core of our being as humans lie paradoxes and dichotomies that contain the whole of existence and encapsulate completeness. In this sense, wholeness involves brokenness as an essential and inherent part of a full life.

Much like Frankl, Elisabeth Lukas reminds us that "what matters are actually never the conditions you find yourself in, but… always the lifework that you were able to build from it" (Lukas 1986). Along the same lines, this volume offers a unique overview of the ingredients and processes that enable us to uncover the hidden beauty and power of the shattered, in which the broken beauty not only survives but thrives. As the various chapters demonstrate, through integrative exploration of theory and practice, when we allow ourselves and others to acknowledge the cracks and wounds, something new is given a space for growth. The potentially destructive can become constructive.

I invite you to delve into the breadth and depth of this volume and to be inspired by its engaging, comprehensive, and much-needed exploration of the human potential to grow and even flourish amidst life's potentially dismantling challenges. The chapters fit together into a rich mosaic that reminds us that human development, as existence itself, is not a static destination to which we should aim but rather a constantly changing, evolving state of becoming. As a whole, the book signals important advances in the understanding and use of positive psychology, resilience, and meaning frameworks to enable human growth and transformation in the wake of traumatic events. Building on varied perspectives, it opens up new academic and clinical as well as personal horizons. Shedding light on aspects of resilience, meaning, spirituality, and growth in the context of natural and technological disasters, this volume presents an integrative discussion that broadens the scope of what it means to be human. The authors and the editor, who have joined their energy and expertise to share novel and promising insights in the rapidly growing area of positive psychology, lead us through a thought-provoking journey. I hope that while reading it, you will see why this book is a vivid reminder that there is something more to human experience than meets the eye, and it is that something more that animates life as we experience it.

Pninit Russo-Netzer, Ph.D. – Positive Psychology Researcher and Senior Lecturer, Diplomate in logotherapy; Coeditor of *Meaning in Positive and Existential Psychology* (Springer), *Clinical Perspectives on Meaning: Positive and Existential Psychotherapy* (Springer), and *Search for Meaning in the Israeli Scene* (Oxford); and Head of the Compass Institute for the Study and Application of Meaning and of the academic training program for logotherapy in Israel.

Dr. Pninit Russo-Netzer
Department of Counseling and Human Development
University of Haifa, Haifa, Israel

School of Advanced Studies Achva Academic College
Shikmim, Israel

References

Frankl, V. E. (1959/1985). *Man's search for meaning* (p. 87). New York: Pocket Books.

Lukas, E. (1986). *Meaning in suffering: Comfort in crisis through logotherapy*. Berkeley: Institute of Logotherapy Press.

Acknowledgments

This volume would not be possible without the support of so many generous, caring people. Thanks to Sharon Panulla, Sofia Geck, and the folks at Springer for their belief in the subject matter and their help throughout the production process. Thanks to each of the authors for their contributions, efforts, expertise, and enthusiasm, as well as for entrusting me with their work. I would like to thank Pninit Russo-Netzer of the University of Haifa for contributing a foreword and Michael F. Steger of Colorado State University for contributing an afterword.

I extend my appreciation to the University of Mississippi for supporting our efforts in developing the Clinical-Disaster Research Center (UM-CDRC), with its focus on disaster mental health and positive psychology, that is, meaning, resilience, and posttraumatic growth with respect to disaster preparedness, mitigation, response, and recovery. I am duly grateful for their support of our efforts to develop and cultivate the Disaster Sciences interdisciplinary minor.

I am indebted to the many colleagues, friends, family, research participants, clients, and graduate and undergraduate students who have shaped my knowledge and thinking over the years. Thanks also to the many individuals who have provided scholarly mentoring in one way or another, at one time or another: Barb Yutrzenka, Rosemary Henrion, Bob Hutzell, Jerry Jacobs, Teri Elliott, Kim Houston, John York, and John L. Webb. This book is also in appreciation to the graduate student members of our research team, Marci Weber, Alexis Liberto, Jeff Pavlacic, Mikaela Raley, Victoria McCutcheon, and Lavina Ho, for challenging me, inspiring me, believing in me, and generally just doing an all-around great job of keeping me on my toes.

With special gratitude, this book would not have been initiated, undertaken, or completed without the love and support of Laura and Ezra – "Whys to the How."

Oxford, MS, USA
September 2019

Stefan E. Schulenberg, Ph.D.

Contents

1 **Positive Psychological Approaches to Disaster: An Introduction** 1
Stefan E. Schulenberg

2 **Resilience and Recovery Following Disasters: The Meaning Making Model** 9
Crystal L. Park and Erin C. Blake

3 **Religion, Spirituality, and Meaning in the Wake of Disasters** 27
Daryl R. Van Tongeren, Jamie D. Aten, Edward B. Davis, Don E. Davis, and Joshua N. Hook

4 **Reconciling Disaster and Deity: Trauma, Spirituality, and Growth in the Context of Natural and Technological Disasters Induced by Climate Change** 45
Mary Beth Werdel

5 **Veterans and Disaster Response Work: The Role of Continued Service in Meaning Making and Recovery** 61
Shannon E. McCaslin, Damian Bramlett, Katherine Juhasz, Margaret Mackintosh, and Shauna Springer

6 **The Hero's Journey to Resilience and Thriving in the Context of Disaster** 81
Bruce W. Smith

7 **Firefighters: An Occupational Case Study of Resilience** 99
Victoria Alicia Torres and Suzy Bird Gulliver

8 **Responding to Adolescents Following Natural and Technological Disasters: The Essential Nature of Hope** 115
Alexis K. Liberto, Emily Thomas Johnson, and Stefan E. Schulenberg

9 Strengths and Application of Response Team vs. Community-Based Models of Psychological First Aid 137
Gerard A. Jacobs

10 Posttraumatic Growth After Disasters 155
Olivia M. Riffle, Paisley R. Lewis, and Richard G. Tedeschi

11 Facilitating Posttraumatic Growth in the Wake of Natural Disasters: Considerations for Crisis Response 169
David N. Sattler and Aaron Smith

12 The Disaster Sciences Interdisciplinary Minor at the University of Mississippi: Positive Psychology in Action 187
Mikaela J. Raley, Marcela C. Weber, Christopher E. Lemon, and Stefan E. Schulenberg

Afterword to Positive Psychological Approaches to Disaster: Meaning, Resilience, and Posttraumatic Growth..................... 199

Index.. 203

About the Editor

Stefan E. Schulenberg received his Ph.D. in Clinical Psychology, with a specialization in Clinical-Disaster Psychology, from the University of South Dakota in 2001. He is a licensed psychologist in the state of Mississippi, a Professor in the University of Mississippi's Psychology Department, and a Logotherapy Diplomate. He is the Director of the University of Mississippi's Clinical-Disaster Research Center (UM-CDRC), an integrated research, teaching, and training center with emphases in disaster mental health and positive psychology. He is also the Director of the University of Mississippi's Interdisciplinary Minor in Disaster Sciences (DSci), a joint effort across the departments of psychology, criminal justice, social work, and sociology.

He has authored/coauthored over 80 peer-reviewed journal articles and chapters in scholarly texts. He is the Editor of *Clarifying and Furthering Existential Psychotherapy: Theories, Methods, and Practices* (2016), the Coeditor of *Clinical Perspectives on Meaning: Positive and Existential Psychotherapy* (2016), and part of the authorship team that produced *Disasters that Shaped Emergency Management: Case Studies for the Homeland Security/Emergency Management Professional* (2018). His research interests include clinical-disaster psychology, positive psychology, and logotherapy, concepts such as perceived meaning, purpose, resilience, posttraumatic stress, and posttraumatic growth. He has conducted research on the effects of Hurricane Katrina, the Deepwater Horizon oil spill, and other disaster-related events (e.g., tornadoes, flooding). He offers workshops and provides training on disaster preparedness, psychological first aid, disaster response, meaning and purpose in life, resilience, and posttraumatic growth.

He has served as a Disaster Mental Health Volunteer and Supervisor in the American Red Cross and has worked previously with various other volunteer organizations, such as the American Foundation for Suicide Prevention. He teaches the graduate cognitive assessment course for the University of Mississippi's doctoral program in clinical psychology. At the undergraduate level, he teaches courses in disaster mental health, positive psychology, and psychology and law.

List of Contributors

Jamie D. Aten, Ph.D. Department of Psychology and Humanitarian Disaster Institute, Wheaton College, Wheaton, IL, USA

Erin C. Blake Department of Psychological Sciences, University of Connecticut, Storrs, CT, USA

Damian Bramlett, M.S. National Center for PTSD, Dissemination and Training Division, VA Palo Alto HCS (MPD), Menlo Park, CA, USA

Don E. Davis, Ph.D. Department of Counseling and Psychological Services, Georgia State University, Atlanta, GA, USA

Edward B. Davis, Psy.D. Department of Psychology, Wheaton College, Wheaton, IL, USA

Suzy Bird Gulliver, Ph.D. Warriors Research Institute, Baylor Scott & White Health, Waco, TX, USA

Texas A&M College of Medicine Health Science Center, Temple, TX, USA

Joshua N. Hook, Ph.D. Department of Psychology, University of North Texas, Denton, TX, USA

Gerard A. Jacobs, Ph.D. Disaster Mental Health Institute, University of South Dakota, Vermillion, SD, USA

Emily Thomas Johnson, Ph.D. Behavior, Attention, and Developmental Disabilities Consultants, Sardis, MS, USA

Katherine Juhasz, M.S. National Center for PTSD, Dissemination and Training Division, VA Palo Alto HCS (MPD), Menlo Park, CA, USA

Christopher E. Lemon Department of Psychology, Clinical-Disaster Research Center, University of Mississippi, Oxford, MS, USA

Paisley R. Lewis, B.A. University of North Carolina at Charlotte, Charlotte, NC, USA

Alexis K. Liberto, M.A. Department of Psychology, Clinical-Disaster Research Center, University of Mississippi, Oxford, MS, USA

Margaret Mackintosh, Ph.D. National Center for PTSD, Dissemination and Training Division, VA Palo Alto HCS (MPD), Menlo Park, CA, USA

Shannon E. McCaslin, Ph.D. National Center for PTSD, Dissemination and Training Division, VA Palo Alto HCS (MPD), Menlo Park, CA, USA

Department of Psychiatry and Behavioral Sciences, Stanford University, Stanford, CA, USA

Crystal L. Park, Ph.D. Department of Psychological Sciences, University of Connecticut, Storrs, CT, USA

Mikaela J. Raley, M.S. Department of Psychology, Clinical-Disaster Research Center, University of Mississippi, Oxford, MS, USA

Olivia M. Riffle, M.A. University of North Carolina at Charlotte, Charlotte, NC, USA

Pninit Russo-Netzer, Ph.D. Department of Counseling and Human Development, University of Haifa, Haifa, Israel

School of Advanced Studies Achva Academic College, Shikmim, Israel

David N. Sattler, Ph.D. Department of Psychology, Western Washington University, Bellingham, WA, USA

Stefan E. Schulenberg, Ph.D. Department of Psychology, Clinical-Disaster Research Center, University of Mississippi, Oxford, MS, USA

Aaron Smith, Ph.D. Department of Psychology, Western Washington University, Bellingham, WA, USA

Bruce W. Smith, Ph.D. Department of Psychology, University of New Mexico, Albuquerque, NM, USA

Shauna Springer, Ph.D. Suicide Prevention Initiatives, Tragedy Assistance Program for Survivors, Arlington, VA, USA

Michael F. Steger, Ph.D. Department of Psychology, Colorado State University, Fort Collins, CO, USA

North-West University, Vanderbijlpark, South Africa

Richard G. Tedeschi, Ph.D. University of North Carolina at Charlotte, Charlotte, NC, USA

Daryl R. Van Tongeren, Ph.D. Department of Psychology, Hope College, Holland, MI, USA

Victoria Alicia Torres, M.A. Department of Psychology, University of Mississippi, Oxford, MS, USA

Marcela C. Weber, M.A. Department of Psychology, Clinical-Disaster Research Center, University of Mississippi, Oxford, MS, USA

Mary Beth Werdel, Ph.D. Department of Pastoral Mental Health Counseling, Fordham University, Bronx, NY, USA

Chapter 1
Positive Psychological Approaches to Disaster: An Introduction

Stefan E. Schulenberg

The concept of this book has been developing over a long period of time, over 20 years or so, tracing it back to studies in logotherapy and disaster mental health while in the clinical training program at the University of South Dakota (USD) in the mid to late 1990s (Schulenberg 2016; Schulenberg, Drescher, and Baczwaski 2014). Just prior to this period, as an undergraduate student at the University of Houston in 1994, I read *Man's Search for Meaning* (Frankl 1959/1985) for the first time, as part of a course in personality theories. By the mid to late 1990s, I was pursuing a doctoral degree in clinical psychology at USD, with specialized training in disaster mental health. I was especially interested in applications of meaning, initially and specifically Viktor Frankl's logotherapy, inspired by *Man's Search for Meaning*, his most popular and influential work (see Hutzell 2006). The first, primary aspect of the book tells of his concentration camp experiences during the Holocaust. The second aspect of the book describes his perspective of logotherapy, which translates to "healing through meaning." It is a therapy, a personality theory, and a guiding life philosophy, one that centers on the significance of meaning and purpose to the human experience, with emphasis on the idea that meaning may be discovered under all circumstances, even those that involve unavoidable suffering (Frankl 1959/1985; Schulenberg 2016; Schulenberg, Hutzell, Nassif, and Rogina 2008).

Frankl's perspective on the essential nature of meaning to the human condition was a revelation, a forerunner to contemporary conceptualizations of meaning making, resilience, and posttraumatic growth (Schulenberg 2016; Schulenberg et al. 2014). His work preceded both disaster mental health and positive psychology (Calhoun and Tedeschi 2008, 2013; Halpern and Tramontin 2007; Schulenberg 2003, 2016; Schulenberg et al. 2014), each of which was developing as its own field in the

---

S. E. Schulenberg (✉)
Department of Psychology, Clinical-Disaster Research Center, University of Mississippi, Oxford, MS, USA
e-mail: sschulen@olemiss.edu

S. E. Schulenberg (ed.), *Positive Psychological Approaches to Disaster*,
https://doi.org/10.1007/978-3-030-32007-2_1

mid to late 1990s (see for example, Jacobs 1995, 2007; Jacobs, Quevillon, and Stricherz 1990; Linley 2013; Seligman and Csikszentmihalyi 2000). While studying these areas simultaneously, two things seemed readily apparent. The first is that logotherapy is essentially *positive psychology*. The second is that logotherapy is essentially *disaster mental health*.

Positive psychology is an applied science that focuses on flourishing – that is, what makes for a good life, a good person, or the best in people (Diener 2009; Lopez and Gallagher 2009; Schulenberg 2016). Positive psychology, as stated by Peterson (2013):

> is the scientific study of what makes life most worth living (Peterson 2006). It is a call for psychological science and practice to be as concerned with strength as with weakness; as interested in building, the best things in life as in repairing the worst; and as concerned with making the lives of normal people fulfilling as with healing pathology. (p. 3)

Disaster mental health refers to the "specialized domain of training, research, and service provision applied to or with individuals, communities, and nations exposed to a disaster" (Yutrzenka and Naifeh 2008, p. 97). Disaster mental health is a rapidly growing applied science comprised of such areas of psychology as clinical, community, multicultural, social, cognitive, neuroscience, etc. (Schulenberg 2016; Schulenberg et al. 2014). Both positive psychology and disaster mental health share a resonance with meaning, resilience, and posttraumatic growth, of which *Man's Search for Meaning* serves as exemplar.

In learning about meaning, disaster mental health, and positive psychology during graduate school, it became evident how these areas fit so well with one another (Schulenberg 2016). By 2002, I was fortunate to have found an academic position as a Visiting Assistant Professor at the University of Mississippi, where I was subsequently retained as a tenure-track Assistant Professor in 2003. Logotherapy was at the heart of my initial research and writing efforts. Meaning was a key aspect to our research team's work, a concept that we studied in a range of contexts.

Both logotherapy and positive psychology share a central perspective of the importance of meaning, as well as its broad applicability with respect to, and appreciation of, values, virtues, and character strengths (see, for instance, Niemiec 2018 and Niemiec and McGrath 2019). Emphasis on the essential nature of meaning was a commonality between logotherapy and positive psychology, as well as related approaches. Meaning becomes even more salient during times of adversity. This was something we were aiming to study as a research team, but it also could not have been more omnipresent given our state being affected by a number of historically significant, culturally-defining disasters in recent years. Among them was Hurricane Katrina (Clements and Casani 2016), which impacted the Mississippi Gulf Coast in 2005, and the Deepwater Horizon oil spill (Baczwaski, Aiena, and Schulenberg 2018), which affected the Mississippi Gulf Coast in 2010. Our team was part of a coordinated research effort with respect to Hurricane Katrina and the Deepwater Horizon oil spill (Schulenberg, Dellinger et al. 2008; Schulenberg, Johnson et al. 2014). As an outgrowth of our work in these areas, we formed the Clinical-Disaster Research Center at the University of Mississippi (UM-CDRC).

The UM-CDRC is an integrated research, teaching, training, and service center with a systematic focus on disaster mental health, positive psychology, and logotherapy. As an extension of this effort, we subsequently developed an interdisciplinary minor in Disaster Sciences as a means of providing students with education as to the disaster mental health and emergency management fields (see Raley, Weber, Lemon, and Schulenberg, this volume). In some ways, the center and the minor serve as our own form of meaning making, resilience, and growth in the context of the culture of disaster that we live in today.

People frequently wonder *why* and *how* such disastrous events could happen. We know this from the research and from real-life experiences. One aspect of meaning is its role in the interpretation of experience. Disasters render people vulnerable to shattered worldviews (Janoff-Bulman 1992; Schulenberg 2014; see also Park 2010 and Park, Currier, Harris, and Slattery 2016). People question their beliefs, their sense of safety and predictability, their spiritual ideals and self-concept. Frankl was right. Meaning is a motivation and driving force behind human thinking and behavior. We know this from different pockets of literature generated from different perspectives (logotherapy, positive psychology, disaster mental health, motivational interviewing, Acceptance and Commitment Therapy). Yet, in fields such as psychology, tunnel vision is sometimes an issue, where one focuses on one pocket of the literature so much so that other pockets are forgotten or ignored. Thus, the evolution of theory, research, and practical application tends to decelerate given a lack of integration of perspectives. Growth is much more likely to occur through the recognition and synthesis of various literatures and disciplines. Not just when considering different paradigms in psychology, but when considering different fields. Exposure and integration should occur across fields, in a true multidisciplinary approach. This was the kind of thinking incorporated into the development of the center and the interdisciplinary minor, where we emphasize meaning, resilience, and posttraumatic growth at the levels of the individual and the community.

One way to look at these concepts is the idea that meaning may catalyze resilience and stimulate posttraumatic growth (Schulenberg 2014; see also Park 2010 and Park et al. 2016). This is certainly a simplification as complexities abound. However, for us it continues to be a useful framework for coordinating a range of research and theoretical projects, whether considering the context of the individual or the larger community. In terms of complexity, an issue in the literature is how concepts such as meaning, resilience, and posttraumatic growth are defined and assessed (Weathers, Aiena, Blackwell, and Schulenberg 2016). As noted above, meaning could relate to the *interpretation* of one's experience. It could have to do with discovering *meaning in the moment*, or one's perceived sense of significance in the larger scheme of things (*ultimate meaning*; Frankl 1959/1985). To what extent do we perceive our lives as mattering? "Meaning provides us with the sense that our lives matter, that they make sense, and that they are more than the sum of our seconds, days, and years" (Steger 2012, p. 165). Meaning is sometimes referred to in terms of *presence* (how much meaning one perceives) or *search* (relating to one's quest for meaning, or *will to meaning*; Frankl 1959/1985). It is often either associated, or used synonymously, with *purpose*, which is goal directed and ideally congruent with one's values, decisions, and behaviors. There are many themes common across various sources with regard to defining meaning:

> (1) meaning underlies a consistent explanatory framework to evaluate life …; (2) meaning is related to setting future goals, creating a sense of utility and excitement …; (3) meaning is a subjective perception that motivates the completion of daily activities; (4) meaning involves actualization of personal values …; (5) the lack of meaning in life, or meaninglessness, results in maladaptive thoughts, feelings, and behaviors …; and (6) even though it is subjective, meaning has been associated with paths common across people (e.g., relationships, service-oriented behavior) … (Florez, Schulenberg, and Stewart 2016, pp. 108–109)

One must be vigilant when studying meaning to recognize in what way the term is being used. The same approach is needed for studying resilience and posttraumatic growth. These concepts are regarded as distinct but related, and there is overlap between them and the concept of meaning. For example, meaning is incorporated into some models of resilience and posttraumatic growth, as part of the definition and/or a means of assessment (Weathers et al. 2016). One must be aware when studying resilience or posttraumatic growth to understand how the respective term is being defined and assessed (e.g., Calhoun and Tedeschi 2008, 2013; Southwick and Charney 2018). We observe each of these concepts in this current, collaborative effort, one that grew out of an initial edited work that explored positive psychology and disaster mental health in a special issue of the *Journal of Clinical Psychology* that appeared in 2016 (Schulenberg 2016). The special issue project serves as a benchmark for the current endeavor.

Overview of the Book

The chapters of the book are organized loosely into three basic sections, focusing on the respective positive psychological concepts of meaning, resilience, and posttraumatic growth. Each grouping of chapters illustrates applications of the concept to disaster mental health. For example, the opening section on meaning, meaning making, and spirituality is consistent with positive psychological character strengths that fall under the virtue of transcendence and wisdom (see, for example, Niemiec 2018 and Niemiec and McGrath 2019). The general content of the book opens with *Resilience and Recovery Following Disasters: The Meaning Making Model*, contributed by Crystal Park and Erin Blake. The selection is followed by *Religion, Spirituality, and Meaning in the Wake of Disasters* by Daryl Van Tongeren, Jamie Aten, and colleagues, and *Reconciling Disaster and Deity: Trauma, Spirituality, and Growth in the Context of Natural and Technological Disasters Induced by Climate Change* by Mary Beth Werdel. The final chapter in this initial grouping of writings is a contribution by Shannon McCaslin, Damian Bramlett, and colleagues, *Veterans and Disaster Response Work: The Role of Continued Service in Meaning Making and Recovery*. The opening section is anticipated by a Foreword written by Pninit Russo-Netzer.

The second section of the book is organized and grouped around the concept of resilience, which is consistent with positive psychological character strengths such as bravery, perseverance, hope, and self-regulation under virtues such as courage, temperance, and transcendence. The opening chapter by Bruce Smith is entitled, *The Hero's Journey to Resilience and Thriving in the Context of Disaster*. Dr. Smith's effort is followed by selections authored by Jerry Jacobs (*Strengths and Application of Response Team vs. Community-Based Models of Psychological First Aid*), Victoria Torres and Suzy Bird Gulliver (*Firefighters: An Occupational Case Study in Resilience*), and Alexis Liberto, Emily Thomas Johnson, and myself (*Responding to Adolescents following Natural and Technological Disasters: The Essential Nature of Hope*).

The third grouping of chapters focuses on posttraumatic growth, which is consistent with positive psychological character strengths such as spirituality (under the virtue of transcendence), perspective (under the virtue of wisdom), perseverance (under the virtue of courage), and love (under the virtue of humanity). The opening chapter in this section is a work by Olivia Riffle, Paisley Lewis, and Richard Tedeschi entitled, *Posttraumatic Growth after Disasters.* The selection is followed by *Facilitating Posttraumatic Growth in the Wake of Natural Disasters: Considerations for Crisis Response* (authored by David Sattler and Aaron Smith), and *The Disaster Sciences Interdisciplinary Minor at the University of Mississippi: Positive Psychology in Action* (authored by Mikaela Raley, Marci Weber, Chris Lemon, and myself). The book concludes with an Afterword by Michael F. Steger.

References

Baczwaski, B. J., Aiena, B. J., & Schulenberg, S. E. (2018). Deepwater Horizon oil spill (2010). In D. H. McElreath, D. A. Doss, R. Nations, J. M. Van Slyke, C. J. Jensen, B. R. Russo, R. C. Tesiero, S. E. Schulenberg, L. S. McElreath, A. Wellman, & A. M. Lindsley (Eds.), *Disasters that shaped emergency management: Case studies for the homeland security/emergency management professional* (pp. 181–189). Dubuque: Kendall Hunt.

Calhoun, L. G., & Tedeschi, R. G. (2008). The paradox of struggling with trauma: Guidelines for practice and directions for research. In S. Joseph & P. A. Linley (Eds.), *Trauma, recovery, and growth: Positive psychological perspectives on posttraumatic stress* (pp. 325–337). Hoboken: John Wiley & Sons.

Calhoun, L. G., & Tedeschi, R. G. (2013). *Posttraumatic growth in clinical practice*. New York: Routledge.

Clements, B. W., & Casani, J. A. P. (2016). *Disasters and public health: Planning and response* (2nd ed.). Oxford: Butterworth-Heinemann.

Diener, E. (2009). Positive psychology: Past, present, and future. In S. J. Lopez & C. R. Snyder (Eds.), *Oxford handbook of positive psychology* (2nd ed., pp. 7–11). New York: Oxford University Press.

Florez, I. A., Schulenberg, S. E., & Stewart, T. L. (2016). Meaning and automatic stereotyping: Advancing an agenda for research. In A. Batthyany (Ed.), *Logotherapy and Existential Analysis: Proceedings of the Viktor Frankl Institute, Vienna* (Vol. 1, pp. 107–124). Switzerland: Springer International Publishing. https://doi.org/10.1007/978-3-319-29424-7_11.

Frankl, V. E. (1959/1985). *Man's search for meaning.* (rev. ed.). New York: Washington Square Press.
Halpern, J., & Tramontin, M. (2007). *Disaster mental health: Theory and practice*. Belmont: Thomson Brooks/Cole.
Hutzell, R. R. (2006, February 1). The continued relevance of *Man's Search for Meaning* [Review of the book *Man's Search for Meaning*: An Introduction to Logotherapy]. *PsycCRITIQUES—Contemporary Psychology: APA Review of Books, 51* (No. 5), Article 19. Retrieved April 6, 2006, from the PsycCRITIQUES database.
Jacobs, G. A. (1995). The development of a national plan for disaster mental health. *Professional Psychology: Research and Practice, 26*, 543–549.
Jacobs, G. A. (2007). The development and maturation of humanitarian psychology. *American Psychologist, 62*, 932–941.
Jacobs, G. A. (2016). *Community-based psychological first aid: A practical guide to helping individuals and communities during difficult times*. Oxford: Butterworth-Heinemann.
Jacobs, G. A., Quevillon, R. P., & Stricherz, M. (1990). Lessons from the aftermath of Flight 232: Practical considerations for the mental health profession's response to air disasters. *American Psychologist, 45*, 1329–1335.
Janoff-Bulman, R. (1992). *Shattered assumptions: Towards a new psychology of trauma*. New York: Free Press.
Linley, P. A. (2013). Positive psychology (history). In S. J. Lopez (Ed.), *The encyclopedia of positive psychology* (pp. 742–746). Chichester: Wiley-Blackwell.
Lopez, S. J., & Gallagher, M. W. (2009). A case for positive psychology. In S. J. Lopez & C. R. Snyder (Eds.), *Oxford handbook of positive psychology* (2nd ed., pp. 3–6). New York: Oxford University Press.
Niemiec, R. M. (2018). *Character strengths interventions: A field guide for practitioners*. Boston: Hogrefe.
Niemiec, R. M., & McGrath, R. E. (2019). *The power of character strengths*. Cincinnati: VIA Institute on Character.
Park, C. L. (2010). Making sense of the meaning literature: An integrative review of meaning making and its effects on adjustment to stressful life events. *Psychological Bulletin, 136*, 257–301. https://doi.org/10.1037/a0018301.
Park, C. L., Currier, J. M., Harris, J. I., & Slattery, J. M. (2016). *Trauma, meaning, and spirituality: Translating research into clinical practice*. Washington, DC: American Psychological Association.
Peterson, C. (2013). *Pursuing the good life: 100 reflections on positive psychology*. New York: Oxford University Press.
Schulenberg, S. E. (2003). Empirical research and logotherapy. *Psychological Reports, 93*, 307–319. https://doi.org/10.2466/PR0.93.5.307-319.
Schulenberg, S. E. (2014, May). *Meaning and disaster mental health*. Paper presented at the 2nd International Conference on Logotherapy & Existential Analysis, Vienna, Austria.
Schulenberg, S. E. (2016). Disaster mental health and positive psychology – Considering the context of natural and technological disasters: An introduction to the special issue. *Journal of Clinical Psychology, 72*, 1223–1233. https://doi.org/10.1002/jclp.22409.
Schulenberg, S. E., Dellinger, K. A., Koestler, A. J., Kinnell, A. M. K., Swanson, D. A., Van Boening, M. V., & Forgette, R. G. (2008). Psychologists and Hurricane Katrina: Natural disaster response through training, public education, and research. *Training and Education in Professional Psychology, 2*, 83–88. https://doi.org/10.1037/1931-3918.2.2.83.
Schulenberg, S. E., Drescher, C. F., & Baczwaski, B. J. (2014). Perceived meaning and disaster mental health: A role for logotherapy in clinical-disaster psychology. In A. Batthyany & P. Russo-Netzer (Eds.), *Meaning in positive and existential psychology* (pp. 251–267). New York: Springer. https://doi.org/10.1007/978-1-4939-0308-5_15.
Schulenberg, S. E., Hutzell, R. R., Nassif, C., & Rogina, J. M. (2008). Logotherapy for clinical practice. *Psychotherapy: Theory, Research, Practice, Training, 45*, 447–463. https://doi.org/10.1037/a0014331.

Schulenberg, S. E., Johnson, L. F., Drescher, C. F., Herzog, J. D., Willoughby, S. G., & Allen, M. (2014). Enhancing graduate student training through collaborative research: Working and learning together in response to the Gulf oil spill. *Training and Education in Professional Psychology, 8*, 312–319. https://doi.org/10.1037/tep0000062.

Seligman, M. E. P., & Csikszentmihalyi, M. (2000). Positive psychology: An introduction. *American Psychologist, 55*, 5–14.

Southwick, S. M., & Charney, D. S. (2018). *Resilience: The science of mastering life's greatest challenges* (2nd ed.). Cambridge: Cambridge University Press.

Steger, M. F. (2012). Experiencing meaning in life: Optimal functioning at the nexus of well-being, psychopathology, and spirituality. In P. T. P. Wong (Ed.), *The human quest for meaning: Theories, research, and applications* (2nd ed., pp. 165–184). New York: Routledge.

Weathers, L. N., Aiena, B. J., Blackwell, M. A., & Schulenberg, S. E. (2016). The significance of meaning to conceptualizations of resilience and posttraumatic growth: Strengthening the foundation for research and practice. In P. Russo-Netzer, S. E. Schulenberg, & A. Batthyany (Eds.), *Clinical perspectives on meaning: Positive and existential psychotherapy* (pp. 149–169). Cham: Springer International Publishing.

Yutrzenka, B. A., & Naifeh, J. A. (2008). Traumatic stress, disaster psychology, and graduate education: Reflections on the special section and recommendations for professional psychology training. *Training and Education in Professional Psychology, 2*, 96–102.

Chapter 2
Resilience and Recovery Following Disasters: The Meaning Making Model

Crystal L. Park and Erin C. Blake

Like terrorist attacks, natural and technological disasters affect whole communities. However, unlike them, disasters are not deliberately caused by other human beings. Conjointly, these two aspects—the community-level impact and the non-intentionality—present a unique set of circumstances for survivors. Every disaster is unique, varying in dimensions such as their scope and the resultant loss, devastation, and displacement (Norris et al. 2002). By definition, however, all disasters are sudden and catastrophic, and survivors often experience substantial distress (Norris et al. 2002). Posttraumatic stress symptoms or disorder (PTSD), along with heightened symptoms of depression, anxiety, and somatic complaints, and excessive alcohol use have been consistently reported, particularly following large-scale disasters (e.g., Fergusson et al. 2014; Nordløkken et al. 2013). Following disasters in which people perceive some element of human responsibility, people often report feelings of uncertainty, distrust, and anger (Norris et al. 2002).

Levels of recovery and resilience following disasters are impressively high, especially when focusing on psychiatric symptoms (Bonanno et al. 2010). For example, following Hurricane Ike, only 8.3% of an exposed sample reported symptoms that met criteria for hurricane-related PTSD and only 20.6% had one or more of the following: suicidality, alcohol abuse, depression, or panic disorder (Pietrzak et al. 2012). Even following the extreme devastation of Hurricane Katrina, the incidence of PTSD in survivors was only 22% (Galea et al. 2008). Yet there may be many other kinds of lingering social and psychological damage following disasters. Although resilience implies a return to baseline (Bonanno et al. 2010), people may return to a new and different "normal" following disasters. Findings from other types of highly stressful situations suggest that survivors often feel profoundly changed afterwards in their views of themselves and the world (e.g., Appleton and

C. L. Park (✉) · E. C. Blake
Department of Psychological Sciences, University of Connecticut, Storrs, CT, USA
e-mail: crystal.park@uconn.edu

S. E. Schulenberg (ed.), *Positive Psychological Approaches to Disaster*,
https://doi.org/10.1007/978-3-030-32007-2_2

Flynn 2014), yet there is little nuanced research in the disaster literature to investigate this possibility. One study of survivors of Typhoon Haiyan found high levels of negative cognitions about oneself and the world (Nalipay and Mordeno 2016), suggesting that their experience had perhaps permanently altered their beliefs.

Understanding how different ways of responding to and recovering from disasters may lead to very different trajectories—thriving, resilience, and recovery or continued distress—as well as the "new normal" that many survivors establish may usefully inform the development of post-disaster interventions. It may even be possible to implement pre-disaster prevention-focused programs to strengthen people *before* encountering disasters, in order to reduce distress and facilitate effective coping in the wake of such occurrences (Park and Slattery 2014). In this chapter, we take a meaning making perspective to investigate how people recover from disasters.

A Model of Meaning and Meaning Making

The meaning making model (Park 2010) provides a useful conceptual framework for considering processes of coping and recovery following stressful events. This model distinguishes two levels of meaning: global and situational. Global meaning concerns individuals' fundamental beliefs—about the world and other people, their identity in that world— as well as their unique hierarchies of goals and values and their sense of meaning and purpose (Park 2010). Situational meaning refers to the influences of global meaning, in conjunction with the context of a particular situation, on one's appraisals of and subsequent responses to that situation. Situational meaning encompasses the meanings assigned to these experiences, the potential discrepancies between global and appraised meaning, the processes involved in reconciling those discrepancies (i.e., "meaning making"), and the changes resulting from these reconciliation processes (i.e., "meaning made"). Figure 2.1 depicts this model as it applies to a specific disaster.

People assign meanings to situations to comprehend the situation's significance to them (Lazarus and Folkman 1984). These appraised meanings are shaped by individuals' global meaning in conjunction with the specifics of a particular situation. For example, those with a strong belief that they have control over their environment may focus on appraising aspects of a situation that they can change, while someone with a strong belief in karma might seek to identify a prior mistake or offense he or she committed.

One type of appraisal that is particularly important in the context of highly stressful events is causal attributions, individuals' understanding of why a particular event occurred. Attributions can have a naturalistic or supernatural religious character (Hood et al. 2009). For example, some individuals may attribute an airplane crash as being due to inclement weather or pilot error, while others may attribute it to God's intentions to punish the victims or to teach a lesson. Often, people make both proximal (immediate reason why) and distal (underlying, teleological reason why)

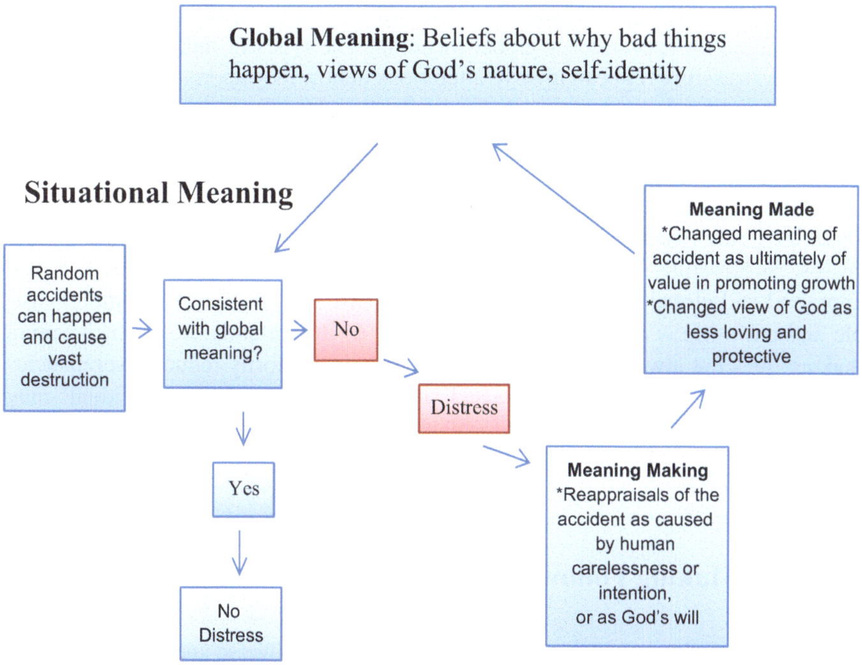

Fig. 2.1 Application of the meaning making model to a widespread technological accident

attributions, with the former more likely to have a naturalistic essence and the latter a religious or metaphysical one (see Park and Folkman 1997).

After appraising an event, individuals determine the extent to which that appraised meaning is consistent with their meaning system (global beliefs and goals). Events can violate or even "shatter" beliefs about how the world works (e.g., events occur in fair and predictable ways) and about themselves (e.g., I am a good person and therefore am invulnerable). Events can also render an individual's goals as no longer attainable (e.g., damage to or loss of key aspects of one's life such as one's health or personal relationships). Events can also threaten individuals' sense of life as meaningful (Janoff-Bulman and Frantz 1997). Such violations typically initiate cognitive and emotional processing efforts to rebuild their meaning systems in a way that reduces the perception of violation between situational and global meaning (Park et al. 2016); this processing is termed "meaning making" (Park and Folkman 1997). Meaning making can take multiple forms (Park 2010): people may try to change their appraised meaning of the stressor to make it less aversive or minimize its impact, thereby assimilating it into their extant meaning system, or they may change their global beliefs and goals to accommodate it. Meaning making can also involve revising their sense of their lives as meaningful or purposeful. Many cognitive and emotional processing theories are based on these meaning making processes (see Park et al. 2016, for a review).

Meaning making processes may result in meanings made, which comprise changes in either appraised or global meaning. The types of meaning individuals make of a stressful event can involve alterations in how they appraise the event (e.g., coming to see it as less damaging than initially thought). Changes in global meaning (e.g., viewing the world as more dangerous or embracing a new life goal, having a lower level of meaning in life), and perceived stress-related or posttraumatic growth (i.e., believing one has grown in positive ways as a result of the stressful experience) (Park 2010) are two such types. These changes arise through meaning making processes. Successfully making meaning reduces perceived discrepancies between appraised and global meanings and restores a sense that the world is comprehensible and one's life is purposeful (Park et al. 2016). Importantly, however, meaning making does not always produce meanings that satisfactorily reduce discrepancies between global meaning and appraised situational meaning, and individuals may become stuck in ruminative cycles of meaning making efforts driven by their distress.

Meaning Making Following Disasters

The meaning making model is useful in integrating the diverse and disparate literature on individuals' processes of responding to and recovering from disasters. Disasters are highly stressful events that can violate beliefs about the fairness and predictability of the world (McElroy-Heltzel et al. 2018). They tend to create cascades of interrelated difficulties and challenges entailing loss of or damage in many key domains of survivors' lives (e.g., family, home, community, work, health), violating their pursuit of important goals and ways of life that they were striving to attain or maintain prior to the disaster. Thus, meaning making processes to reduce those violations of global beliefs and goals likely play critical roles throughout survivors' recoveries.

Global Meaning and Disasters

Global beliefs have been shown to be closely associated with individuals' responses to and recovery from disasters. Probably most widely-studied in this regard is beliefs in one's ability to cope with a specified disaster (self-efficacy). Self-efficacy for coping after disaster has been associated with lower levels of post-disaster distress in many populations, including survivors of hurricanes, volcano eruptions, wildfires, and earthquakes (see Luszczynska et al. 2009, for a review).

Although less well-studied in the context of disaster, other global beliefs also appear to be important to post-disaster distress. For example, survivors of a flood in Germany who had higher beliefs in a just world—a belief that negative events are distributed in a predictable and fair way—reported lower levels of anxiety, depression and general psychological distress, but not PTSD symptoms (Otto et al. 2006). A study of survivors of the Sri Lankan tsunami found that those who had a generally pessimistic explanatory style (perceiving negative events as having internal, stable, and global causes) had more PTSD symptoms and poorer health (Levy et al. 2009). Maintaining global beliefs that the world is controllable and fair and that one can competently handle the disaster may allow survivors to feel more agency and thus cope more effectively with the difficulties posed by the disaster. However, these mediational linkages have rarely been tested (cf. Benight et al. 1999).

One such global belief, purpose in life, is a strong correlate of post-disaster resilience. In survivors of the 2005 Pakistan earthquake, nearly two-thirds of whom scored on a questionnaire as meeting criteria for PTSD, higher purpose in life was associated with lower PTSD symptom levels and higher positive emotions (Feder et al. 2013). In individuals seeking clinical services following the Gulf Oil Spill, higher sense of purpose in life was strongly correlated with life satisfaction (Drescher et al. 2012). In a prospective study of mostly non-Hispanic Black low-income mothers living in or near New Orleans, purpose in life assessed 1 year *prior to* Hurricane Katrina predicted perceived posttraumatic growth—but not PTSD—1 and 2 years after the hurricane (Lowe et al. 2013). All of these samples were comprised of survivors experiencing subjective post-disaster distress, and it appears that their ability to maintain a sense that they had valuable goals to accomplish may have allowed them to persevere and to find sustenance in the midst of catastrophic circumstances (Iacoviello and Charney 2014). The prospective study of Katrina survivors, however, suggests that a sense of purpose may not project forward to protect survivors from distress; concurrent assessments of purpose and distress may have yielded different findings.

Religiousness and spirituality have also been implicated as aspects of global meaning influencing disaster recovery. In a sample of survivors of the 2005 Pakistani earthquake, 3 years afterwards being "religious-minded" was independently related to lower PTSD symptoms (Ali et al. 2012), suggesting salutary effects of a global religious life. However, some types of religiousness/spirituality are related to poorer recovery. In a sample of Sri Lankan survivors 6 months after the 2004 Asian Tsunami, belief in karma was associated with poor health, although not with PTSD symptoms (Levy et al. 2009). Still other studies found no relationship between religiousness/spirituality and post-disaster adjustment. For example, in a large sample of college students in areas affected by Hurricanes Katrina and Rita in 2005, religiousness was unrelated to trauma symptoms (Pecchioni et al. 2011). Survivors of the L'Aquila (Italy) Earthquake who reported being high in religiosity had the lowest levels of PTSD symptomatology, while high spirituality was related to higher levels of symptomatology (Stratta et al. 2013), suggesting a protective value for organizational and ritual aspects of religiousness but a potential liability for spirituality per se. Further, in that sample, spiritual struggle, but not other aspects of religiousness or spirituality, was related to higher levels of PTSD symptomatology and suicidality (Stratta et al. 2012). Finally, another analysis of the prospective data collected from low-income mothers following Hurricane Katrina (described previously) found that pre-disaster religiousness did not have a direct effect on post-disaster distress, but it did predict less post-disaster distress through a heightened sense of purpose and optimism (Chan et al. 2012). For survivors of the 2016 Louisiana Flood, beliefs in theodicies of a suffering God and providence were *positively* related to PTSD symptoms. However, these same beliefs in benevolent theodicies buffered the link between perceptions of the flood as violating global beliefs and PTSD symptoms (McElroy-Heltzel et al. 2018). This study suggests positive theodicies might create vulnerabilities to violation when encountering extreme stressors but may also be comforting; perhaps, as individuals make meaning of disasters, more salutary effects of benevolent theodicies might emerge. Buffering effects of spirituality were also found in other samples of survivors of Hurricane Katrina. One study found survivors who reported experiencing higher spiritual meaning following the disaster also reported less severe PTSD symptoms in response to resource loss, relative to survivors who reported lower spiritual meaning (Haynes et al. 2017), while another found that religious comfort and struggle were (inversely) related to positive outcomes, but religious comfort also buffered the negative effects of resource loss on emotional health (Cook et al. 2013).

As is true of most of the disaster literature (and broader trauma literature), these findings are somewhat difficult to interpret because almost all of these studies were conducted *after* the disaster, in many cases long afterward, using retrospective study designs. Because aspects of global meaning may, and in fact likely often do, shift following traumatic experiences, measuring elements of individuals' global meaning after a disaster may be more reflective of outcomes (i.e., meaning made) than of pre-disaster resources that influenced adjustment processes.

Situational Meaning of Disasters

Appraisals of the Disaster

According to the meaning making model, survivors' appraised meanings of the disaster will inform their perceptions of global meaning violation and, thus, their post-disaster distress. For example, among family members and close friends who lost loved ones in the Mount Saint Helens volcanic eruption, appraising the death as preventable predicted *increased* distress up to 3 years later (Chenell and Murphy 1992). Other types of appraised meanings assigned to disaster are associated with posttraumatic stress symptoms as well. For survivors of the 2011 Japanese earthquake/tsunami/nuclear disaster, appraisals of harm and threat were related to more distress and lower quality of life, while challenge appraisals were related to less distress and higher perceptions of growth from the disaster and quality of life (Kyutoku et al. 2012). Similarly, appraisals of threat/harm/low control were related to depression, anxiety, and PTSD symptoms in survivors of the 1993 Perth (Australia) Flood (Morgan et al. 1995), and in survivors of the 2008 Wenchuan (China) Earthquake. Similar to the larger literature on appraised meanings of stressors, these disaster-specific findings demonstrate that appraising the disaster as threatening and uncontrollable is distressing, while appraising the disaster as low in threat and high in challenge is less so. Although research specifically in the context of disasters has not studied the impact of appraisals on subsequent coping, the broader coping literature shows that appraisals of high challenge and low threat are related to more active and engaged coping (Aldwin 2007).

Much of the research on post-disaster situational appraisals and recovery has focused on attributions. Unlike intentionally inflicted traumatic events, natural disasters have no perpetrator. Because it is difficult to incorporate the knowledge that "some people will intentionally inflict terrible harm upon me" into one's meaning system, trauma intentionality relates to higher PTSD symptoms (Santiago et al. 2013). However, because of their non-intentional nature, natural disasters create a gap in one's understanding of why such a devastating event occurred. Natural disasters thus have been historically considered "acts of God" (Steinberg 2000). However, technological and even natural disasters are increasingly seen as lying in an attributional gray zone, because although they may not have been deliberately caused, survivors can perceive elements of human negligence or lack of planning/anticipation of problems that create the conditions leading to disaster or exacerbating its negative effects (Blocker and Sherkat 1992; Kumagai et al. 2006). Exemplifying this gray zone is Hurricane Katrina (Squires and Hartman 2006). This devastating hurricane was not human-made, but the extent of damage in its aftermath was largely due to mistakes and neglect by large corporate and government entities as well as entrenched racism and poverty (Labib and Read 2015). Not only did the levees break due to poor design and maintenance and poor hurricane risk management policies, increasing the resulting flood damage, but the emergency response efforts were also woefully under-resourced (Labib and Read 2015). In hindsight, these factors can be partly blamed for the hundreds of lives lost in this disaster. However, a corporation or governmental entity may still not be enough to bridge the gap of intentional vs. "act of God".

Gaps in understanding why disasters occur may account for the fact that religious attributions—and subsequent religious coping—are common following natural and technological disasters. For example, a study of two major natural disasters—Hurricane Katrina in 2005 and the Chilean earthquake in 2010—found that describing the disasters as an act of God was among the most common explanations. Further, the more that survivors encountered *extreme hardship*—unpredictable, disruptive, and uncontrollable experiences—the more likely they were to explain the hurricane or earthquake as an act of God (Stephens et al. 2013). However, in a highly religious sample of survivors of the Haiti earthquake, 64.7% considered the quake to be a natural phenomenon and only 9% ascribed a divine origin while 23.4% reported not knowing the origin (Blanc et al. 2016).

One's general religiousness influences the likelihood that one will make religious attributions. The aforementioned study of college students in the area affected by Hurricanes Katrina and Rita asked participants why events like these happen. Those high in religiosity mostly identified the cause as God's plan, while those low in religiosity were more likely to attribute the event to a freak of nature, the law of averages, or a random natural event (Pecchioni et al. 2011).

Further, religious attributions often predict better recovery. In a sample of women who survived the 2004 Indonesian Tsunami studied 3 years after the disaster, attributions to karma were negatively related to depressive or PTSD symptoms (Banford et al. 2014). Similarly, in the study of undergraduates after Katrina and Rita, those who attributed such disasters to God's plan, random natural events, and law of averages had significantly lower levels of PTSD symptoms than did those who selected freak of nature, moral karma, and payback (Pecchioni et al. 2011). Nearly half of the women surveyed near the site of the South East Anatolian (Turkey) earthquake explained the quake as the will and guidance of God, while 41% considered it a natural event and 9% blamed human irresponsibility. Women who blamed other humans' irresponsibility for the disaster reported higher levels of depressive, somatization and paranoid symptoms than did those explaining it as God's will or as a natural event (Sezgin and Punamäki 2012).

Not all religious attributions are benign, however, and the specifics of the attribution influence its associations with recovery. For example, in the abovementioned sample of survivors of the Pakistani earthquake, one type of religious appraisal for the disaster, feeling punished by God for one's sins or lack of spirituality, was, perhaps not surprisingly, associated with higher stress levels and negative emotions (Feder et al. 2013). Similarly, for survivors of the 1993 Midwest (US) Flood, attributing the flood to God's love or reward was associated with better psychological adjustment and higher religious well-being, but attributions to God's anger or punishment were associated with greater distress (Smith et al. 2000). On the other hand, in a sample of Hurricane Katrina survivors who were displaced to a shelter in Texas within several weeks of the storm, perceiving God as in control and perceiving the hurricane as punishment were both related to higher levels of PTSD symptoms (Park et al. in press). Thus, attributions can have important implications for the perceptions of discrepancies with global meaning and therefore with long-term recovery. Some attributions may reinforce survivors' beliefs that the world is predictable and comprehensible and that God loves and protects them, while others may leave survivors feeling vulnerable and lacking control.

Making Meaning of Disaster

Survivors of disasters commonly report employing many types of coping with its aftermath, including active problem-solving and seeking social support (Wadsworth et al. 2009). Although these types of coping can be helpful, meaning making is often the best or even the *only* option for recovery from the profound damage and loss left in the wake of a disaster (Hollifield et al. 2008; Park 2016). Meaning making involves changing the meaning one assigns to the disaster and changing one's global beliefs or goals to reduce discrepancies between one's appraisals of the disaster and his or her global meaning (Park 2016). Changes in one (or both) aspects are necessary to restore harmony between their global meaning and their experience of disaster.

Reappraising or reframing a stressful situation to see it in less threatening ways that render it more consistent with one's global meaning is among the most common ways to make meaning of a highly stressful event (Park 2010). Reappraisal is quite common and often highly effective in ongoing stressful situations, such as in the aftermath of disasters, when many interrelated stressors remain for extended periods of time (Aldwin 2007). Through reappraisal, survivors can create new, less threatening ways of viewing the disaster and its consequences, and these reappraised meanings should facilitate the reduction of discrepancies with global meaning. For example, an early study of a technological disaster (partial nuclear meltdown) found that for people living near Three Mile Island, positive reappraisal coping was associated with less distress and lower levels of norepinephrine, a biomarker of stress (Collins et al. 1983). A study of members of the U. S. Embassy Tokyo community in the months following the March 2011 earthquake, tsunami, and nuclear crisis in Japan found that although self-reported *use* of positive reappraisal was not associated with psychological functioning, *success* using reappraisal as assessed on a performance-based experimental task, was associated with fewer symptoms of depression and PTSD (Cavanagh et al. 2014). A study of survivors of the 2010 Chilean earthquake/tsunami demonstrated that cognitive processing involving brooding rumination but not deliberate meaning making mediated associations between exposure severity and PTSD symptoms, while deliberate meaning making mediated the link between severity and perceived growth (García et al. 2015).

In some instances, meaning making may be usefully employed along with more active coping strategies. For example, in a longitudinal study of displaced and relocated adult survivors of Hurricane Katrina, those who employed both direct problem-solving and seeking of social support along with acceptance and reappraisal demonstrated the most resilient trajectories of recovery (Wadsworth et al. 2009). Such conjoint coping seems to best meet the needs of coping with broad existential concerns concurrently with demands to create new post-disaster lives that require direct action.

Religious coping— actions related to God or a higher power taken to deal with stressful experiences— is very common following disasters (Davis et al. 2019; Marks et al. 2009) and has long been a common approach to understanding and coping with disasters in many cultures around the world (Gaillard and Texier 2010). Further, religious coping appears to be the primary mechanism through which global religiousness/spirituality influences post-disaster psychological adjustment (Wadsworth et al. 2009). Thus, a fair amount of disaster-related research has examined the role of religious coping.

Positive religious coping, which includes coping efforts such as attempting to gain comfort, intimacy, and closeness with God, is generally associated with fewer symptoms of psychological distress and greater reports of psychological growth after traumatic events, although the effects are somewhat inconsistent (Pargament et al. 2011). On the other hand, negative religious coping, which includes reappraising the event as punishment from God and questioning God's power, is consistently related to higher levels of distress and poorer adjustment (Pargament et al. 2011).

Some studies have demonstrated favorable relations between religious coping and post-disaster adjustment. For example, in one sample of survivors displaced by Hurricane Katrina, prayer was associated with fewer stress symptoms (Spence et al. 2007), and in the abovementioned study of survivors of the 1993 Midwest (US) Flood (Smith et al. 2000) as well as a large sample of Hurricane Katrina survivors (Henslee et al. 2015), positive religious coping was associated with better psychological adjustment and functioning while negative religious coping was associated with greater distress and poorer functioning.

However, religious coping with disaster is not always helpful. In a sample of survivors within 2 years of the 2004 Asian tsunami, respondents' use of their religious practices to cope was strongly associated with anxiety and diagnosed PTSD (Hollifield et al. 2008). In a sample of survivors of the 2005 Pakistani earthquake, positive religious coping was unrelated to PTSD (Ahmad et al. 2010). In two studies of displaced Hurricane Katrina survivors, positive religious coping was unrelated to PTSD or depressive symptoms, while negative religious coping was positively related to distress (Park et al. in press; Wadsworth et al. 2009). These inconsistent findings from research on religious coping specifically with disasters parallel those in the broader literature: religious coping is sometimes associated with better functioning following a range of stressors, but is often unrelated or even inversely related (e.g., Pargament et al. 2011).

Meanings Made from the Disaster

Meanings made, the outcomes of the meaning making process, have been documented following disasters. One type of meaning made involves making changes in global meaning, such as changes in global beliefs or religiousness and spirituality. *Perceptions of changes* in global meaning suggest that such perceptions are common. For example, a longitudinal study of Norwegian tourists who had experienced the 2004 tsunami were asked to report on their current global beliefs and their beliefs 6 months prior, shortly before the tsunami. Difference scores indicated that participants reported, on average, experiencing changes on all beliefs measured in a negative direction, including invulnerability, just world, predictable world, controllable world, good and benevolent world, and meaningful life. Perceived changes to a lower belief in a just world were related to lower quality of life and higher PTSD symptoms assessed 2 years later, while perceived changes toward lower meaningfulness of life were associated with lower levels of quality of life but not with PTSD symptoms (Nygaard and Heir 2012).

Changes in religiousness and spirituality are a commonly studied type of meanings made following traumatic events (e.g., Falsetti et al. 2003), and again, self-reported changes are common. For example in the abovementioned sample of Norwegian tourists who experienced the 2004 Asian tsunami, 8% reported strengthening and 5% reported weakening of their religious beliefs. Perceived changes in either direction were associated with higher levels of posttraumatic stress compared to those whose strength of religious beliefs remained unchanged (Hussain et al. 2011). In-depth qualitative interviews with a highly religious sample of adult survivors of the 2016 Louisiana flood documented high levels of religious meanings made, including renewed beliefs and experiences of God's benevolence and providence (Davis et al. 2019).

However, due to retrospective bias, the validity of people's reports of changes in global meaning must be regarded with skepticism; comparison studies may yield a more accurate picture. For example, a sample of people who had experienced the L'Aquila (Italy) Earthquake, compared to a matched sample of people from nearby unaffected areas, reported lower levels of spirituality and higher levels of spiritual struggle (Stratta et al. 2012). However, no differences in religiousness between groups were noted. Another study compared global belief scores reported by a sample of adults exposed to the Icelandic earthquakes to those of a sample of non-exposed adults. The groups differed in beliefs about luck, with the exposed group reporting feeling luckier than did those in the control group, but no differences were noted between the groups in beliefs about the benevolence of other people or the world, justness or fairness of the world, or controllability (Bödvarsdóttir and Elklit 2004).

In addition to changing one's global meaning, meaning making can result in changes in how one understands the situation. Among the commonly studied situational outcomes of meaning making are perceptions that the event led to *posttraumatic growth*, positive changes one attributes to a traumatic event (Park 2010). People often report the event led them to grow, including having a greater appreciation for life, more effective coping skills, closer relationships with others, and increased compassion, life meaning, and spirituality (Park 2009). High levels of perceived growth have been reported following many types of disasters, including earthquakes (e.g., Xu and Liao 2011), tsunamis (e.g., Tang 2006), and hurricanes (e.g., Lowe et al. 2013). For example, some survivors of the 2013 Colorado Floods stated that the floods gave them the push "to make a fresh start and to commit to being open to new possibilities, options, and various routes in life" (Dursun et al. 2016). While these perceptions of positive changes can result from meaning making (i.e., constitute meanings made), reporting positive changes may also constitute efforts towards actively reappraising how one understands the disaster—thus, these reframing efforts would represent the process of meaning making rather than a product (i.e., meaning made; Park 2010).

In spite of the hundreds of studies focusing on it, the meaning of perceived growth is unclear (Jayawickreme and Blackie 2014). Some researchers consider these reports to constitute a positive outcome of stressful experiences (e.g., Shakespeare-Finch and Lurie-Beck 2014). Many others, including those focused specifically on disaster survivors, have demonstrated that perceived posttraumatic growth is often *positively* associated with PTSD symptoms and other symptoms of distress. For example, in the prospective study of low income mothers after Katrina, posttraumatic growth was moderately to strongly positively associated with PTSD symptoms at both 2 and 3 years out (Lowe et al. 2013). Similarly, posttraumatic growth was highly correlated with posttraumatic stress symptoms in samples of adult survivors 1 year following the 2008 Sichuan Earthquake (Xu and Liao 2011) and survivors of the 2004 tsunami 6 months (Tang 2006) and even 6 years afterwards (Michélsen et al. 2017). Yet perceived growth is not always adversely related to adjustment following disasters. For example, in survivors of the Japanese tsunami/earthquake/nuclear disaster, perceived growth was positively associated with anxiety but also negatively to depressive symptoms and positively to quality of life, perhaps due to some underlying positivity or optimism personality characteristic (Kyutoku et al. 2012). Importantly, the fact that perceived growth is often positively associated with distress does not mean that survivors do not grow or experience positive changes following disasters—many likely do—just that self-report measures may be a poor way to assess post-disaster growth (Frazier et al. 2009).

One implication of the meaning making model and the efforts survivors make to restore consistency between global and situational meaning is that sometimes the meanings made may reduce discrepancies, thus alleviating the distress, but are themselves negative in valence. For example, through making meaning of disasters, some people may come to think of themselves as having deserved their fate (e.g., Baum et al. 1983) or to see the universe as harsh and unpredictable (Janoff-Bulman and Morgan 1994). Thus, although discrepancy may be lessened between situational and global meaning, this newfound understanding of the world may in itself create distress. In considering meanings made, then, it is important to attend to their content as well as to their ability to reduce discrepancy (Park 2010).

Summary and Conclusions

The meaning making model usefully describes individuals' post-disaster recovery. Increasing research attention has led to knowledge regarding how survivors' global meaning, particularly their religiousness/spirituality and sense of meaning, and the appraisals and meaning making in which they engage following the disaster, influence their post-disaster distress and resilience. Meanings made in the form of changes in global beliefs and perceived growth are commonly reported but inconsistently related to psychological well-being. Findings to date, however, are far from conclusive. Because the very nature of disasters as unexpected and highly chaotic makes conducting well-planned research close to the event difficult, most studies of meaning in the context of disaster have been conducted long after its occurrence. By the time of assessment, much meaning making has already likely taken place. Further, post-disaster studies are typically conducted using cross-sectional designs, an understandable choice given the challenges of following disaster survivors who may have been relocated and often live in remote geographic areas using longitudinal designs. However, cross-sectional studies are of limited use in discerning the temporal ordering among study variables (e.g., do changes in global beliefs lead to distress, or does distress lead to changes in global beliefs)?

Even more challenging, truly understanding meaning making following a disaster requires pre-disaster baseline data. For example, studies of disaster that assessed individuals' global beliefs, such as in a just or fair world, a benevolent God, or controllability, are virtually non-existent. Yet understanding which types of pre-existing global meaning leave people relatively vulnerable and which types lead to resilience and thriving would be extremely useful in developing prevention approaches aiming to foster resilience. Finally, the present review focused only on individual meaning making. Yet a defining feature of disasters is their community-wide impact, and survivors' recovery processes unfold in the context of social relationships—families, congregations, communities (Patterson et al. 2010). To better understand disaster recovery, more comprehensive research is needed to examine these interrelations between individual and broader social processes of coping and meaning making.

Given the acceleration of both technology and climate change, the likelihood of future natural and technological disasters is increasing (Wisner 2010). These unfortunate occurrences both provide researchers with opportunities to conduct better research and amplify the need for a better understanding of how to help those affected. Helping efforts may comprise both intervention efforts following disasters (e.g., Schulenberg et al. 2014) and prevention or preparedness efforts to facilitate recovery in the event of a future disaster (Park and Slattery 2014).

References

Ahmad, S., Feder, A., Lee, E. J., Wang, Y., Southwick, S. M., Schlackman, E., et al. (2010). Earthquake impact in a remote South Asian population: Psychosocial factors and posttraumatic symptoms. *Journal of Traumatic Stress, 23*, 408–412.

Aldwin, C. M. (2007). *Stress, coping, and development: An integrative perspective* (2nd ed.). New York, NY: The Guilford Press.

Ali, M., Farooq, N., Bhatti, M. A., & Kuroiwa, C. (2012). Assessment of prevalence and determinants of posttraumatic stress disorder in survivors of earthquake in Pakistan using Davidson Trauma scale. *Journal of Affective Disorders, 136*, 238–243.

Appleton, L., & Flynn, M. (2014). Searching for the new normal: Exploring the role of language and metaphors in becoming a cancer survivor. *European Journal of Oncology Nursing, 18*, 378–384.

Banford, A. J., Wickrama, T., & Ketring, S. A. (2014). Physical health problem intrusion linking religious attributions to marital satisfaction in survivors of the 2004 tsunami. *Journal of Geography and Natural Disasters, 4*, 118.

Baum, A., Fleming, R., & Singer, J. E. (1983). Coping with victimization by technological disaster. *Journal of Social Issues, 39*, 117–138.

Benight, C. C., Ironson, G., Carver, C. S., Wynings, C., Burnett, K., & Greenwood, D. (1999). Conservation of resources and coping self-efficacy predicting distress following a natural disaster: A causal model analysis where the environment meets the mind. *Anxiety, Stress, and Coping, 12*, 107–126.

Blanc, J., Rahill, G. J., Laconi, S., & Mouchenik, Y. (2016). Religious beliefs, PTSD, depression and resilience in survivors of the 2010 Haiti earthquake. *Journal of Affective Disorders, 190*, 697–703.

Blocker, T. J., & Sherkat, D. E. (1992). In the eyes of the beholder: Technological and naturalistic interpretations of a disaster. *Organization & Environment, 6*, 153–166.

Bödvarsdóttir, I., & Elklit, A. (2004). Psychological reactions in Icelandic earthquake survivors. *Scandinavian Journal of Psychology, 45*, 3–13.

Bonanno, G. A., Brewin, C. R., Kaniasty, K., & La Greca, A. M. (2010). Weighing the costs of disaster consequences, risks, and resilience in individuals, families, and communities. *Psychological Science in the Public Interest, 11*, 1–49.

Cavanagh, S. R., Fitzgerald, E. J., & Urry, H. L. (2014). Emotion reactivity and regulation are associated with psychological functioning following the 2011 earthquake, tsunami, and nuclear crisis in Japan. *Emotion, 14*, 235–240.

Chan, C. S., Rhodes, J. E., & Pérez, J. E. (2012). A prospective study of religiousness and psychological distress among female survivors of Hurricanes Katrina and Rita. *American Journal of Community Psychology, 49*, 168–181.

Chenell, S. L., & Murphy, S. A. (1992). Beliefs of preventability of death among the disaster bereaved. *Western Journal of Nursing Research, 14*, 576–594.

Collins, D. L., Baum, A., & Singer, J. E. (1983). Coping with chronic stress at Three Mile Island: Psychological and biochemical evidence. *Health Psychology, 2*, 149–166.

Cook, S. W., Aten, J. D., Moore, M., Hook, J. N., & Davis, D. E. (2013). Resource loss, religiousness, health, and posttraumatic growth following Hurricane Katrina. *Mental Health, Religion, & Culture, 16*, 352–366.

Davis, E. B., Kimball, C. N., Aten, J. D., Andrews, B., Van Tongeren, D. R., Hook, J. N., Davis, D. E., Granqvist, P., & Park, C. L. (2019). Religious meaning making and attachment in a disaster context: A longitudinal qualitative study of flood survivors. *Journal of Positive Psychology, 14*, 659–671.

Drescher, C. F., Baczwaski, B. J., Walters, A. B., Aiena, B. J., Schulenberg, S. E., & Johnson, L. R. (2012). Coping with an ecological disaster: The role of perceived meaning in life and self-efficacy following the Gulf oil spill. *Ecopsychology, 4*, 56–63.

Dursun, P., Steger, M. F., Bentele, C., & Schulenberg, S. E. (2016). Meaning and posttraumatic growth among survivors of the September 2013 Colorado floods. *Journal of Clinical Psychology, 72*, 1247–1263.

Falsetti, S. A., Resick, P. A., & Davis, J. L. (2003). Changes in religious beliefs following trauma. *Journal of Traumatic Stress, 16*, 391–398.

Feder, A., Ahmad, S., Lee, E. J., Morgan, J. E., Singh, R., Smith, B. W., et al. (2013). Coping and PTSD symptoms in Pakistani earthquake survivors: Purpose in life, religious coping and social support. *Journal of Affective Disorders, 147*, 156–163.

Fergusson, D. M., Horwood, L. J., Boden, J. M., & Mulder, R. T. (2014). Impact of a major disaster on the mental health of a well-studied cohort. *JAMA Psychiatry, 71*, 1025–1031.

Frazier, P., Tennen, H., Gavian, M., Park, C. L., Tomich, P., & Tashiro, T. (2009). Does self-reported post-traumatic growth reflect genuine positive change? *Psychological Science, 20*, 912–919.

Gaillard, J. C., & Texier, P. (2010). Religions, natural hazards, and disasters: An introduction. *Religion, 40*, 81–84.

Galea, S., Tracy, M., Norris, F., & Coffey, S. F. (2008). Financial and social circumstances and the incidence and course of PTSD in Mississippi during the first two years after Hurricane Katrina. *Journal of Traumatic Stress, 21*, 357–368.

García, F. E., Cova, F., Rincón, P., & Vázquez, C. (2015). Trauma or growth after a natural disaster? The mediating role of rumination processes. *European Journal of Psychotraumatology, 6*(1), 26557.

Haynes, W. C., Van Tongeren, D. R., Aten, J., Davis, E. B., Davis, D. E., Hook, J. N., et al. (2017). The meaning as a buffer hypothesis: Spiritual meaning attenuates the effect of disaster-related resource loss on posttraumatic stress. *Psychology of Religion and Spirituality, 9*, 446–453.

Henslee, A. M., Coffey, S. F., Schumacher, J. A., Tracy, M., Norris, F. H., & Galea, S. (2015). Religious coping and psychological and behavioral adjustment after Hurricane Katrina. *The Journal of Psychology, 149*, 630–642.

Hollifield, M., Hewage, C., Gunawardena, C. N., Kodituwakku, P., Bopagoda, K., & Weerarathnege, K. (2008). Symptoms and coping in Sri Lanka 20–21 months after the 2004 tsunami. *The British Journal of Psychiatry, 192*, 39–44.

Hood, R. W., Hill, P. C., & Spilka, B. (2009). *The psychology of religion: An empirical approach* (4th ed.). New York: Guilford.
Hussain, A., Weisaeth, L., & Heir, T. (2011). Changes in religious beliefs and the relation of religiosity to posttraumatic stress and life satisfaction after a natural disaster. *Social Psychiatry and Psychiatric Epidemiology, 46*, 1027–1032.
Iacoviello, B. M., & Charney, D. S. (2014). Psychosocial facets of resilience: Implications for preventing post-trauma psychopathology, treating trauma survivors, and enhancing community resilience. *European Journal of Psychotraumatology, 5*, 23970.
Janoff-Bulman, R., & Frantz, C. M. (1997). The impact of trauma on meaning: From meaningless world to meaningful life. In M. J. Power & C. R. Brewin (Eds.), *The transformation of meaning in psychological therapies: Integrating theory and practice* (pp. 91–106). Hoboken: Wiley.
Janoff-Bulman, R., & Morgan, H. J. (1994). Victims' responses to traumatic life events: An unjust world or an uncaring world? *Social Justice Research, 7*, 47–68.
Jayawickreme, E., & Blackie, L. E. (2014). Post-traumatic growth as positive personality change: Evidence, controversies and future directions. *European Journal of Personality, 28*, 312–331.
Kumagai, Y., Edwards, J., & Carroll, M. S. (2006). Why are natural disasters not "natural" for victims? *Environmental Impact Assessment Review, 26*, 106–119.
Kyutoku, Y., Tada, R., Umeyama, T., Harada, K., Kikuchi, S., Watanabe, E., et al. (2012). Cognitive and psychological reactions of the general population three months after the 2011 Tohoku earthquake and tsunami. *PLoS One, 7*(2), e31014.
Labib, A., & Read, M. (2015). A hybrid model for learning from failures: The Hurricane Katrina disaster. *Expert Systems with Applications, 42*, 7869–7881.
Lazarus, R. S., & Folkman, S. (1984). *Stress, appraisal, & coping*. New York: Springer.
Levy, B. R., Slade, M. D., & Ranasinghe, P. (2009). Causal thinking after a tsunami wave: Karma beliefs, pessimistic explanatory style and health among Sri Lankan survivors. *Journal of Religion and Health, 48*, 38–45.
Lowe, S. R., Manove, E. E., & Rhodes, J. E. (2013). Posttraumatic stress and posttraumatic growth among low-income mothers who survived Hurricane Katrina. *Journal of Consulting and Clinical Psychology, 81*, 877–889.
Luszczynska, A., Benight, C., & Cieslak, R. (2009). Self-efficacy and health-related outcomes of collective trauma: A systematic review. *European Psychologist, 14*, 51–62.
Marks, L. D., Cherry, K. E., & Silva, J. L. (2009). Faith, crisis, coping, and meaning making after Katrina: A qualitative, cross-cohort examination. In K. E. Cherry (Ed.), *Lifespan perspectives on natural disasters* (pp. 195–215). New York: Springer.
McElroy-Heltzel, S. E., Davis, E. B., Davis, D. E., Aten, J. D., Van Tongeren, D. R., Hook, J. N., & Hwang, J. (2018). Benevolent theodicies protect against PTSD following a natural disaster. *Journal of Psychology & Christianity, 37*, 6–16.
Michélsen, H., Therup-Svedenlöf, C., Backheden, M., & Schulman, A. (2017). Posttraumatic growth and depreciation six years after the 2004 tsunami. *European Journal of Psychotraumatology, 8*, 1302691.
Morgan, I. A., Matthews, G., & Winton, M. (1995). Coping and personality as predictors of post-traumatic intrusions, numbing, avoidance and general distress: A study of victims of the Perth flood. *Behavioural and Cognitive Psychotherapy, 23*, 251–264.
Nalipay, M. J. N., & Mordeno, I. G. (2016). Emotional intensity of trauma memory as moderator of the relationship between posttraumatic cognitions and PTSD symptoms. *Journal of Pacific Rim Psychology, 10*, e7.
Nordløkken, A., Pape, H., Wentzel-Larsen, T., & Heir, T. (2013). Changes in alcohol consumption after a natural disaster: A study of Norwegian survivors after the 2004 Southeast Asia tsunami. *BMC Public Health, 13*(1), 58.
Norris, F. H., Friedman, M. J., Watson, P. J., Byrne, C. M., Diaz, E., & Kaniasty, K. (2002). 60,000 disaster victims speak: Part I. An empirical review of the empirical literature, 1981—2001. *Psychiatry, 65*, 207–239.
Nygaard, E., & Heir, T. (2012). World assumptions, posttraumatic stress and quality of life after a natural disaster: A longitudinal study. *Health and Quality of Life Outcomes, 10*, 76.

Otto, K., Boos, A., Dalbert, C., Schöps, D., & Hoyer, J. (2006). Posttraumatic symptoms, depression, and anxiety of flood victims: The impact of the belief in a just world. *Personality and Individual Differences, 40*, 1075–1084.

Pargament, K., Feuille, M., & Burdzy, D. (2011). The brief RCOPE: Current psychometric status of a short measure of religious coping. *Religions, 2*, 51–76.

Park, C. L. (2009). Overview of theoretical perspectives. In C. L. Park, S. Lechner, M. H. Antoni, & A. Stanton (Eds.), *Positive life change in the context of medical illness: Can the experience of serious illness lead to transformation?* (pp. 11–30). Washington, DC: American Psychological Association.

Park, C. L. (2010). Making sense of the meaning literature: An integrative review of meaning making and its effects on adjustment to stressful life events. *Psychological Bulletin, 136*, 257–301.

Park, C. L. (2016). Meaning making in the context of disasters. *Journal of Clinical Psychology, 72*, 1234–1246.

Park, C. L., & Folkman, S. (1997). The role of meaning in the context of stress and coping. *Review of General Psychology, 1*, 115–144.

Park, C. L., Riley, K. E., George, L. S., Gutierrez, I. A., Hale, A. E., Cho, D., & Braun, T. D. (2016). Assessing disruptions in meaning: Development of the global meaning violation scale. *Cognitive Therapy and Research, 40*, 831–846.

Park, C. L., Sacco, S. J., & Mills, M. A. (in press). Do religious resources help in the immediate aftermath of a crisis? Hurricane Katrina evacuees' religious habits, appraisals, and coping. *Psychological Trauma, 11*, 563–570.

Park, C. L., & Slattery, J. M. (2014). Resilience interventions with a focus on meaning and values. In M. Kent, M. C. Davis, & J. W. Reich (Eds.), *The resilience handbook: Approaches to stress and trauma* (pp. 370–382). New York: Routledge.

Patterson, O., Weil, F., & Patel, K. (2010). The role of community in disaster response: Conceptual models. *Population Research and Policy Review, 29*, 127–141.

Pecchioni, L. L., Edwards, R., & Grey, S. H. (2011). The effects of religiosity and religious affiliation on trauma and interpretations following Hurricanes Katrina and Rita. *Journal of Communication and Religion, 34*, 37–58.

Pietrzak, R. H., Tracy, M., Galea, S., Kilpatrick, D. G., Ruggiero, K. J., Hamblen, J. L., et al. (2012). Resilience in the face of disaster: Prevalence and longitudinal course of mental disorders following Hurricane Ike. *PLoS One, 7*(6), e38964.

Santiago, P. N., Ursano, R. J., Gray, C. L., Pynoos, R. S., Spiegel, D., Lewis-Fernandez, R., et al. (2013). A systematic review of PTSD prevalence and trajectories in DSM-5 defined trauma exposed populations: Intentional and non-intentional traumatic events. *PLoS One, 8*(4), e59236.

Schulenberg, S. E., Drescher, C. F., & Baczwaski, B. J. (2014). Perceived meaning and disaster mental health: A role for logotherapy in clinical-disaster psychology. In P. Russo-Netzer & A. Batthyany (Eds.), *Meaning in positive and existential psychology* (pp. 251–267). New York: Springer.

Sezgin, U., & Punamäki, R. L. (2012). Earthquake trauma and causal explanation associating with PTSD and other psychiatric disorders among South East Anatolian women. *Journal of Affective Disorders, 141*, 432–440.

Shakespeare-Finch, J., & Lurie-Beck, J. (2014). A meta-analytic clarification of the relationship between posttraumatic growth and symptoms of posttraumatic distress disorder. *Journal of Anxiety Disorders, 28*, 223–229.

Smith, B. W., Pargament, K. I., Brant, C., & Oliver, J. M. (2000). Noah revisited: Religious coping by church members and the impact of the 1993 Midwest flood. *Journal of Community Psychology, 28*, 169–186.

Spence, P. R., Lachlan, K. A., & Burke, J. M. (2007). Adjusting to uncertainty: Coping strategies among the displaced after Hurricane Katrina. *Sociological Spectrum, 27*, 653–678.

Squires, G. D., & Hartman, C. W. (2006). Pre-Katrina, Post-Katrina. In G. D. Squires & C. W. Hartman (Eds.), *There is no such thing as a natural disaster: Race, class, and Hurricane Katrina* (pp. 1–11). New York: Routledge.

Steinberg, T. (2000). *Acts of God: The unnatural history of natural disaster in America*. New York: Oxford University Press.

Stephens, N. M., Fryberg, S. A., Markus, H. R., & Hamedani, M. G. (2013). Who explains Hurricane Katrina and the Chilean earthquake as an act of God? The experience of extreme hardship predicts religious meaning-making. *Journal of Cross-Cultural Psychology, 44*, 606–619.

Stratta, P., Capanna, C., Riccardi, I., Carmassi, C., Piccinni, A., Dell'Osso, L., & Rossi, A. (2012). Suicidal intention and negative spiritual coping one year after the earthquake of L'Aquila (Italy). *Journal of Affective Disorders, 136*, 1227–1231.

Stratta, P., Capanna, C., Riccardi, I., Perugi, G., Toni, C., Dell'Osso, L., & Rossi, A. (2013). Spirituality and religiosity in the aftermath of a natural catastrophe in Italy. *Journal of Religion and Health, 52*, 1029–1037.

Tang, C. S. K. (2006). Positive and negative postdisaster psychological adjustment among adult survivors of the Southeast Asian earthquake–tsunami. *Journal of Psychosomatic Research, 61*, 699–705.

Wadsworth, M. E., Santiago, C. D., & Einhorn, L. (2009). Coping with displacement from Hurricane Katrina: Predictors of one-year post-traumatic stress and depression symptom trajectories. *Anxiety, Stress, & Coping, 22*, 413–432.

Wisner, B. (2010). Untapped potential of the world's religious communities for disaster reduction in an age of accelerated climate change: An epilogue & prologue. *Religion, 40*, 128–131.

Xu, J., & Liao, Q. (2011). Prevalence and predictors of posttraumatic growth among adult survivors one year following 2008 Sichuan Earthquake. *Journal of Affective Disorders, 133*, 274–280.

Chapter 3
Religion, Spirituality, and Meaning in the Wake of Disasters

Daryl R. Van Tongeren, Jamie D. Aten, Edward B. Davis, Don E. Davis, and Joshua N. Hook

In September 2017, the cover of *Time* magazine depicted Doppler images of hurricanes overlain on a map of the United States, with the title "The Storms Keep Getting Stronger. And So Do We." (*Time* 2017). This image and tagline underscored two sentiments felt across the U.S. First, disasters are increasing in their frequency, intensity, and impact (CRED 2016; EM-DAT n.d.), and they are having an increasing effect on the daily lives of Americans. Second, in the face of this barrage of disasters, Americans are responding with resilience, fortitude, and grit. This inspiring human response to disasters has captured the interest of both researchers and the public, and as the incidence and impact of disasters continues to intensify, more resources will presumably be poured into studying, preparing for, responding to, and recovering from disasters. At the same time, because of global warming, more people will be affected by disasters than ever before. Accordingly, understanding the psychological and spiritual effects of disasters is an important endeavor.

Preparation for this chapter was made possible through the support of a grant from the John Templeton Foundation (Grant #44040). The opinions expressed in this publication are those of the authors and do not necessarily reflect the views of the John Templeton Foundation.

D. R. Van Tongeren (✉)
Department of Psychology, Hope College, Holland, MI, USA
e-mail: vantongeren@hope.edu

J. D. Aten
Department of Psychology and Humanitarian Disaster Institute, Wheaton College, Wheaton, IL, USA

E. B. Davis
Department of Psychology, Wheaton College, Wheaton, IL, USA

D. E. Davis
Department of Counseling and Psychological Services, Georgia State University, Atlanta, GA, USA

J. N. Hook
Department of Psychology, University of North Texas, Denton, TX, USA

S. E. Schulenberg (ed.), *Positive Psychological Approaches to Disaster*,
https://doi.org/10.1007/978-3-030-32007-2_3

A Religious Meaning-Based Approach to Disasters

Disasters are a multifaceted threat to meaning. Survivors may experience considerable distress as they attempt to make sense of the disaster experience, understand how these experiences fit with their broader understanding and set of beliefs about how the world works, and reestablish a sense of purpose and direction in the wake of the disaster. Moreover, the considerable physical and psychological losses associated with disasters often make even the most basic of tasks—such as finding food, water, and shelter—more challenging, making other motivational needs feel less pressing (see Maslow 1943). Thus, in the wake of disasters, survivors often draw from various coping resources to help restore a sense of meaning that the disaster has disrupted.

Religion is an important aspect of life for many individuals. Worldwide, 84% of individuals report a religious affiliation (Pew 2015). For many, religion/spirituality (R/S) is a prominent source of meaning (Emmons 2005; Vail et al. 2010; Van Tongeren et al. 2013b), especially in the context of coping with adverse life events (McIntosh 1995; Park 2005, 2010). Following a disaster, people may rely on their R/S beliefs to help them make sense of the unexpected and negative event, restore a sense of meaning and significance in life, and regain or redefine their sense of purpose or direction.

Below, we propose a theory of religious meaning in the context of disasters. First, we define meaning. Next, we explain how R/S provides meaning. Then, we discuss situations in which R/S can sometimes impede one's ability to cope effectively in the wake of a disaster. Finally, we consider theory and research from positive psychology that might inform how individuals, relationships, and societies can draw on faith to grow stronger in response to the growing frequency and intensity of disasters.

Defining Meaning

Psychological research on meaning in life has accelerated in recent years. Despite conceptual ambiguity about what meaning is, researchers have begun converging on a definition of meaning that recognizes its three core aspects: coherence, significance, and purpose (George and Park 2016; Heintzelman and King 2014b; Martela and Steger 2016). Specifically, *meaning in life* refers to "the extent to which one's life is experienced as making sense, as being directed and motivated by valued goals, and as mattering in the world" (George and Park 2016, p. 206). Disasters often disrupt people's sense of meaning across each of these dimensions.

Coherence

Coherence is the degree to which people understand and comprehend their lives and the world around them (George and Park 2016, 2017; Heintzelman and King 2014b; Martela and Steger 2016). Broadly speaking, when things are predictable and there are reliable associations in the world (e.g., good things happen to good people [i.e., just world theory]; God is benevolent), life makes sense and seems meaningful (Heintzelman and King 2014a). Violations of these predicted, reliable associations provide valuable environmental information (via feelings of meaninglessness) about how to shift one's behavior to address these disruptions. For example, before a disaster, if life is going generally well, life feels coherent and meaningful. But if a disaster destroys your home and community, this experience is inconsistent and incoherent with what you expect (e.g., good things *did not* happen to me; my loved ones and God *did not* protect me and my community), so life probably does not make much coherent sense to you at present. Such a disruption in meaning pulls you to address this discrepancy and attempt to regain a coherent understanding of the world, yourself, and others, including God (see Park 2010).

Usually, life is perceived as pretty meaningful (Heintzelman and King 2014a). However, unexpected, negative events such as disasters can threaten this sense of coherence and meaning. People experience a sense of coherence when their interpretation of an event (i.e., situational meaning) matches their global beliefs about the way the world works (i.e., global meaning; Park 2010). At such times, the congruence between one's broad worldview beliefs and a particular outcome makes coherent sense and feels meaningful. Meaning is disrupted when events are unexpected, inconsistent with, or discrepant from how one assumes the world should work. Disasters may disrupt coherence when one's particular beliefs are violated, such as if people hold the belief that God is all-knowing (i.e., omniscient), all-powerful (i.e., omnipotent), and all-loving (i.e., benevolent). These beliefs about God cause people to wrestle with questions such as "Where was God during the disaster?" or "What was God's state of mind?" Perhaps God allowed—or even caused—the disaster for some reason. Sometimes a cruel and punishing, but consistent God may seem preferable to an entirely arbitrary and unpredictable God.

This tension between beliefs (e.g., God is good) and experience (e.g., God failed to protect me) creates distress, which motivates people to negotiate their beliefs. Any number of adjustments in beliefs about God might ease the dissonance. For example, some people may cling to God's loving intent, but reduce their conviction that God is powerful and engaged in influencing events such as disasters. Other people may cling to God's power and engagement, but wonder about the goodness or justice of God. Still others may preserve a sense of God's power and benevolence through intuiting the mind of God towards the victims, filling in stories about how the victims deserved their plight. For instance, after both natural (e.g., Hurricane Katrina) and human-made disasters (e.g., 9/11), some religious leaders in the U.S. asserted that sin and moral corruption (e.g., homosexuality) led to, or caused, these disasters

(ABC News 2001; CNN 2010). Indeed, the difficulty making sense of an incoherent event can upend people's perceived meaning, and it can motivate them to alter their religious cognitions and attributions.

Significance

Significance is the feeling that one matters and has value and importance in the world (George and Park 2016, 2017; Heintzelman and King 2014b; Martela and Steger 2016). People feel significant when they have a sense that they deeply matter to others. A lack of perceived significance is related to depression and a variety of other mental health concerns (George and Park 2017). For many, feelings of significance emerge relatively naturally when they feel well-connected to others or have a strong religious faith (i.e., they feel they matter to God).

Disasters often disrupt one's feelings of significance. Disasters can remind people about the fragility of life, threatening their sense of control over events and over their own lives. When mortality is salient, people may begin to rethink their place in the world, as they perceive they are merely a small and seemingly insignificant individual in the grand scope of nature (Pyszczynski et al. 2010). Indeed, death and meaning are intricately related (Landau et al. 2006; Van Tongeren and Green 2018). Many studies have examined how reminders of death challenge people's sense of significance and can cause people to seek to restore a sense of mattering to others (see Solomon et al. 2004).

In terms of religious cognition, perhaps the crisis of meaning that occurs involves a shaking of people's sense that they matter to God. The logic may go something like this: "If I matter to God, how can I understand that God did not take steps to protect me in this situation? A loving parent would not allow irreparable harm to occur, yet I can imagine no good coming from this, so whatever the reason, God has abandoned me and left me unprotected."

Purpose

Purpose is "the extent to which individuals experience life as being directed and motivated by valued life goals" (George and Park 2016, p. 206; see also Heintzelman and King 2014b; Martela and Steger 2016). Often, these goals involve commitments to roles (e.g., marriage, parent) or broader relationship systems (e.g., calling within a career). Purpose involves both the proximal actions (e.g., having a job, being responsible for a pet) and distal aspirations (e.g., advancing science, curing a disease, making money) that shape one's daily decisions. When people feel they are working toward a larger goal, they feel purposeful. Conversely, when they lack specific, concrete goals, they feel purposeless. Purpose helps people transcend their ordinary life and connect with something bigger and presumably greater than themselves. Moreover, purpose may be found by being embedded in and committed to a community. In short, relationships or causes beyond oneself often provide purpose.

Disasters can threaten people's sense of purpose by destroying many of the things that make life purposeful. For example, if people find purpose in going to a job, caring for a pet, or making a difference in the lives of others, disasters can rob them of such opportunities when their place of work is demolished, their pet is lost in the storm, or their ability to thrive is severely impaired by the high degree of resource loss they experienced because of a disaster. The daily actions of survivors might suddenly narrow from the magnificent to the mundane; their central focus might shift toward finding food and water, securing shelter, and beginning to rebuild their lives. After a disaster, it may take people quite some time to restore some of the habits and routines of investment in major life pursuits or strivings (Emmons 2005). At the same time, for people embedded within a functioning R/S community, the great need caused by the disaster may provide a period of communal focus that helps to bolster a sense of purpose.

R/S as a Source of Meaning

R/S has long been considered a source of meaning (Emmons 2005; Newton and McIntosh 2013; Park 2005, 2010; Vail et al. 2010; Van Tongeren et al. 2013b). People rely on R/S beliefs to meet a host of needs, ranging from basic to existential (Batson and Stocks 2004). However, there are important individual differences in the orientation people adopt toward R/S (e.g., Allport and Ross 1967), particularly in the degree to which R/S beliefs offer people security in the wake of a meaning threat (Beck 2004, 2006; Van Tongeren et al. 2013a, b) or motivate people toward growth (Van Tongeren et al. 2016). After a disaster, R/S beliefs can help survivors maintain or restore a sense of meaning by aiding them in making sense of the event (i.e., coherence), preserving a sense they matter (i.e., significance), and providing a broader goal (i.e., purpose).

R/S and Coherence

Following a disaster, R/S beliefs can help individuals make sense of any losses that they, their loved ones, or their community have experienced. R/S can even be viewed as a schema (i.e., interpretative framework) people use to understand and cope with stressful life events (McIntosh 1995; Park et al. 2017). Indeed, following unsettling or upsetting events, people often turn toward their R/S beliefs as a way to find meaning. For example, among parents whose infant child suddenly died, finding meaning in the death of their child was associated with greater future well-being (McIntosh et al. 1993).

R/S can offer believers a coherent worldview and cognitive structure for interpreting adverse events they have experienced. To illustrate, prior work has suggested that among patients with brain tumors (and their relatives), finding a sense of coherence offers an important link between one's R/S beliefs and ability to cope (Strang and Strang 2001). Religious certainty also has a strong effect on well-being (Ellison 1991), underscoring the important role of R/S in offering a structure through which one can reliably interpret the world. For instance, R/S can help people make sense of a tragic loss by offering a certain, organized, and predictable interpretative lens through which they can extract meaning. This feeling of meaning and security can help facilitate individuals' coping. For example, following a disaster, survivors with higher R/S meaning reported experiencing fewer posttraumatic stress disorder symptoms, even when their actual loss was high (Haynes et al. 2017). Indeed, disaster survivors often turn to R/S to help make sense of events and losses they have experienced, and, in doing so, they frequently restore a sense of meaning and coherence in their lives (Park 2016).

R/S and Significance

R/S can also help individuals maintain a sense of significance. Disasters are a potent reminder of human mortality. When mortality is made salient, people's sense of significance and meaning is often threatened, leaving them clinging to beliefs or structures that imbue their life with significance (Pyszczynski et al. 2010). R/S is perfectly suited to address the existential fear of death (Vail et al. 2010), in part by offering promises of literal immortality (Dechesne et al. 2003). One of the ways people manage anxiety-provoking thoughts about their own death is by adopting R/S beliefs that provide them with literal immortality (Van Tongeren and Green 2018). With promises of literal immortality, R/S beliefs can offer meaning (and a web of relationships) that transcends death, thereby contributing to greater meaning (Van Tongeren et al. 2013a, b), and this sense of meaning can help manage fears related to death (Van Tongeren et al. 2017b). That is, R/S beliefs often assure and remind people that they are significant, loved, and important. They are part of a community that will last forever, and in the scope of eternity, transitory suffering may not loom quite as large. They matter, not only in this life, but also in the next. A higher power, often God, loves and cares for them so much that they will live on forever. Thus, in the wake of disasters (which can threaten life and remind survivors how fragile and unpredictable life is), R/S can offer assurance individuals will be protected and preserved—even if only in life after death. A powerful R/S answer to the problem of suffering is that "all will be made well" after a relatively short period of difficulty.

R/S and Purpose

Following a disaster, some individuals may begin to question their purpose or calling, especially if they have experienced considerable loss. How should they orient their lives? Toward what should they be directing their effort and energy? R/S beliefs can help provide individuals with a sense of purpose, derived from a broader set of goals (Emmons 2005). This may happen on both a proximal and a distal level. Proximally, in the immediate aftermath of a disaster, it could mean reorienting oneself toward helping survivors in dire need. Exposure to trauma leads some people to engage in prosocial behavior as a path to well-being (Frazier et al. 2013), and prior work has demonstrated the causal link between R/S and prosociality, primarily for religious individuals (Shariff et al. 2016). This might suggest a noble purpose immediately following a disaster may be engaging one's R/S values to act prosocially and help those in need.

More distally, disaster survivors might turn toward R/S beliefs to help them reorganize their broader sense of purpose (Park 2005, 2016; Sibley and Bulbulia 2012). Indeed, following disruptions to meaning, people tend to report increased religiousness yet decreased religious uncertainty or doubt (Van Tongeren and Green 2010), suggesting the type of R/S beliefs that are most helpful in navigating adversity involve the certainty of a clear path or plan (see also Van Tongeren et al. 2013b, 2016). Through the process of sanctification, people can orient their life to sacred callings or purposes (Pargament et al. 2005). In so doing, R/S can help survivors restore meaning by providing them a sense of purpose, both in the immediate aftermath of the disaster, as well as during the longer process of recovery.

Variations in Religious Cognitions and Attributions Following a Disaster

In the wake of disasters, how R/S survivors engage their R/S beliefs can affect how they cope with the disaster and its aftermath. For such persons, we suspect both the *content* of their R/S beliefs and the *style* with which they hold these beliefs will affect how they respond to and cope with the disaster. Below, we describe how variation in these features of R/S beliefs may interact and alter how they cope.

The content of R/S beliefs can play an important role in people's responses to disasters. Previous work has highlighted how people are strongly motivated to maintain cognitive consistency among their various beliefs and attitudes. Cognitive dissonance theory (Festinger 1957) posits that individuals are most comfortable when they experience cognitive consistency—that is, their beliefs or attitudes are congruent with their behavior and with one another. When there is a discrepancy between attitudes or between one's attitudes and behaviors, individuals experience dissonance, which is a motivating state that impels one to reduce this discrepancy. The central feature of this theoretical model is that people thrive when their beliefs are congruent and aligned, and they are motivated to rectify imbalances or dissonances in their beliefs. Accordingly, disaster survivors may normatively assess the degree to which their experiences match with what they believe about God. When there is a consistency, they might feel comfortable; however, when there is a discrepancy, they may be motivated to address this discrepancy by shifting their beliefs or reinterpreting the situation (Park 2010, 2016).

Two central components of the content of religious cognitions may directly affect how people respond following a disaster: (a) people's views of or beliefs regarding God (or some other supernatural agent), and (b) the degree to which individuals believe that God (or some supernatural agent) caused the disaster.

Regarding people's views about God, people likely apply the same schematic perception processes to God that they use to perceive and understand humans. For instance, similar to how individuals usually perceive other people in terms of how warm/cold and agentic/passive they are, individuals may tend to perceive God in terms of how warm/cold (i.e., benevolent/cruel) and agentic/passive (i.e., active/passive) God is. Previous sociological research suggests that viewing God across these dimensions yields four different "gods" people perceive: authoritarian, benevolent, critical, and distant (Froese and Bader 2010).

Thus, drawing from person-perception research and prior sociological work on god perception, we conceptualize two dimensions of religious cognitions related to the nature and character of God, yielding four possible combinations of perceptions of God (see Fig. 3.1): (A) active and benevolent, (B) passive and benevolent, (C) passive and cruel, or (D) active and cruel. It is likely that these beliefs may interact with supernatural attributions to affect peoples' responses to disasters. *Supernatural attributions* refer to the perceived causality for particular events (e.g., are naturalistic factors, some god, fate/chance, or the devil responsible for this earthquake?). For example, believing that a malevolent supernatural agent caused a hurricane likely results in greater psychological tension than believing that a benevolent supernatural agent is trying to protect one from the damages of a hurricane that was caused by naturalistic factors. Thus, the content of one's religious cognitions likely matters greatly.

The style with which disaster survivors hold their R/S beliefs can also affect how they respond following the disaster. Previous work has suggested that people who are more open to doubt and questioning—such as individuals with a quest religious

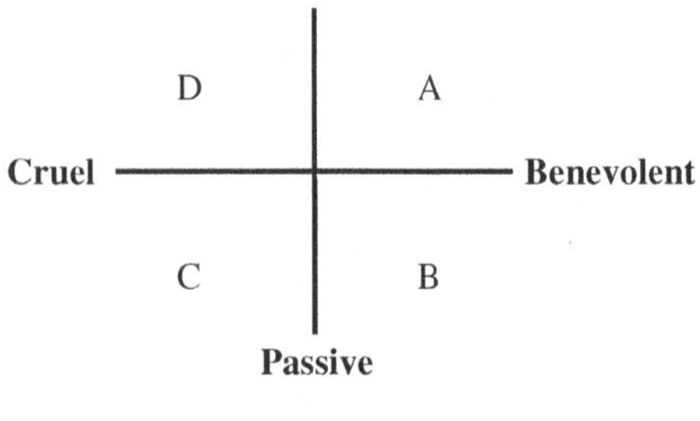

Fig. 3.1 Beliefs about supernatural agents may fall along the dimensions of benevolent/cruel and active/passive, yielding (at least) four views: active and benevolent (**A**), passive and benevolent (**B**), passive and cruel (**C**), and active and cruel (**D**)

orientation—may be more tolerant and open-minded in the absence of threat, but such beliefs may be ill-suited to deal with the existential threat of disasters (Van Tongeren et al. 2013b). For example, participants with security-providing beliefs, such as defensive theological beliefs or religious fundamentalism, were not affected by meaning threats to the degree that those high in quest religion were; the latter demonstrated significantly more death anxiety following threats to meaning. This finding suggests that one's way of holding R/S beliefs may provide one with some degree of protection from the negative effects of meaning threats. Likewise, following interpersonal or ideological threats, individuals who engage humbly with the threat, are less likely to get defensive, even when controlling for orthodoxy of beliefs (Van Tongeren, Stafford et al. 2016). These findings suggest that, besides the *content* of people's R/S beliefs, the *style* of their beliefs may play a role in how they respond to threats.

Taken together, it can be argued that, in the wake of disasters, perhaps the ideal set of R/S beliefs are *strategically flexible*. Whereas the core features of one's beliefs may be security-providing and likely need to be held with certainty (e.g., relational components, such as the belief that God loves and protects me), other features may need to be adapted or modified in the face of conflicting evidence. For example, if one believes that God is benevolent and protecting (which may serve a buffering function after a disaster), believing that God is responsible for one's misfortune (i.e., caused the hurricane) may strain one's R/S beliefs, leaving one prone to existential anxiety and associated adverse mental health effects. On the other hand, if people shift responsibility away from God (i.e., the hurricane was primarily caused by human factors, such as global warming), they may be able to preserve the security-providing features of their R/S beliefs while viewing the world in an epistemically reasonable way that does not create additional tension or discrepancy among their beliefs. More research in this area would help advance understanding of the nuanced processes by which people explain adverse events (e.g., disasters), as well as how religious cognitions interact with such attributions.

What Makes R/S Meaning Special?

People find meaning in a variety of ways. Many draw on their cultural worldviews (Pyszczynski et al. 2010), which can be religious or irreligious. Adverse life experiences such as disasters can impel people to try to make meaning of their situation, and these meaning-making efforts often involve R/S beliefs and practices (Park 2016; Park et al. 2017). With all the possible ways people can derive meaning after a disaster, what is special about R/S? We contend that three features of R/S make it especially likely that people may turn toward such beliefs in the wake of a disaster: (a) R/S addresses existential issues, (b) R/S communities provide social support and consensual validation, and (c) R/S helps answer attributional questions (see also Park 2016; Park et al. 2017).

First, R/S helps address existential fears. In fact, some have argued that R/S is perfectly suited to meet needs across motivational levels, including existential needs (Batson and Stocks 2004). Put differently, God or the supernatural can be evoked at every level, such as finding food and meeting physiological needs, securing safety, finding shelter, communing with others, developing a sense of esteem and self-worth, and finding one's unique calling or identity. Moreover, R/S beliefs often address existential fears, such as death (Vail et al. 2010). Prior work has shown that cognitively activating R/S schemas decreases death-related anxiety for individuals for whom religion is central (Van Tongeren, McIntosh et al. 2013). Moreover, following reminders of death, those high in intrinsic religiousness, for whom religion is an important and defining feature, are less reactive and defensive (Jonas and Fischer 2006).

Disasters may evoke existential fears, including making mortality salient. Indeed, following 9/11 (a terrorist disaster), church attendance in the U.S. peaked for a year, as many people turned to R/S to seek comfort and existential solace (Pyszczynski et al. 2003). R/S beliefs offer promises of immortality (embeddedness within a community that will never suffer the pain of separation again), which helps make life feel more meaningful and death feel less terrifying (Van Tongeren and Green 2018). To the degree disasters are an existential threat, R/S is a helpful existential solution.

Second, people may turn toward R/S because R/S communities offer networks for giving and receiving social and existential support. Socially, people can give and receive the benefits that come from being in close, interdependent relationships (e.g., they can give and receive practical and emotional support). Part of the meaning-providing functions people derive from R/S beliefs include the ways people express their R/S commitments through relationships with other members of their R/S community (see Van Tongeren et al. 2013b). Indeed, research has provided evidence of a strong religious in-group helping norm (Galen 2012). That is, R/S people show a strong preference toward helping other members of their R/S group. In a disaster context, members of a faith community may offer emotional support or practical support to disaster-affected members of their community (e.g., bringing them a meal; watching their children; or helping them unbury their belongings, sift through rubble, repair their home, and rebuild their lives).

In the wake of a disaster, R/S communities can also offer existential support. They can help provide a consensually validated way of making sense of the event and of the world in its aftermath. Other members of the community can help disaster-affected individuals and families come to terms with their losses in ways that feel authentic to their shared R/S worldview, beliefs, and values. They might draw on religious scriptures describing God's love, nearness, and comfort, especially during times of suffering and tragedy (e.g., disasters). Alternatively, members of the R/S community can help survivors affirm their shared R/S beliefs during a time of existential strain, offering a helpful buttress for the doubt and chaos that often ensues following a disaster. When other people see the world the same way you do, you feel less anxious and more affirmed that your way of seeing the world is right, and this certainty can help quell existential anxieties (Yalom 1980).

Third, R/S can help answer attributional questions about the disaster. In the wake of adversity, people normatively ask why it happened, and R/S beliefs allow for faith in one or more powerful supernatural agents that can actively affect humans' well-being. When trying to explain unexplained events, people often turn toward supernatural accounts (Stephens et al. 2013). People developed cognitive proficiency in detecting agency as a way of increasing chances for survival (Guthrie 1993). When a bush moves, those that assumed an agent (e.g., predator) caused that action were more likely to act (e.g., run away) and survive. Thus, humans are equipped with the ability to infer causal agency. However, according to some theorists, these patterns are hyperactive among some, yielding assumptions of agency when there is no reasonable cause. This can lead to belief in supernatural forces in the absence of plausible explanations (Gray and Wegner 2010). R/S is a ready resource for answering why things occurred, perhaps because God either caused or allowed it to happen.

Is There a Dark Side of R/S Meaning?

Although R/S can be a powerful source of meaning, there are likely situations in which R/S beliefs act as an impediment to coping with a natural disaster. That is, there are times when R/S can help and other times when it can hurt (Griffin 2010). In what follows, we outline some examples of the dark side of R/S meaning.

First, following an adversity like a disaster, some R/S beliefs may increase stress and impair coping. For instance, if someone believes God is loving and protecting, disasters may disrupt such conceptualizations of God. How could an all-powerful, all-knowing, and all-loving God cause or allow such a tragic event to occur? Without a flexible way of applying these beliefs (or nuances in the beliefs themselves), individuals are likely to feel increased discrepancy and stress (Park 2010, 2016). For example, disasters may put pressure on the omnipotence, omniscience, and omnibenevolence of God's character. Because of the dissonance created (Festinger 1957), survivors may alter their attitude regarding how powerful, knowledgeable, and good God is. Alternatively, they may have to add cognitions to help recreate a balance; for example, following human-made disasters (e.g., 9/11; ABC News 2001) and natural disasters (e.g., Hurricane Katrina or the 2010 Haiti earthquake; CNN 2010), religious leaders conjectured that humans' sinful actions led to these disasters' horrific destruction. Such claims bolster beliefs that God is loving and protecting—but only toward people who love and serve God, whereas God is perceived as just and punishing toward people who do not. In some cases, rigid R/S belief structures may make it difficult to cope with uncertain or unexplainable events that run counter to longstanding assumptions about God or the nature of the world, perhaps requiring people to do mental gymnastics to maintain a sense of coherence.

Second, although R/S communities can offer considerable support following tragedy, they can also offer well-intentioned but misguided and hurtful platitudes to disaster-affected members. Psychologically, such explanations commonly seem to function as a way for community members either to resolve their own cognitive dissonance about the disaster or assuage their own anxiety about experiencing pain and loss. For example, when trying to comfort a survivor whose family member died in a disaster, a fellow member of the survivor's R/S community might say, "God works out everything for good." Although well-intentioned, this statement may feel theologically inauthentic and psychologically painful to survivors. Such claims can delegitimize survivors' experiences of grief, loss, and pain, fostering feelings of isolation and possibly contributing to mental health problems (e.g., depression).

A third way R/S meaning can strain postdisaster coping is in the domain of supernatural attributions. Supernatural attributions refer to whom or what one assigns as the cause(s) of the disaster. Following disasters, people regularly make supernatural attributions (Stephens et al. 2013). However, there are many unanswered questions about how supernatural attributions affect people's coping responses to disasters. How can people make sense of a tragic event when they believe that God is all-powerful? Did God *cause* the event, *allow* the event to occur, or is God *distant and disengaged*? These attributions likely relate strongly to beliefs about God's agency and character. Moreover, to what degree is God's response interrelated and interdependent with humans' actions? From a different perspective, was the devil or other demonic forces responsible for this disaster? How people think about the cause of the disaster may put increased pressure on their belief structure and thereby hinder their postdisaster coping efforts. For instance, when people endure R/S struggles, they may begin to experience God differently, and they may revise their theological beliefs about God to fit these new experiences (Van Tongeren et al. 2017c).

For many disaster survivors, R/S helps them cope by helping them find and regain a sense of meaning (Park 2016). But for other survivors, R/S meaning can lead to unintended negative consequences. The problem of evil and suffering in the world has long been a troubling aspect of religious theology, and disasters are no exception. More research is needed to advance understanding of the ways R/S meaning can help survivors in their postdisaster coping efforts, as well as the ways certain religious cognitions and attributions might impede or impair healthy postdisaster coping.

Toward a Positive Psychology of Disasters

To this point, we have surveyed theory and research generally pointing to ways that disasters may undermine, at least temporarily, people's sense of coherence, significance, and purpose. R/S can provide people with resources to respond to these threats to meaning. However, drawing on the positive psychology framework, we wonder if disasters can also instigate certain processes that solidify and consolidate meaning in people's lives. Positive psychology focuses on how individuals flourish across multiple domains (Seligman and Csikszentmihalyi 2000). Positive psychology has focused on positive features of human life, such as character strengths, virtues, meaning, and R/S. We see these responses to be particularly important in the wake of the adversity of disasters. Although some work is being conducted in these domains, we see many useful areas for future research at these intersections. Below, we briefly explain a few additional areas in which positive psychology might catalyze research on disasters.

Character Strengths

How do people respond in the face of adversity? The entire Western tradition of virtue suggests that character forms gradually through many choices, and severe stress can reveal, test, and sometimes prove character. Situations when a positive response is the most difficult (e.g., cases of extreme fear and danger) may be the very situations where a positive response is most needed (e.g., courage). Most religious traditions reinforce this fact that the best and the worst of people comes out under duress.

Recent research has focused on spiritual fortitude as one such character strength in the wake of adversity. Spiritual fortitude assesses the confidence that people have that they possess sufficient spiritual resources to deal with adversity, such as a disaster (Van Tongeren et al. 2017a). This character strength, which is unique from grit and resilience, assesses spiritual resources across three dimensions: spiritual endurance (to withstand adversity), spiritual enterprise (to act virtuously in the midst of adversity), and redemptive purpose (to find meaning in adversity). Preliminary research has found that spiritual fortitude is associated with greater meaning in life and spiritual well-being, as well as lower adversity-related anxiety, over and above the associations with grit and resilience (Van Tongeren et al. 2017a). Thus, in the wake of adversity, people may be able to draw on character strengths that are rooted in their R/S beliefs, thereby metabolizing adversity in ways that can lead to healthy outcomes.

Virtues

For people embedded within faith traditions that view suffering as an opportunity to grow, the stress of disasters provides a crucial period of training in virtue. Severe strain provides people with a chance to expand their sense of their human limitations through drawing on the unlimited resources of God through prayer and community engagement. They can learn that their prior view of themselves was arbitrary and narrowly circumscribed, and within a community, they can see various exemplars who have experienced similar transformations during periods of transition or crisis. Prior work has demonstrated how trauma exposure is associated with prosocial behavior (Frazier et al. 2013). Other work has focused on how exposure to an earthquake increases children's altruistic behavior (Li et al. 2013). For some, there appears to be a natural prosocial response to the adversity of disasters. However, we suspect that other virtuous responses may be affected by disasters. For example, prior work has demonstrated how reminders of death increase forgiveness of close others (Van Tongeren et al. 2013a). Given the role of forgiveness in restoring a sense of meaning (Van Tongeren et al. 2015), virtues that help repair or sustain relationship functioning (e.g., forgiveness) may be particularly useful in the wake of disasters. Similarly, we suspect that individual differences in humility, gratitude, compassion, and wisdom may alter how individuals respond to adversity. Alternatively, exposure to disasters might affect one's humility, the degree to which one is grateful, how compassionately one responds, or how one seeks to act wisely.

Religious and Nonreligious Meaning

We have already explained how disasters are a multifaceted threat to meaning, as well as how R/S meaning may play a central role in how people cope with such adversity. However, meaning systems need not be religious. Many people find meaning in relationships, affiliation with larger (secular) groups or countries, work, nature, individual performance or achievement, hobbies or activities, or nonreligious spiritualities. Moreover, many nonreligious beliefs, such as belief in a just world or assumptions about the nature of humanity and the way the world works, help people frame an understanding of the world that does not rely on religious faith. In the same way that these beliefs may be threatened by inconsistent information (Park 2010), many of the processes we explain above are likely relevant, including shifting one's attitudes to achieve greater alignment between the sense assigned to the situation and the larger framework of beliefs that offers an interpretive lens through which one understands one's social world. However, other dimensions of a nonreligious meaning system may be less disrupted in the wake of disasters. For example, when tragedy strikes, nonreligious survivors would not have to explain the role of the supernatural. More work should explore how nonreligious meaning systems function in the wake of adversity such as disasters.

Open Questions

Given the promise of positive psychology to help explicate a full account of how disasters affect individuals' sense of meaning and R/S beliefs, as well as how these processes affect their mental health, we see several promising open questions for future research.

- **Which features of religious cognition are most strongly related to positive coping?** Prior work has highlighted the important role of R/S in making meaning following disasters. For example, R/S meaning acts as a buffer following the loss associated with a natural disaster (Haynes et al. 2017). More questions remain. Are there particular beliefs that lead to better mental health outcomes? Are certain styles of belief more likely to buffer the negative emotional and psychological effects of disasters? Which particular beliefs about God's character, nature, and relationship with humans are most predictive of successful or unsuccessful coping?

- **What is the role of supernatural attributions?** We have briefly explained how people turn toward supernatural causes to explain disasters (Stephens et al. 2013); however, more work is needed. How do people decide whether God, or another supernatural agent, is responsible for the disaster? Do R/S beliefs affect attributions, or do attributions shift R/S beliefs? How do these processes change over time, especially when in relationship with members of the individual's broader R/S community? When can supernatural attributions be helpful or harmful in coping?
- **What role do virtues play in responses to disasters?** Initial work on the relationship between virtues and disaster is promising (Li et al. 2013), but we suspect that work in this area has a very bright future. We see several fruitful areas of future work. Does humility, forgiveness, or gratitude help survivors, or those working with survivors, better adjust to and recover from the disaster? How can virtues be cultivated in the wake of such adversity? How does the practice of virtues affect relationships following periods of intense stress?
- **When, and how, does *real* growth occur?** Prior research has highlighted methodological limitations in research studying perceived and actual posttraumatic growth (PTG), suggesting that PTG may not be as common as previous research suggests (Jayawickreme and Blackie 2014). Future work needs to employ prospective longitudinal designs that can capture assessments of individuals before and after disasters. Although methodologically and practically challenging, such data would be rich for addressing more directly the degree to which actual growth occurs, and what predicts such growth.
- **How can methodological diversity improve disaster research?** Most research on disasters is retrospective. This makes intuitive sense; researchers wait for a disaster to occur, study the survivors, and then draw conclusions. However, this retrospective, cross-sectional data has limitations. Accordingly, we suggest researchers adopt a variety of approaches to address these limitations. Experimental work could explore how exposure to disaster-related stimuli affect participants' psychological responses. Alternatively, the effectiveness of different psychological and R/S interventions with disaster survivors could be evaluated, such as meaning-focused interventions (e.g., expressive writing tasks). Prospective longitudinal research with disaster survivors could examine their R/S meaning making over time. Moreover, daily-dairy studies and experience-sampling studies could provide a finer point of assessment for disaster researchers. We encourage future researchers to use all the methodological approaches available to them to capture the richest understanding of disasters, including the intersections of meaning, R/S, and virtues in the wake of disasters.

Conclusion

Disasters have become an increasingly salient part of American life. As individuals try to make sense of why the disaster occurred, what it means for them individually, and how it affects their broader sense of purpose and meaning, many turn toward R/S to provide a framework for interpreting such events and regaining a sense of psychological equanimity. Future research that seeks to understand these processes will surely help improve the lives and well-being of disaster survivors and will better equip the people and organizations who serve them in the wake of disasters.

References

ABC News. (2001). Falwell suggests gays to blame for attacks. Retrieved from http://abcnews.go.com/Politics/story?id=121322&page=1.

Allport, G. W., & Ross, J. M. (1967). Personal religious orientation and prejudice. *Journal of Personality and Social Psychology, 5*(4), 432–443.

Batson, C. D., & Stocks, E. L. (2004). Religion: Its core psychological functions. In J. Greenberg, S. Koole, & T. Pyszczynski (Eds.), *Handbook of experimental existential psychology* (pp. 141–155). New York, NY: Guilford Press.

Beck, R. (2004). The function of religious belief: Defensive versus existential religion. *Journal of Psychology and Christianity, 23*, 208–218.

Beck, R. (2006). Defensive versus existential religion: Is religious defensiveness predictive of worldview defense? *Journal of Psychology and Theology, 34*, 143–153.

Centre of Research on the Epidemiology of Disaster (CRED). (2016). *The human cost of weather related disasters*. Geneva, Switzerland. Retrieved from https://www.unisdr.org/.

CNN. (2010). Pat Robertson says Haiti paying for 'pact to the devil.' Retrieved from http://www.cnn.com/2010/US/01/13/haiti.pat.robertson/index.html?iref=allsearch.

Dechesne, M., Pyszczynski, T., Arndt, J., Ransom, S., Sheldon, K. M., van Knippenberg, A., & Janssen, J. (2003). Literal and symbolic immortality: The effect of evidence of literal immortality on self-esteem strivings in response to mortality salience. *Journal of Personality and Social Psychology, 84*, 722–737.

Ellison, C. G. (1991). Religious involvement and well-being. *Journal of Health and Social Behavior, 32*, 80–99.

EM-DAT. (n.d.). *The OFDA/CRED International disaster database*. Brussels: Universite Catholique de Louvain, Brussels. Retrieved from www.emdat.be.

Emmons, R. A. (2005). Striving for the sacred: Personal goals, life meaning, and religion. *Journal of Social Issues, 61*, 731–745.

Festinger, L. (1957). *A theory of cognitive dissonance*. California: Stanford University Press.

Frazier, P., Greer, C., Gabrielsen, S., Tennen, H., Park, C., & Tomich, P. (2013). The relationship between trauma exposure and prosocial behavior. *Psychological Trauma, 5*, 286–294.

Froese, P., & Bader, C. (2010). America's four gods: What we say about God and what that says about us. Oxford, UK: Oxford University Press.

Galen, L. W. (2012). Does religious belief promote prosociality? A critical examination. *Psychological Bulletin, 138*, 876–906.

George, L. S., & Park, C. L. (2016). Meaning in life as comprehension, purpose, and mattering: Toward integration and new research questions. *Review of General Psychology, 20*, 205–220.

George, L. S., & Park, C. L. (2017). The Multidimensional Existential Meaning Scale: A tripartite approach to measuring meaning in life. *Journal of Positive Psychology, 12*, 613–627.

Gray, K., & Wegner, D. M. (2010). Blaming god for our pain: Human suffering and the divine mind. *Personality and Social Psychology Review, 14*, 7–16.

Griffin, J. L. (2010). *Religion that heals, religion that harms*. New York: Guilford Press.

Guthrie, S. E. (1993). *Faces in the clouds: A new theory of religion*. New York: Oxford University Press.

Haynes, W. C., Van Tongeren, D. R., Aten, J., Davis, E. B., Davis, D. E., Hook, J. N., Boan, D., & Johnson, T. (2017). The meaning as a buffer hypothesis: Spiritual meaning attenuates the effect of disaster exposure on posttraumatic stress. *Psychology of Religion and Spirituality, 9*, 446–453.

Heintzelman, S. J., & King, L. A. (2014a). Life is pretty meaningful. *American Psychologist, 69*, 561–574.

Heintzelman, S. J., & King, L. A. (2014b). (The feeling of) meaning-as-information. *Personality and Social Psychology Review, 18*, 153–167.

Jayawickreme, E., & Blackie, L. E. (2014). Post-traumatic growth as positive personality change: Evidence, controversies and future directions. *European Journal of Personality, 28*, 312–331.

Jonas, E., & Fischer, P. (2006). Terror management and religion: Evidence that intrinsic religiousness mitigates worldview defense following mortality salience. *Journal of Personality and Social Psychology, 91*, 553–567.

Landau, M. J., Greenberg, J., Solomon, S., Pyszczynski, T., & Martens, A. (2006). Windows into nothingness: Terror management, meaninglessness, and negative reactions to modern art. *Journal of Personality and Social Psychology, 90*, 879–892.

Li, Y., Li, H., Decety, J., & Lee, K. (2013). Experiencing a natural disaster alters children's altruistic giving. *Psychological Science, 24*, 1686–1695.

Martela, F., & Steger, M. (2016). The three meanings of meaning in life: Distinguishing coherence, purpose, and significance. *The Journal of Positive Psychology, 11*, 531–545.

Maslow, A. H. (1943). A theory of human motivation. *Psychological Review, 50*, 370–396. https://doi.org/10.1037/h0054346.

McIntosh, D. N. (1995). Religion as schema, with implications for the relation between religion and coping. *The International Journal for the Psychology of Religion, 5*, 1–16.

McIntosh, D. N., Silver, R. C., & Wortman, C. B. (1993). Religion's role in adjustment to a negative life event: Coping with the loss of a child. *Journal of Personality and Social Psychology, 65*, 812–821. https://doi.org/10.1037/0022-3514.65.4.812.

Newton, A. T., & McIntosh, D. N. (2013). Unique contributions of religion to meaning. In J. A. Hicks & C. Routledge (Eds.), *The experience of meaning in life: Classical perspectives, emerging themes, and controversies* (pp. 257–269). New York: Springer.

Pargament, K. I., Magyar-Russell, G. M., & Murray-Swank, N. A. (2005). The sacred and the search for significance: Religion as a unique process. *Journal of Social Issues, 61*, 665–687.

Park, C. L. (2005). Religion as a meaning-making framework in coping with life stress. *Journal of Social Issues, 61*, 707–729.

Park, C. L. (2010). Making sense of the meaning literature: An integrative review of meaning making and its effects on adjustment to stressful life events. *Psychological Bulletin, 136*, 255–301.

Park, C. L. (2016). Meaning making in the context of disasters. *Journal of Clinical Psychology, 72*, 1234–1246.

Park, C. L., Currier, J. M., Harris, J. I., & Slattery, J. M. (2017). *Trauma, meaning, and spirituality: Translating research into clinical practice*. Washington: American Psychological Association.

Pew Research Center. (2015, April 2). The future of world religions: Population growth projections, 2010-2050. http://www.pewforum.org/2015/04/02/religious-projections-2010-2050/.

Pyszczynski, T., Greenberg, J., & Goldenberg, J. (2003). Freedom versus fear: On the defense, growth, and expansion of the self. In M. Leary & J. Tangney (Eds.), *Handbook of self and identity* (pp. 314–343). New York: Guilford Press.

Pyszczynski, T., Greenberg, J., Koole, S., & Solomon, S. (2010). Experimental existential psychology: Coping with the facts of life. In S. Fiske & D. Gilbert (Eds.), *Handbook of social psychology* (Vol. 1, 8th ed., pp. 724–757). New York: Wiley.

Seligman, M. E. P., & Csikszentmihalyi, M. (2000). Positive psychology: An introduction. *American Psychologist, 55*, 5–14. https://doi.org/10.1037/0003-066x.55.1.5.

Shariff, A. F., Willard, A. K., Andersen, T., & Norenzayan, N. (2016). Religious priming: A meta-analysis with a focus on prosociality. *Personality and Social Psychology Review, 20*, 27–48.

Sibley, C. B., & Bulbulia, J. (2012). Faith after an earthquake: A longitudinal study of religion and perceived health before and after the 2011 Christchurch New Zealand earthquake. *PLoS One, 7*, 1–10.

Solomon, S., Greenberg, J., & Pyszczynski, T. (2004). The cultural animal: Twenty years of terror management theory and research. In J. Greenberg, S. Koole, & T. Pyszczynski (Eds.), *Handbook of experimental existential psychology* (pp. 13–34). New York: Guilford Press.

Stephens, N. M., Fryberg, S. A., Markus, H. R., & Hamedani, M. G. (2013). Who explains Hurricane Katrina and the Chilean earthquake as an act of God? The experience of extreme hardship predicts religious meaning-making. *Journal of Cross-Cultural Psychology, 44*, 606–619.

Strang, S., & Strang, P. (2001). Spiritual thoughts, coping and 'sense of coherence' in brain tumour patients and their spouses. *Palliative Medicine, 15*, 127–134.

Time. (2017). The angels of Irma. Retrieved from: http://time.com/magazine/us/4941004/september-25th-2017-vol-190-no-12-u-s/.

Vail, K. E., Rothschild, Z. K., Weise, D. R., Solomon, S., Pyszczynski, T., & Greenberg, J. (2010). A terror management analysis of the psychological functions of religion. *Personality and Social Psychology Review, 14*, 84–94.

Van Tongeren, D. R., Aten, J. D., McElroy, S. Davis, D. E., Shannonhouse, L., Davis, E. B., & Hook, J. N. (2017a). *Development and validation of a measure of spiritual fortitude*. Unpublished manuscript under editorial review.

Van Tongeren, D. R., Davis, D. E., Hook, J. N., & Johnson, K. A. (2016). Security versus growth: Existential tradeoffs of various religious perspectives. *Psychology of Religion and Spirituality, 8*, 77–88.

Van Tongeren, D. R., & Green, J. D. (2018). Meaning and death-thought accessibility. *British Journal of Social Psychology, 57*, 230–239.

Van Tongeren, D. R., & Green, J. D. (2010). Combating meaninglessness: On the automatic defense of meaning. *Personality and Social Psychology Bulletin, 36*, 1372–1384.

Van Tongeren, D. R., Green, J. D., Davis, D. E., Worthington, E. L., Jr., & Reid, C. A. (2013a). Till death do us part: Terror management and forgiveness in close relationships. *Personal Relationships, 20*, 755–768.

Van Tongeren, D. R., Green, J. D., Hook, J. N., Davis, D. E., Davis, J. L., & Ramos, M. (2015). Forgiveness increases meaning in life. *Social Psychological and Personality Science, 6*, 47–55.

Van Tongeren, D. R., Hook, J. N., & Davis, D. E. (2013b). Defensive religion as a source of meaning in life: A dual mediational model. *Psychology of Religion and Spirituality, 5*, 227–232.

Van Tongeren, D. R., McIntosh, D. N., Raad, J., & Pae, J. (2013). The existential function of intrinsic religiousness: Moderation of effects of priming religion on intercultural tolerance and afterlife anxiety. *Journal for the Scientific Study of Religion, 52*, 508–523.

Van Tongeren, D. R., Pennington, A., McIntosh, D. N., Newton, A. T., Green, J. D., Davis, D. E., & Hook, J. N. (2017b). Where, o death, is thy sting? The meaning-providing function of beliefs in literal immortality. *Mental Health, Religion, and Culture, 20*, 413–427.

Van Tongeren, D. R., Sanders, M., Edwards, M., Davis, E. B., Aten, J. D., Ranter, J. M., Tsarouhis, A., Short, A., Cuthbert, A., Hook. J. N., & Davis, D. E. (2017c). *Religious and spiritual struggles alter God representations*. Unpublished manuscript under editorial review.

Van Tongeren, D. R., Stafford, J., Hook, J. N., Green, J. D., Davis, D. E., & Johnson, K. A. (2016). Humility attenuates negative attitudes and behaviors toward religious outgroup members. *The Journal of Positive Psychology, 11*, 199–208.

Yalom, I. (1980). *Existential psychotherapy*. New York: Basic Books.

Chapter 4
Reconciling Disaster and Deity: Trauma, Spirituality, and Growth in the Context of Natural and Technological Disasters Induced by Climate Change

Mary Beth Werdel

> *I form the light, and create darkness: I make peace, and create evil: I the LORD do all these things (Isaiah 47:5).*

Research provides strong evidence to suggest that climate change is imminent and, at minimum, partially irreversible. Rising air temperature and sea levels will result in increased severity of natural and technological disasters that involve extreme weather changes such as tropical storms and variable rainfall patterns. This will lead to flooding and droughts, famine from crop and livestock destruction, polluted drinking water, and increased illness and disease (IPCC 2007). As climate change increases the rate of disasters (IPCC 2007), the effects on human psychological illness and flourishing from both the threat and lived experience of natural and technological disasters will likely become more pervasive as well. Subsequently, the area of disaster mental health will become a critical mental health area in the years to come.

As the physical ground is unearthed in disaster, so too may a person's psychological ground grow unsteady and remain unsteady for years. Disasters can result in a decreased sense of predictability and control that can lead to experiences of psychological dysfunction such as acute stress and anxiety (Moser 2007), depression (Dar et al. 2018), and posttraumatic stress disorder (PTSD; Doherty and Clayton 2011). Research suggests that individuals will experience increased stress and decreased well-being in the face of climate change (Weissbecker 2011). There is research to suggest that PTSD symptoms following a natural disaster endure for some people. For example, in a study of survivors of the 2004 Indian Ocean disaster in Southeast Asia, researchers found a six-year prevalence rate of 11.3% for PTSD and a current rate of 4.2% (Arnberg et al. 2013).

PTSD symptoms may be experienced by disaster survivors as well as by front-line first responders charged with saving physical lives and property (Levy-Gigi et al. 2014). Moreover, mental health workers charged with attempting to reconstruct

M. B. Werdel (✉)
Department of Pastoral Mental Health Counseling, Fordham University, Bronx, NY, USA
e-mail: mwerdel@fordham.edu

S. E. Schulenberg (ed.), *Positive Psychological Approaches to Disaster*,
https://doi.org/10.1007/978-3-030-32007-2_4

healthy emotional worlds may also experience PTSD symptoms through vicarious trauma (Baird and Kracen 2006).

The potential for trauma reactions ripples out from the epicenter of individual disasters to the wider global community. As a result, humans are connected not only by a shared climate, but also by a web of potential climate change-induced trauma reactions that cannot and should not be ignored. Thus, there is a significant risk to neglecting mental health concerns associated with climate change (Gifford 2008; Moser 2007; Weissbecker 2011). Mental health professionals will have an important role to play in answering the questions of how to psychologically manage, make sense of, and care for mental health-related reactions to something as pervasive as climate change.

For those who claim a sense of a transcendence, the overwhelming nature of catastrophic events such as natural and technological disasters may bring up questions that straddle the disciplines of psychology and spirituality. The field of theology has long examined the idea of a theodicy: how is it that an all-powerful God allows suffering? No one clear answer is given in religious texts and spiritual writings; however, many possibilities have been considered. Does God shelter or protect people from suffering? Does God cause suffering such as suggested in the above verse from Isaiah? Is suffering intrinsically bad and therefore should be avoided at all cost? Or is suffering intrinsically good in that it brings one closer to God? Did God start—and is now watching—a human free-will experiment, able, but choosing not to intervene in times of suffering?

Religious and spiritual belief systems are ways in which people are mentored into forming meaning related to why a "good" God allows "bad" things to happen. In difficult times, religion and spirituality may play a critical role in the meaning-making process (Pargament et al. 2006; Park 2016). Religion can orient a person in times of stress (Calhoun et al. 2000). Some ways of engaging religious meaning allow for experiences of psychological growth (Pargament et al. 2004), but for others, engaging religious meaning will result in distress (Pargament et al. 2006), psychological stagnation, and decline. In this time of "accelerated climate change," religious communities may provide "untapped potential" (Wisner 2010, p. 128) for those attempting to reorient, adapt, and even grow.

In this chapter, the unique role that the experience of transcendence plays in the process of meaning making and positive growth in the context of natural and technological disasters influenced by climate change will be explored. Using Park's (2016) meaning-making model of coping in times of disaster, three points will be argued. First, the literature in the area of positive psychology broadly, and posttraumatic growth specifically, can and should inform disaster mental health. Second, natural disasters hold spiritual questions that have psychological implications; thus they must be explored together by mental health professionals. Lastly, competencies in the psychological treatment after natural and technological disaster must be growth oriented and spiritually informed.

Positive Psychology and Posttraumatic Growth's Essential Role

The examination of positive psychology and posttraumatic growth must be deliberate. Traditional psychological work is poised to consider negative symptoms related to mental health but not to psychological flourishing and growth. Rooted in the medical model, this psychological framework has encouraged the question of how to best help people manage distress and debilitating symptoms such as anxiety and PTSD after enduring disasters. Psychological darkness is typically considered first, as there is great and enduring darkness created from disasters. For example, take Hurricane Mitch in 1998, a slow moving Category 5 hurricane with wind speeds recorded over 175 mph. Hurricane Mitch is currently the second deadliest Atlantic hurricane on record. Mitch was responsible for over 11,000 fatalities in Central America; 7,000 of the fatalities occurred in the extremely poor and vulnerable country of Honduras. Beyond the persistent rain and hurricane winds, extreme flooding due to lack of modern infrastructure enveloped whole communities. On a trip I took in 2003 to a small rural village just outside of San Francisco de la Paz, Honduras—a community only recently equipped with access to ground water through a human-powered pump and still without electricity—I met a man named Guillermo. As he shared stories of his life in Honduras, he began to speak about Hurricane Mitch unprompted.

Guillermo shared that Hurricane Mitch decimated his community. Homes became unrecognizable piles of stone and mud. Dirt roads became impassable, even by boats. Multiple members of his community died, first in the storm and later from lack of food, water, and health care. Fifteen years after the storm had passed, Guillermo's eyes still readily watered from the grief associated with such profound traumatic loss. His reaction makes sense, as research has evidenced that traumatic events have a strong and enduring hold on our emotional worlds (Steel et al. 2002). While even in the most horrific of situations, houses can be rebuilt, roads can be repaired, and electricity restored—such as with Hurricane Mitch in Honduras—the time it takes to restore our physical landscape can be small compared to the time it takes to reconstruct our emotional landscape. The repair of our interior lives can take years—if it happens at all.

Perhaps the most concerning result of disaster on our inner world is the experience of PTSD. Multiple studies suggest that PTSD is a potential result of disaster, and that the rate of PTSD is likely higher when there is disaster that is a centripetal event (Arnberg et al. 2013). Research indicates social support is a protective factor in mediating the effects of PTSD after disasters (Dar et al. 2018). However, when a centripetal disaster such as Hurricane Mitch impacts large numbers of people in the same community, social and family supports may not be available in the same way as when a stress or trauma is experienced by one person. Thus for people like Guillermo, whose social losses are counted in the tens if not hundreds, negative symptoms persist.

The study of the negative consequences of disaster is essential to ethical mental health care. Research must continue to explore disaster from the traditional medical model. Yet it is imperative to remember two points. First, examining negative symptoms will only result in research related to negative symptoms. Research that provides data on "what is going wrong" will never be able to answer questions related to "what is going right" (Werdel and Wicks 2012). Secondly, with the data that exist to support unavoidable climate change and related increased rates of disaster, the mental health field cannot afford to wait to consider how to treat negative symptoms. Waiting will result in more care needed in the wake of disasters than caretakers available. The mental health field must find ways to best prepare people's interior worlds before disasters occur. Positive psychology, which seeks to understand how personal character strengths can not only help support a person in moving through challenges, but also offers insight into how one can move more easily through—or even flourish—after stress and trauma. One specific area of positive psychology that is essential to disaster mental health is the area of posttraumatic growth.

Over the last 25 years, an abundance of research suggests that while negative symptoms of trauma such as PTSD are real, enduring extreme stress and moving through extreme stress can have positive psychological consequences that are also real. The most widely recognized term used to describe the phenomena is posttraumatic growth (PTG; Calhoun and Tedeschi 2006). PTG literature highlights that the act of enduring stress can set a person on a quest for meaning that encourages a major reconstruction of their global assumptions. This can result in the transformation of a person's experience of themselves, others, or the world. The implication of current research is that people can prepare for climate change by proactively working to increase resiliency. Additionally, research suggests that when people are faced with disaster, enduring the associated stress and trauma can be a gateway to growth.

Park's Meaning-Making Model of Coping

The search for meaning is an essential component of being human, and is a basic human motivation (Frankl 1969). The presence of meaning is related to multiple factors associated with well-being (Dezutter et al. 2013); conversely, the absence of meaning is related to multiple factors associated with psychopathology and distress (Bryan et al. 2013). Meaning in life is a concept one often does not consider until a crisis moment seeks to erase or causes one to question the meaning that they hold. Crisis is like a spotlight that draws attention to the meaning and assumptions that a person has adopted and that—often without awareness—guide the way they think and feel. Sometimes one's meaning in life can sustain and help move them through a crisis situation. Other times, moving through crisis reveals a sense of meaninglessness and resultant distress. This absence of meaning may cause one to enter a search process.

Park's (2016) meaning-making model of coping provides a framework for the meaning-making process in times of stress and trauma (Park 2005, 2008) and in the specific context of natural disasters (Park 2016). Briefly, while coping research often identifies the role that problem solving or emotion-focused coping serve after experiences of stressful life events, in cases of extreme stress and trauma, such as a natural disaster, more than coping is needed. Park (2005) suggests that events such as natural disasters demand the involvement of an intrapsychic cognitive process of meaning making (Park 2005). Only through cognitive adaptation can a person transform intensely stressful life experiences. As Park (2005) writes, "The meaning-making model of coping emphasizes the dynamic, meaning-making aspects of coping, which are particularly relevant in situations that are not solvable or reparable, such as trauma or loss" (p. 710).

Park articulates that every person has two sets of meanings. First, there is global meaning, a combination of global beliefs, goals, and assumptions that can be considered as a person's overall meaning of life. Global meanings translate into daily meaning in the way they influence interpretations of the world, daily strivings and projects, and a subjective sense of meaningfulness associated with feelings of life satisfaction and positive affect (Park 2005). Secondly, there is situational meaning, a meaning that a person gives to a specific life event they experience (Park 2005), such as a hurricane, flood, or other natural disaster. If one's situational meaning contradicts their global meaning, they will experience a sense of distress. This distress acts as the fire that fuels the intrapsychic meaning-making process.

Meaning making is a cognitive processing of life events that involves either the reappraisal of situational meaning or the altering of one's global beliefs to accommodate the possibility of the distressing event. Accommodation of global beliefs can be in either the positive or negative direction. Distress dissipates when there is no longer conflicting forms of meaning, thus ending the meaning-making process (Park 2016).

Janoff-Bulman (1992) suggests there are three global assumptions a person needs to hold in order to experience mental health and well-being: the world is benevolent; the world is meaningful; and the self is worthy. However, when a person experiences extreme stress or trauma, as is the case in natural disasters, the three aforementioned assumptions are shattered. The world is not experienced as benevolent when a tsunami can swallow an entire village without warning. The world is not meaningful when hurricanes can bury teachers and children under the desks, chairs, roofs, and walls of a formerly beloved school. The self is not worthy when saving a brother, a mother, a child, or a neighbor from a wild fire is not possible before narrowly escaping flames engulfing one's home.

When global assumptions are shattered, the rebuilding process allows for three possible experiences. First, a person may not be able to restore assumptions that are key to mental well-being, resulting in continued psychological distress. A second possibility is that a person is able to restore previously held assumptions and thus returns to a baseline level of functioning of mental health. The third possibility is that a person may experience new levels of functioning that are higher than baseline: new ways of experiencing the self, relating to others, or connections to the world or to transcendence. This last possibility has been conceptualized as posttraumatic growth (Tedeschi and Calhoun 2009) or stress-related growth (Park 2005). The two ideas, while conceptualized slightly differently, both carry with them that bad things happen and that by moving through the bad things, one can find intrinsically positive experiences. Both capture the idea that growth is possible not in spite of, but because of, a feeling of brokenness. A negative event such as a disaster is allowed to stay—as it should—intrinsically negative. However, by moving through the stressful situation, one discovers something new about themselves, the world, or others that is intrinsically positive.

There are hundreds of studies that support meaning making and the process of PTG across multiple contexts. Currently, there is a growing body of research that examines psychological growth in the specific context of natural and technological disaster and highlights the importance of meaning making to well-being. For example, in an interpretive phenomenological study of six farming women who experienced the 2010–2011 flooding in a rural section of Victoria, Australia, Carra and Curtin (2017) found that all women moved from a place of helplessness to adapting to change, and finally to experiencing self-discovery. The women who engaged in activities they found meaningful (e.g., photography, community work, farming, and gardening) reported experiences of positive psychological change. Similarly, after evaluating a sample of 57 survivors of the 2013 Colorado floods, Dursun et al. (2016) found evidence that meaning in life—and specifically the search for meaning in life after natural disasters—is related to the process of PTG. More support for meaning and PTG is evidenced by Guo et al. (2013) in a study of 339 adolescents who experienced the 2008 Sichuan earthquake in China. Their results found that meaning-focused coping was positively associated with a measure of PTG and related to positive mental health outcomes.

Evidence is accumulating that suggests it very well may be unethical for caretakers to ignore the role that positive psychology and PTG can play in preparing people for natural and technological disasters. Undoubtedly, an understanding of the meaning-making model and the pathways to posttraumatic growth will not stop climate change or disasters. However, the meaning-making paradigm can allow for an understanding of how psychology may be able to prepare a person for the disasters that will most certainly come. For example, if space can be made in one's global assumptions for climate change, and meaning can be made related to impending disasters before such an event, some negative psychological effects may be mitigated through the resiliency this process affords. Mental health professionals can encourage the development of factors related to PTG such as openness, optimism, self-efficacy, social support, and forgiveness in a person or in a community as another type of pre-disaster intervention. The literature on meaning in life and posttraumatic growth also provides post-disaster hope for people such as Guillermo and the millions of others who will be at some point asked to endure one if not multiple disasters. This research suggests that while one may not be able to make the world anew, one may be able to make themselves anew in positive ways and to create people and communities who may be weary but also wise. As Frankl (1969) reminds us, "when we are no longer able to change a situation…we are challenged to change ourselves" (p. 112).

Spirituality, Disaster, and Growth

Perhaps the most readily available and pre-packaged meaning-making systems are given to people through organized religion. Religion is one way a person is mentored into finding meaning. Religion has been considered from the psychological writings of Frankl (2000) as the search for the ultimate meaning. Thus it makes sense that religion and the related factor of spirituality would be variables of interest to a disaster mental health field considering meaning making and growth, especially given the ultimate meaning of the disaster is often what survivors question.

The field of positive psychology engaged world religions and moral philosophies in the process of identifying six core virtues that promote human goodness and flourishing: wisdom, courage, humility, justice, temperance, and transcendence (Peterson and Seligman 2004). Under the six core virtues, researchers identified 24 strengths of character that are pathways to the six core virtues (Niemiec 2013). It has been suggested that the 24 strengths of character are stable personality traits that can and do change after significant life events (Niemiec 2013). This has important implications for mental health care providers, as disaster is a significant life event that can encourage or discourage the development of character strengths. Strengths of character that have associations to trauma, meaning making, and growth include hope, forgiveness, gratitude, self-regulation, and most notably spirituality (Calhoun et al. 2000; Pargament et al. 2004; Park 2005; Werdel et al. 2014).

Spirituality has the potential to frame a person's life experience. For a person who claims a sense of spirituality, moving through experiences of great stress such as natural disasters will evoke not only psychological but spiritual questions that will be integrated into their meaning-making process. While psychologists and theologians may separate their fields of study, a person attempting to make sense of a disaster may not be so inclined to separate these factors in their search for meaning.

The potential for integrating spirituality and psychology is supported by a recent study by the Pew Research Center (2015) that found that almost 77% of Americans identify with a religion. This means that the majority of people who experience disaster claim a religion. Additionally, research suggests that people with a predisaster religiosity who continue to engage with religion have lower levels of psychological distress (Chan and Rhodes 2013). Ali et al. (2012) found that three years post-disaster, self-reports of being "religious minded" correlated with lower PTSD symptoms in a sample of survivors of the 2005 Pakistani earthquake. Similarly, Chan and Rhodes (2013) found that in a sample of 386 low-income mothers surveyed before, one year after, and four years after Hurricane Katrina, negative religious coping was associated with psychological distress, and positive religious coping was associated with PTG. Their research also found that religious participants who engaged in church prior to the hurricane and who continued to remain engaged in church experienced psychological growth. The relationship between pre- and post-disaster religiousness and post-disaster PTG is accounted for in part by positive religious coping, or the experience of "a secure relationship with a transcendent force, a sense of spiritual connectedness with others, and a benevolent world view" (Pargament et al. 2011, p. 51). However, positive religious coping is not the only way to engage religion in times of stress and trauma. Negative religious coping, or the feeling of being punished or abandoned by God, is another possible response and is found to have a negative association with well-being after stressful life events (Werdel et al. 2014).

It has been suggested that in times of extreme stress and trauma, religion may be the most unfailing way to make meaning (Park 2005); therefore, understanding the nuances of religious coping is important in disaster work. Spiritual and religious texts consider the question of the existence of suffering. Why does suffering exist? What is our role and relationship to suffering? What is the meaning and purpose of suffering? While no one answer exists, religion and spirituality engage the question of suffering in a way that psychology does not. While psychology can provide understandings of processes and outcomes of stress and trauma, "in regard to why stress and trauma exist in the life of a person sitting across from the therapist, the silence can be deafening at times" (Werdel and Wicks 2012, p. 159). In such times of suffering, the question of the goodness of a silent ultimate spirit or God may readily be raised.

That this question might be raised by anyone who has experienced a natural disaster is to be expected. Anyone who has looked at pictures from before and after Category 5 hurricanes ripped through homes, or who has been asked to don protective gear before returning to piles of broken 2×4's, nails, and carpet to find barely recognizable matter, understandably questions the existence of God. Anyone who has been asked to have a funeral for a spouse, a sister, a mother, a father, or a brother when no recognizable body was recoverable from flood waters that potentially graved them in mud piles understandably questions the benevolent God. Anyone who has read a story of mass graves after earthquakes destroyed too many bodies to bury as unique people understandably questions an all-powerful deity. Natural disasters, by token of their profound desecration, hold for survivors many questions of how to reconcile disaster and a deity.

A theodicy is an attempt to make sense of evil and suffering in the world and the presence of God. A theodicy "explores five interrelated theological-philosophical questions: (1) the origin of evil; (2) the nature of evil; (3) the problem of evil; (4) the reason for evil; and (5) the end of evil" (Scott 2015, p. 65). Research has provided evidence for the idea that spirituality is multifaceted and that it includes both positive and negative factors and associations with well-being. For some who claim a deity, the face of God is comforting. For others, the face of God is questioned. For others still, theirs is both a comforting and a punishing God. One's image of God may reveal one's underlining assumptions of how to answer a theodicy (Doka 2002). A person's theodicy can alter their perception of stressful life experiences; consequently, it also influences their emotional experiences such as satisfaction with life (Hall and Johnson 2001; Musick 2000). A theodicy formed from a person's spiritual or religious perspective may provide meaning and purpose in a world filled with existential anxiety produced by life's unanswerable questions (Crews 1986). Or a person's theodicy may fuel loneliness, guilt, shame, anxiety, or depression.

While the term theodicy can be considered the realm of theology, psychology has examined the mental health implications of theodicies as well (Wilt et al. 2016). Hale-Smith et al. (2012) developed the Views of Suffering Scale (VOSS), a 30-item instrument to measure a person's belief about suffering and God. The scale captures theodicies and beliefs grounded predominately in the Judeo-Christian perspective, but also includes other theisms including Buddhism, Hinduism, and Atheism (Hale-Smith et al. 2012). Ten subscales are captured in the VOSS:

1. Encounter: a belief that God is encountered by experiencing and questioning suffering;
2. Soul-building: a belief that God uses suffering to build people's character and virtues;
3. Overcoming: a belief that God is good and that humans can diminish personal suffering through turning to God in faith, prayer, and good deeds;
4. Providence: a belief that God has providential control over suffering and that suffering is part of God's plan for good purposes;
5. Suffering-God: a belief that God suffers along with them and through this gives suffering meaning;
6. Divine Responsibility: a belief in free will and that God is all-good and all-powerful and can change suffering within chosen boundaries;
7. Limited Knowledge: a belief that God does not have knowledge of the future and so cannot prevent suffering;
8. Retribution: a belief that suffering is linked to past wrongdoings;
9. Random: a belief that suffering is random and without purpose; and
10. Unorthodox: a belief that God permits or causes suffering.

Empirical research on theodicy suggests important connections to mental health. In a recent study by Harris et al. (2018), the relationship between a retribution theodicy and spiritual distress was examined in a sample of 214 veterans seeking spiritually-integrated care for PTSD and moral injury. Retribution theodicy, defined as "a belief that evil is punishment for sins in a just world" (Harris et al. 2018, p. 240), was a significant predictor of spiritual distress. The implications suggest that the ways a person thinks about God's relationship to suffering has connections to their well-being.

Exline et al. (2017), in a sample of 454 Christian U.S. undergraduates, found evidence to support that benevolent theodicies, a belief in a loving God, and religious engagement and experiences of positive relationships with God predicted psychological growth. In a study by McElroy-Heltzel et al. (2018), 466 adult survivors of the 2016 Louisiana flood completed measures of benevolent theodicies, belief violations, and post-disaster PTSD symptoms. Results evidenced that a person's belief violations positively correlated to PTSD symptoms. This suggests that when a natural disaster such as a flood disrupts global meaning in life, negative psychological implications will follow. However, the research also evidenced that when survivors had a benevolent theodicy (providence theodicy, a suffering-God theodicy, or a soul-building theodicy), PTSD symptoms were buffered.

Research is still needed to more deeply understand the relationships between theodicies, religious meaning making, and posttraumatic growth. However, the evidence to date suggests that the way a person attempts to make sense of evil and suffering in the world and the presence of God is not a question for theologians alone. Confronting the question of suffering is a core task of religion; however, psychology must also engage the implications of using religion to confront suffering in the context of meaning making. In the case of natural disasters, this need for engagement may be especially true. Therefore, it will be essential to disaster mental health care providers to understand not only the psychological research on theodicy but also the broader connections of images of God, religious coping, and posttraumatic growth.

Certainly, psychology is not religion and religion is not psychotherapy. Perhaps Frankl (2000) said it best when he wrote, "whoever tries to make psychotherapy into an *ancilla theologiae*…not only robs it of the dignity of an autonomous science but also takes away the potential value it might have for religion" (p. 81). However, research exists that suggests people use religion in the meaning-making process and that religious forms of coping have psychological implications that can encourage or discourage post-disaster growth. At minimum, mental health workers must be aware of the relationships between religion and meaning in coping. At best, the mental health field will develop in ways that will be growth focused and spiritually informed.

Growth-Focused and Spiritually-Informed Practices and Competencies

Existing research presents an argument for growth-focused and spirituality-informed practices and competencies to be included in disaster mental health. For interventions and competencies to be growth-focused, research suggests a need for the infusion of positive psychology broadly, and posttraumatic growth specifically, into training and practice. This would include pre-disaster training that encourages promotion of strengths of character such as self-regulation, gratitude, forgiveness, and spirituality and post-disaster interventions that include PTG work.

Researchers have highlighted the need for mental health practitioners to work in developing competencies related to adaption to climate change (Doherty and Clayton 2011; Kazdin 2009). Such interventions could include the infusion of meaning making and growth. Tedeschi and Calhoun (2009) have argued that PTG work is not a new form of therapy but rather that it seeks to integrate evidence-based practices with a growth-oriented approach. Direct interventions to encourage PTG are believed to have negative effects rather than positive so then rather than search for or encourage growth directly, 10 principles best direct the role of expert companion (Tedeschi and Calhoun 2009, pp. 224–225):

1. Acknowledge the difficulty of the situation.
2. To the extent possible, be there through the difficulties.
3. Be willing to listen to the hard parts of the story.

4. Relate to the client through his or her world view.
5. Accept apparent "illusions" as useful to the client.
6. Help the client manage anxiety and other emotions.
7. Help the client move from brooding rumination to more constructive reflection.
8. Notice and remark about the strengths and changes that come from the struggle.
9. Do not offer platitudes.
10. Listen in a way that allows you to be changed.

When considering the application to post-disaster clinical work, growth-oriented ideas may readily be integrated into care if the clinician is aware of the utility of doing so. However, without direction, integration of growth-oriented approaches, such as those outlined by the PTG literature, may be integrated poorly if at all.

For interventions and competencies to be spiritually informed suggests not that all spiritual content needs to be outsourced to religious communities, but rather to consider the place for mental health workers to guide people in religious or spiritual meaning making as it relates to psychological well-being. While religious communities can have a vital role to play in disaster work (Wisner 2010), the mental health component of disaster work cannot be outsourced to religious leaders if they are not trained to consider the psychological implications of using religious and spiritual meaning making after stress and trauma.

Research has begun to outline some of the ways that disaster work may be spiritually informed pre- and post-disaster. Aten et al. (2014) suggest five specific interventions that can be used to integrate spirituality into care in times of disaster (p. 90):

1. Creating a disaster clergy/mental health professional collaboration: a process by which mental health practitioners engage spiritual leaders in the community to build collaborative relationships that will be in place in times of disaster;
2. Disaster planning in which mental health professionals assist religious professionals when disaster happens to engage in response planning;
3. Psychological first aid for the religious community;
4. Consultation, outreach, and advocacy in which mental health practitioners provide training to religious leaders;
5. Clinical services that integrate spirituality into treatment.

The five suggestions proposed demand an integrative care approach in which religious leaders and mental health professionals are in intentional dialogue and practice. This approach is holistic, interdisciplinary, and both community- and person-centered. This approach also aligns with the reality of natural and technological disasters in which the impacts are varied, widespread, and idiosyncratic.

Drawing upon both psychological first aid literature and religious coping literature, Aten et al. (2018) developed Spiritual First Aid (SFA), a spiritually-informed disaster mental health intervention. SFA is "an evidence-informed intervention designed to facilitate survivors' holistic wellness and improve their post-disaster trajectory of recovery" (McElroy-Heltzel et al. 2018, p. 14). Grounded in research that suggests positive religious coping can prevent or buffer post-disaster distress, this approach takes a strengths-based approach to spiritual distress by encouraging people who claim a sense of religiosity or spirituality to access positive spiritual resources such as benevolent theodicies (McElroy-Heltzel et al. 2018). However, this work is possible only when disaster mental health workers are spiritually informed. Like the implications in the growth-oriented literature, there is a need for mental health professionals to recognize the importance of spirituality in mental health and to have the desire and ability to respond.

The research work at the level of intervention is at an early stage. There is great space available to develop interventions encouraging growth and resiliency by drawing upon the research literature on positive psychology and strengths of character such as self-regulation, gratitude, forgiveness, and spirituality. Such interventions hold the promise of promoting psychological flourishing and human goodness in the context of disaster. Space still exists in psychological preparations and interventions for working with the tension of the question of how human suffering evokes the question of a deity. While certainly theologians have work to do in reflection on climate change, it is unethical for religious content to be completely outsourced to traditional religious leaders, churches, synagogues, and other sacred spaces. Mental health professionals have an ethical obligation to address multicultural needs of clients in ways that integrate psychological and spiritual questions. The experience of God is not reserved for theological questions and reflection. The question is not one of how we as care professionals can integrate growth-oriented literature and spirituality into treatment, but how can we provide sound ethical care if we do not?

Conclusion

French existentialist Jean-Paul Sartre (1943/1989) wrote that "human life begins on the far side of despair" (p. 119). Sartre suggests that authentic living demands a sense of transformation that comes only from having moved through profound sadness. Without encountering despair and moving through it, one never encounters true existence. Sartre and positive psychological literature alike suggest that while natural and technological disasters are intrinsically negative, for the person who finds a way to walk through the destruction, there—on the other side of the despair—is the possibility of an authentically different and positively transformed life. The way a person engages deity in response to destruction and how they reconcile theism and suffering will in part determine on which end of despair they land.

Climate change is intrinsically negative. As the earth warms, the sea levels rise, and extreme weather patterns cause the sky to drown the earth in fits of rain, transforming once passable dirt roads into heaps of mud, some people in some communities will be swallowed whole. Some people in some communities will survive, wait for water levels to diminish, and continue life as it was before the floods. Some people in some communities will see that the road can no longer be salvaged as a road. Rather than attempt to do so, they will use their energy and resources to slowly and deliberately build a new road and a new way out. They will develop the eyes to see the heaps of mud and pools of flooded water as something new. For some people on the other side of despair, the pools of thick mud in destroyed roadways will be claimed as the sacred place where lotus flowers may one day root, grow, and perhaps bloom.

References

Ali, M., Farooq, N., Bhatti, M. A., & Kuroiwa, C. (2012). Assessment of prevalence and determinants of posttraumatic stress disorder in survivors of earthquake in Pakistan using Davidson Trauma Scale. *Journal of Affective Disorders, 136*(3), 238–243. https://doi.org/10.1016/j.jad.2011.12.023.

Arnberg, F. K., Johannesson, K. B., & Michel, P. (2013). Prevalence and duration of PTSD in survivors 6 years after a natural disaster. *Journal of Anxiety Disorders, 27*(3), 347–352. https://doi.org/10.1016/j.janxdis.2013.03.011.

Aten, J. D., O'Grady, K. A., Milstein, G., Boan, D., & Schruba, A. (2014). Spiritually oriented disaster psychology. *Spirituality in Clinical Practice, 1*(1), 20–28. https://doi.org/10.1037/scp0000008.

Aten, J. D., Shannonhouse, L., Davis, D. E., Davis, E. B., Hook, J. N., Van Tongeren, D. R., & Leonard, L. (2018). *Spiritual first aid*. Manuscript in preparation.

Baird, K., & Kracen, A. C. (2006). Vicarious traumatization and secondary traumatic stress: A research synthesis. *Counseling Psychology Quarterly, 19*(2), 181–188. https://doi.org/10.1080/09515070600811899.

Bryan, C. J., Elder, W. B., McNaughton-Cassill, M., Osman, A., Hernandez, A. M., & Allison, S. (2013). Meaning in life, emotional distress, suicidal ideation, and life functioning in an active duty military sample. *The Journal of Positive Psychology, 8*(5), 444–452. https://doi.org/10.1080/17439760.2013.823557.

Calhoun, L. G., Cann, A., Tedeschi, R. G., & McMillan, J. (2000). A correlational test of the relationship between posttraumatic growth, religion, and cognitive processing. *Journal of Traumatic Stress, 13*(3), 521–527. https://doi.org/10.1023/A:1007745627077.

Calhoun, L. G., & Tedeschi, R. G. (Eds.). (2006). *Handbook of posttraumatic growth: Research and practice*. Mahwah: Erlbaum.

Carra, K. A., & Curtin, M. (2017). Posttraumatic growth among Australian farming women after a flood. *Journal of Loss and Trauma, 22*(5), 453–463. https://doi.org/10.1080/15325024.2017.1310506.

Chan, C. S., & Rhodes, J. E. (2013). Religious coping, posttraumatic stress, psychological distress, and posttraumatic growth among female survivors four years after Hurricane Katrina. *Journal of Traumatic Stress, 26*(2), 257–263. https://doi.org/10.1002/jts.21801.

Crews, C. F. (1986). *Ultimate questions: A theological primer*. Mahwah: Paulist Press.

Dar, K. A., Iqbal, N., Prakash, A., & Paul, M. A. (2018). PTSD and depression in adult survivors of flood fury in Kashmir: The payoffs of social support. *Psychiatry Research, 261*, 449–455. https://doi.org/10.1016/j.psychres.2018.01.023.

Dezutter, J., Casalin, S., Wachholtz, A., Luyckx, K., Hekking, J., & Vandewiele, W. (2013). Meaning in life: An important factor for the psychological well-being of chronically ill patients? *Rehabilitation Psychology, 58*(4), 334–341. https://doi.org/10.1037/a0034393.

Doherty, T. J., & Clayton, S. (2011). The psychological impacts of global climate change. *American Psychologist, 66*(4), 265–276. https://doi.org/10.1037/a0023141.

Doka, K. (2002). How could God? In J. Kauffman (Ed.), *Loss of the assumptive world: A theory of traumatic loss* (pp. 49–54). New York: Brunner-Routledge.
Dursun, P., Steger, M. F., Bentele, C., & Schulenberg, S. E. (2016). Meaning and posttraumatic growth among survivors of the September 2013 Colorado floods. *Journal of Clinical Psychology, 72*(12), 1247–1263. https://doi.org/10.1002/jclp.22344.
Exline, J. E., Hall, T. W., Pargament, K. I., & Harriott, V. A. (2017). Predictors of growth from spiritual struggle among Christian undergraduates: Religious coping and perceptions of helpful action by God are both important. *The Journal of Positive Psychology, 12*(5), 501–508. https://doi.org/10.1080/17439760.2016.1228007.
Frankl, V. (1969). *The will to meaning: Foundations and applications of logotherapy*. New York: Penguin.
Frankl, V. (2000). *Man's search for ultimate meaning*. New York: Basic Books.
Gifford, R. (2008). Psychology's essential role in alleviating the impacts of climate change. *Canadian Psychology, 49*(4), 273–280. https://doi.org/10.1037/a0013234.
Guo, M., Gan, Y., & Tong, J. (2013). The role of meaning-focused coping in significant loss. *Anxiety, Stress, & Coping: An International Journal, 26*(1), 87–102. https://doi.org/10.1080/10615806.2011.627507.
Hale-Smith, A., Park, C. L., & Edmondson, D. (2012). Measuring beliefs about suffering: Development of the Views of Suffering Scale. *Psychological Assessment, 24*(4), 855–866. https://doi.org/10.1037/a0027399.
Hall, M. E. L., & Johnson, E. L. (2001). Theodicy and therapy: Philosophical/theological contributions to the problem of suffering. *Journal of Psychology and Christianity, 20*(1), 5–17.
Harris, J. I., Usset, T., & Cheng, Z. H. (2018). Theodicy and spiritual distress among veterans managing posttraumatic stress. *Spirituality in Clinical Practice, 5*(4), 240–250. https://doi.org/10.1037/scp0000170.
Intergovernmental Panel on Climate Change. (2007). *Climate change 2007: The physical science basis. Contributions of working group I to the fourth assessment report of the intergovernmental panel on climate change*. Cambridge: Cambridge University Press.
Janoff-Bulman, R. (1992). *Shattered assumptions: Towards a new psychology of trauma*. New York: Simon & Schuster.
Kazdin, A. E. (2009). Psychological science's contributions to a sustainable environment: Extending our reach to a grand challenge of society. *American Psychologist, 64*(5), 339–356. https://doi.org/10.1037/a0015685.
Levy-Gigi, E., Richter-Levin, G., & Szabolcs, K. (2014). The hidden price of repeated traumatic exposure: Different cognitive deficits in different first-responders. *Frontiers in Behavioral Neuroscience, 8*, 281. https://doi.org/10.3389/fnbeh.2014.00281.
McElroy-Heltzel, S. E., Davis, E. B., Davis, D. E., Aten, J. D., Hook, J. N., Van Tongeren, D. R., & Hwang, J. (2018). Benevolent theodicies protect against PTSD following a natural disaster. *Journal of Psychology & Christianity, 37*(1), 6–16.
Moser, S. C. (2007). More bad news: The risk of neglecting emotional responses to climate change information. In S. C. Moser & L. Dilling (Eds.), *Creating a climate for change: Communicating climate change and facilitating social change* (pp. 64–80). New York: Cambridge University Press.
Musick, M. A. (2000). Theodicy and life satisfaction among Black and White Americans. *Sociology of Religion, 61*(3), 267–287. https://doi.org/10.2307/3712579.
Niemiec, R. M. (2013). VIA character strengths: Research and practice (the first 10 years). In H. H. Knoop & A. Delle Fave (Eds.), *Cross-cultural advancements in positive psychology: Vol. 3. Well-being and cultures: Perspectives from positive psychology* (pp. 11–29). New York: Springer.
Pargament, K. I., Desai, K. M., & McConnell, K. M. (2006). Spirituality: A pathway to posttraumatic growth or decline? In L. G. Calhoun & R. G. Tedeschi (Eds.), *Handbook of posttraumatic growth: Research and practice* (pp. 121–137). Mahwah: Erlbaum.

Pargament, K. I., Feuille, M., & Burdzy, D. (2011). The brief RCOPE: Current psychometric status of a short measure of religious coping. *Religions, 21*(1), 51–76. https://doi.org/10.3390/rel2010051.

Pargament, K. I., Koenig, H. G., Tarakeshwar, N., & Hann, J. (2004). Religious coping methods as predictors of psychological, physical and spiritual outcomes among medically ill elderly patients: A two-year longitudinal study. *Journal of Health Psychology, 9*(6), 713–730. https://doi.org/10.1177/1359105304045366.

Park, C. L. (2005). Religion as a meaning-making framework in coping with life stress. *Journal of Social Issues, 61*(4), 707–729. https://doi.org/10.1111/j.1540-4560.2005.00428.x.

Park, C. L. (2008). Testing the meaning making model of coping with loss. *Journal of Social & Clinical Psychology, 27*(9), 970–994. https://doi.org/10.1521/jscp.2008.27.9.970.

Park, C. L. (2016). Meaning making in the context of disasters. *Journal of Clinical Psychology, 72*(12), 1234–1246. https://doi.org/10.1002/jclp.22270.

Peterson, C., & Seligman, M. E. P. (2004). *Character strengths and virtues: A handbook and classification.* Washington: American Psychological Association.

Pew Research Center. (2015). *America's changing religious landscape.* Washington: Pew Forum on Religion and Public Life.

Sartre, J. P. (1943/1989). *No exit and three other plays.* New York: Vintage.

Scott, M. S. M. (2015). *Pathways in theodicy: An introduction to the problem of evil.* Minneapolis: Fortress Press.

Steel, Z., Silove, D., Phan, T., & Bauman, A. (2002). Long-term effect of psychological trauma on the mental health of Vietnamese refugees resettled in Australia: A population-based study. *The Lancet, 360*, 1056–1062. https://doi.org/10.1016/S0140-6736(02)11142-1.

Tedeschi, R. G., & Calhoun, L. G. (2009). The clinician as expert companion. In C. L. Park, S. C. Lechner, M. H. Antoni, & A. L. Stanton (Eds.), *Medical illness and positive life change: Can crisis lead to personal transformation?* (pp. 215–235). Washington: American Psychological Association.

Weissbecker, I. (2011). Introduction: Climate change and human well-being. In I. Weissbecker (Ed.), *Climate change and human well-being: Global challenges and opportunities* (pp. 1–15). New York: Springer.

Werdel, M. B., Dy-Liacco, G. S., Ciarrochhi, J. W., Wicks, R. J., & Breslford, G. M. (2014). The unique role of spirituality in the process of growth following stress and trauma. *Pastoral Psychology, 63*(1), 57–71. https://doi.org/10.1007/s11089-013-0538-4.

Werdel, M. B., & Wicks, R. J. (2012). *Primer on posttraumatic growth: An introduction and guide.* Hoboken: Wiley.

Wilt, J. A., Exline, J. J., Grubbs, J. B., Park, C. L., & Pargament, K. I. (2016). God's role in suffering: Theodicies, divine struggle, and mental health. *Psychology of Religion and Spirituality, 8*(4), 352–362. https://doi.org/10.1037/rel0000058.

Wisner, B. (2010). Untapped potential of the world's religious communities for disaster reduction in an age of accelerated climate change: An epilogue & prologue. *Religion, 40*(2), 128–131. https://doi.org/10.1016/j.religion.2009.12.006.

Chapter 5
Veterans and Disaster Response Work: The Role of Continued Service in Meaning Making and Recovery

Shannon E. McCaslin, Damian Bramlett, Katherine Juhasz, Margaret Mackintosh, and Shauna Springer

The consequences of natural and technological disasters often demand an organized and skilled response to manage chaotic and stressful conditions. In the wake of such disasters, responders are given the opportunity to support and positively impact individuals and communities in tangible ways that may be felt not only in the immediate days post-event, but in subsequent months and even years afterward. Military veterans possess skills and abilities that may make them uniquely suited for contributing to effective disaster response. Additionally, continued service through disaster work may provide an opportunity for veterans to engage in meaningful activity and to connect with veteran and civilian peers, as well as the greater community, as they transition out of military service. This chapter explores the "fit" of veterans for disaster response work through the lens of positive psychology, which emphasizes strengths, values, growth, and meaning making (Schulenberg 2016). Further, we review how engagement in disaster response work may be beneficial for veterans coping with challenges encountered during the transition from the military to civilian settings and with mental health conditions.

Military veterans comprise less than 10% of the U.S. population (National Center for Veterans Analysis and Statistics 2018; Parker et al. 2017). Approximately 90% of veterans are male; however, the number of women enlisting in the military is

S. E. McCaslin (✉)
National Center for PTSD, Dissemination and Training Division, VA Palo Alto HCS (MPD), Menlo Park, CA, USA

Department of Psychiatry and Behavioral Sciences, Stanford University, Stanford, CA, USA
e-mail: Shannon.McCaslin@va.gov

D. Bramlett · K. Juhasz · M. Mackintosh
National Center for PTSD, Dissemination and Training Division, VA Palo Alto HCS (MPD), Menlo Park, CA, USA

S. Springer
Suicide Prevention Initiatives, Tragedy Assistance Program for Survivors, Arlington, VA, USA

S. E. Schulenberg (ed.), *Positive Psychological Approaches to Disaster*,
https://doi.org/10.1007/978-3-030-32007-2_5

increasing, resulting in a growing number of women veterans (National Center for Veterans Analysis and Statistics 2018). Nearly three-quarters of veterans are over the age of 50 (Parker et al. 2017). Veterans who served during the Gulf War and Vietnam era currently comprise the largest cohort (approximately 13,900,000), followed by veterans who served post-9/11 (approximately 2,800,000) (National Center for Veterans Analysis and Statistics 2018).

As in the general population, a minority of veterans have been diagnosed with a mental health condition (Kessler et al. 2005; Kessler et al. 1995). Prevalence estimates of mental health conditions among veterans vary considerably depending on methodological factors, such as study sample (e.g., patient versus general population sample), type of assessment (e.g., diagnostic interview versus self-report questionnaire), and service characteristics (e.g., combat versus non-combat, era of service) (Kok et al. 2012). In one study of over four million physical and mental health treatment seeking U.S. veterans, 25.7% met criteria for one or more mental health conditions (Trivedi et al. 2015). Conditions examined included depression (13.5%), posttraumatic stress disorder (PTSD; 9.3%), substance use disorder (8.3%), anxiety disorder (4.8%), and serious mental illness (SMI; 3.7%). Trivedi et al. (2015) also reported that comorbidity among mental health conditions was extremely common. For example, 92.7% of those veterans with PTSD, 83.8% of those with depression, and 87.9% of those with substance use disorders were diagnosed with at least one additional mental health condition.

In recent decades, studies of PTSD among veterans have proliferated. Among the first studies to carefully examine rates of mental health diagnoses among veterans, the National Vietnam Veterans Readjustment Study (NVVRS; Kulka et al. 1990) recruited a nationally representative sample of Vietnam era veterans and civilians and found higher rates of current prevalence of PTSD (15.2% for men, 8.5% for women) among those who had served in combat. These estimates of PTSD compared to current PTSD rates of 2.5% found for non-combat theater Vietnam era male veterans, 1.2% for male Vietnam era civilians, 1.1% for women veterans, and 0.3% for women civilians (Kulka et al. 1990). Moreover, the rates of PTSD were significantly higher among those with high levels of combat exposure, with 35.8% of men and 17.5% of women meeting criteria for PTSD (Kulka et al. 1990). In further analyses of this sample, rates for other psychiatric conditions, such as depression and substance use, were also found to be higher among veterans with high combat exposure (Jordan et al. 1991). Later follow-up with a subsample of the NVVRS Vietnam theater veterans (n = 699, the National Vietnam Veterans Longitudinal Study; NVVLS) found that PTSD scores remained stable over time for most veterans, with 16% reporting an exacerbation in symptoms and 8% reporting an improvement in symptoms (Steenkamp et al. 2017).

In a sample of over 2,500 Gulf War veterans, rates of PTSD assessed by self-report varied by time of assessment (Wolfe et al. 1999). At approximately 1 week following redeployment to the U.S., the rate of PTSD was 3%. When re-assessed approximately 18–24 months later, rates of PTSD in this sample had increased to 8%. Kok et al. (2012) conducted a meta-analysis of studies examining PTSD prevalence among non-treatment seeking or injured military personnel that had served in

Iraq and Afghanistan, finding average PTSD prevalence rates of 3% pre-deployment and 5% at post-deployment. In contrast, a meta-analysis of post-9/11 veteran studies, which included a broader range of participants (i.e., both treatment-seeking and non-treatment-seeking veterans), estimated a PTSD prevalence rate of 23% (Fulton et al. 2015). Thus, it is important to consider the immense variability in the sociodemographic factors, historical contexts, and personal experiences of servicemember and veteran populations when considering rates of psychological conditions in these populations.

The study of moral injury and its impact on veterans' psychological well-being also has increased sharply over the past decade. Moral injury is a term that has been used to refer to events encountered (i.e., participated in, witnessed, or learned about) during military service, which conflict with or violate the servicemembers' held moral values or ethical beliefs (Drescher et al. 2011; Litz et al. 2009). Events range broadly in type and include harming or killing others in war (e.g., enemy combatants or civilians), failing to act, witnessing or learning about harm done to others, or betrayal by fellow servicemembers. Broader conceptualizations, wherein the emotional and psychological sequelae are less tied to a specific event, have also been put forth (e.g., Springer 2018). In a nationally representative sample of 564 U.S. combat veterans, 10.8% acknowledged perpetrating events that met criteria for moral injury, 25.5% endorsed having experienced or witnessed transgressions (things seen as morally wrong; e.g., harming of civilians or enemy prisoners) by others, and 25.5% endorsed betrayal by others. In this study, endorsement of these types of events were positively associated with combat severity, and the perpetration of acts by one's self was related to an increased risk for current mental health conditions and suicidal ideation (Wisco et al. 2017). Additionally, the experience of betrayal was associated with post-deployment suicide attempts. Experience of moral injury is often related to reports of shame and guilt (Held et al. 2018; Jinkerson 2016; Litz et al. 2009). The experience contributes to increased psychological distress, exacerbates symptomatology (e.g., PTSD), and can lead to a sense of struggle regarding one's identity and/or spirituality (Drescher and Foy 2008; Held et al. 2018; Litz et al. 2009; Maguen et al. 2009). Combat-related guilt has also been linked to suicidal ideation among Vietnam combat veterans with PTSD (Hendin and Haas 1991). Further, exposure to morally injurious events has been associated with social withdrawal and isolation and a loss of, and search for, meaning and purpose (Currier et al. 2015; Drescher et al. 2011; Held et al. 2018).

Research on healing from moral injury noted that, along with mental health treatment, attempts at reparation or repair (e.g., participation in prosocial undertakings) and peer support may play important roles in meaning making and recovery (Held et al. 2018). Drescher and Foy (2008) emphasized that engagement in activities that are consistent with one's values can be healing and can contribute to a restored sense of meaning. Indeed, approaches that have been developed for the treatment of moral injury incorporate assessment of values and engaging in actions aligned with one's personal values (Litz et al. 2009; Springer 2018). Restoring a sense of meaning in one's life through these types of activities can have implications for recovery from mental illness. Positive sense of meaning in one's life has been linked to lower

PTSD severity among a sample of 174 veterans who served during a variety of eras, with this relationship being strongest among those with lower versus higher levels of depression (Owens et al. 2009). Adaptive meaning making of traumatic experiences was found to partially mediate the relationship between morally injurious event exposure and mental health outcomes among 131 veterans who served in Iraq and/or Afghanistan (Currier et al. 2015). The authors emphasized the importance of examining meaning-oriented interventions to help veterans recover their sense of purpose. Volunteerism, and within this, disaster response work, may be a path through which a sense of meaning can be restored.

While a small proportion of veterans will experience mental health symptoms severe enough and for long enough to be diagnosed with a current psychiatric disorder, many veterans experience transient symptoms related to separation from the military and transition to the civilian setting (Koenig et al. 2014). The shift from active duty servicemember (e.g., living and working amongst other servicemembers) to veteran (e.g., served honorably on active duty in the U.S. Armed Forces) can mean the loss of a structured and familiar military cultural context, in which one's role is well-defined, as well as the loss of a strong and supportive social network. The distinctiveness of military culture is reflected in the values and beliefs that are reinforced throughout military service and often continue to remain a part of one's identity even after separation from military service. For example, servicemembers are expected to put mission and country above self, which often contrasts with the individualism of broader American culture. Servicemembers often experience a deep sense of camaraderie, fostered by long periods of being away from home and family, and training that explicitly focuses on unit cohesion and trust building, both of which are critical for optimal performance (Ahern et al. 2015; Goodwin et al. 2018). Moreover, while entry into military service and culture can be an intense and consuming experience over an extended period of time (e.g., basic training, which ranges from 6–16 weeks depending on service branch, occupation, and era; "Length of Basic Training" 2019), the transition out of military service stands in stark contrast, often taking mere days. It is not surprising that although separation from military service may allow servicemembers greater personal control over their lives, it may also simultaneously lead to feelings of disconnection and isolation.

Professionally, while serving in the military, individuals acquire job-related skills and often hold positions that require high levels of responsibility and astute responsiveness to changing environments (e.g., leading personnel in combat missions while ensuring their safety and well-being, handling highly sensitive documents and information, adapting to frequently changing situations). Moreover, many of the character strengths explicated in the field of positive psychology (Niemiec 2014, 2018; Niemiec and McGrath 2019; Peterson and Seligman 2004) are also those that are developed and reinforced over the course of military service. These include bravery, persistence, authenticity/honesty, citizenship, leadership, self-regulation, humor, and gratitude. These strengths, skills, and abilities often go unrecognized in the civilian context, which is in contrast to the experience while serving, where achievements and honors may be explicitly recognized through medals, pins, or patches displayed on one's uniform (McCaslin et al. 2015). In addition, learned skills may not easily translate to a civilian occupation. However, the combination of military cultural values, character strengths, and skills acquired during military service can make veterans an ideal fit for work within the volunteer service sector, which may provide additional opportunities for validation of skills and achievements.

Continued Service Through Volunteer Opportunities

Selfless service is a core military value and one which many servicemembers continue to view as important even following separation from military service. However, opportunities for continued engagement in service-related activities may not be readily apparent to veterans who have the capacity and desire to serve. The importance of providing pathways to continued service for veterans in areas such as disaster response, emergency services, and health care professions, has been emphasized (Brock et al. 2013). Continued service opportunities can also be an avenue through which veterans utilize their specialized skills and connect with veteran peers. Moreover, service opportunities may facilitate healthy community reintegration through increased connection with civilian peers and the greater community (Kranke et al. 2017a, b).

In the general population, volunteer service is associated with positive psychosocial and mental health outcomes (for reviews see Adams and Boscarino 2015; Jenkinson et al. 2013; and Thoits and Hewitt 2001). Decreases in depression and improved well-being have been demonstrated among older adults, with a notable relationship between volunteer service and improved mortality (Lum and Lightfoot 2005; Morrow-Howell et al. 2003; Musick et al. 1999). In these studies, increased opportunity for social interaction was suggested as one avenue through which volunteer service may impact mortality. Jenkinson et al. (2013) conducted a systematic review of 40 published investigations of the impact of volunteerism on mental and physical health outcomes. The studies compared those who volunteered with non-volunteers and were varied with regards to design, including cohort studies ($n = 17$) and a smaller number of randomized clinical trials (RCTs; $n = 7$) and non-RCTs ($n = 4$). The observational (cohort) studies demonstrated that volunteer service had a positive impact on depression, life satisfaction, and general well-being, but did not impact physical health. These positive effects were not replicated in the controlled studies, although the authors noted that methodological issues might have played a role (e.g., small sample size), prompting a call from the authors for more rigorous research in this area. In a national sample of 2,681 adults, Thoits and Hewitt (2001) found a reciprocal relationship of well-being to volunteerism: those with higher well-being were more likely to volunteer and volunteering led to increased well-being. Given the potential benefits of volunteer service on psychological health and well-being, consideration of the potential benefits of continued meaningful service for veterans should be further explored.

Although there is a relative lack of research examining the impact of volunteerism on veterans' mental health and well-being, two recent studies have suggested that these types of opportunities hold promise to benefit veterans in multiple ways (Lawrence et al. 2017; Matthieu et al. 2017). Matthieu et al. (2017) examined the impact of participation in a national civic service program among 346 post-9/11 veterans. Veterans participated in a structured fellowship program that was a component of a national non-profit organization called "The Mission Continues" (see Table 5.1 for a description). Participation resulted in significant improvement across mental health and well-being outcomes including improvements in overall health, decreased PTSD and depression symptoms, and decreased difficulty in everyday functioning due to emotional health concerns (Matthieu et al. 2017). Additionally, perceptions of social isolation and loneliness decreased while perceived social support, self-efficacy, and the belief that "life holds purpose and meaning" increased. Veterans with depression symptoms showed the most benefit in terms of having a positive purpose in life, enhanced social support, and decreased feelings of loneliness, while those meeting criteria for probable PTSD at the beginning of the study were more likely to show improvements in self-efficacy. Another study of 67 post-9/11 veterans with traumatic brain injury (TBI) who had participated in a similar "The Mission Continues" program found similar benefits (Lawrence et al. 2017). Veterans with PTSD demonstrated decreases in PTSD symptoms, decreases in feelings of isolation and loneliness, and increases in perceptions of self-efficacy and the availability of social support. In particular, the PTSD symptoms of numbness and detachment from others, activities, or surroundings appeared to drive the overall decrease in PTSD scores. The authors concluded

Table 5.1 Examples of veteran-focused volunteer and disaster response relevant organizations

Name	Mission type	Mission objectives	Website
Team Rubicon[a]	Disaster response	Brings skilled and experienced veterans and first responders together for disaster response.	https://teamrubiconusa.org/
The Mission Continues	Community service	Empowers veterans to find purpose through community service.	https://missioncontinues.org/
Tragedy Assistance Program for Survivors (TAPS)	Community service	Veterans serve as volunteer mentors for children who have lost a loved one during military service.	https://www.taps.org/
Travis Manion Foundation	Community service	Veterans serve as ambassadors to help young adults develop character and leadership skills.	https://www.travismanion.org/

[a]This organization primarily focuses on disaster relief. The organizations included are examples of organizations that may provide volunteer opportunities. Inclusion does not constitute an endorsement of any of the organizations, or of one organization over another.

that increased social support played a key role in improved psychological outcomes among this group of veterans.

The following vignette is fictional and one example of a veteran participating in volunteer disaster relief work. It is provided to illustrate the various points made throughout the chapter.

Cynthia spent 4 years on active duty in motor transportation (truck driver) in the U.S. Marine Corps. While in the Marines, she was deployed on tours in both Afghanistan and Iraq. During her deployments, she experienced multiple losses and witnessed serious injuries of both close friends and leaders. After completing her term of service, she decided to separate from the military and pursue a college degree at a local university. However, soon after transitioning out of military service, she frequently felt as if she did not fit into the college setting. She experienced sadness from no longer having the close relationships and a sense of purpose she had while serving. The other students were often younger and many did not even seem aware that there were military servicemembers deployed to ongoing wars and conflicts. She felt as if there was a huge gap between her experiences and theirs.

While in college, Cynthia joined the campus' Student Veteran Organization; this organization gave her a sense of belonging and camaraderie that she had not experienced since separating from the Marine Corps. Through various service projects that the veteran organization conducted during the school year, Cynthia discovered she had a passion for helping others in their time of need, finding that this resonated with her time in the military. She found her leadership and organizational abilities, honed during her military service, made her an asset during these activities. As she neared graduation, Cynthia started to look for other ways that she could be involved in activities that provided the same type of camaraderie and opportunities to make a difference as those she had experienced on campus. A fellow student veteran mentioned that he was a member of a disaster response volunteer organization and shared with her how his affiliation with this organization was meaningful to him: he had forged relationships with community members and was able to use the skills he had learned in the military to help disaster survivors, which gave him a renewed sense of purpose.

Cynthia was excited to hear about his experiences and started the membership application process for this organization online. She completed the required training modules, to include a background check and creating a personal profile, which highlighted some of her military skills and experiences. Cynthia began to receive requests to deploy to disaster sites but she found it hard to get time off from her new job or to make the deployments fit her schedule. After a few months, Cynthia finally received a disaster deployment request that worked with her schedule, and she had enough vacation time saved up to deploy. Within 72 hours of sending her availability, Cynthia was on a plane for a week-long deployment to assist with recent flooding in a large U.S. city.

Veteran Engagement in Disaster Work

The opportunities that disaster response work, and more broadly volunteer service, afford for veterans may be congruent with the ways in which their military service influenced their global sense of meaning (e.g., fundamental beliefs about themselves and their world and sense of purpose; Park 2016). For example, valuing service to one's community and country is a value consistent across both military and volunteer service. Disaster response work may provide a venue through which they can serve in a meaningful capacity while simultaneously utilizing their skills and abilities (Wilson 2012). Moreover, through such work, veterans may find social connection and support. Veterans often have rigorous and specialized training in areas relevant to successful disaster response work, including the abilities to manage and lead groups, and to prepare and react to stressful or threatening work environments, as well as training in foreign languages, medical skills, and logistics (e.g., Hardison et al. 2017). Following separation from the military, veterans may find that their specialized experience and skills become "invisible" and there are few opportunities to utilize the training they have received. Disaster response is a context in which these kinds of skills and training are critically needed and highly valued. Disaster-affected communities benefit when responders are highly skilled in areas such as completing threat assessments, organizing group-based efforts, establishing leadership structures, creating communication networks and developing effective logistical systems. Veterans often have these skills and may become assets to disaster-affected communities as they can rapidly organize components of a disaster response plan and work effectively as members of a team.

Previous research has found that veterans are more prepared than non-veterans for disasters (e.g., maintain a complete emergency preparedness kit; Der-Martirosian et al. 2014; Geiger 2016) and they have a greater willingness to provide direction and leadership to others during an emergency (Geiger 2016). Perhaps due to their increased self-efficacy in the area of disaster response, research also has demonstrated that veterans were less likely to "leave their community during a mandatory evacuation" (Der-Martirosian et al. 2014). While this might place them at an increased risk of harm, it also suggests that veterans may have a greater sense of being able to cope with these types of situations based on previous experiences (e.g., having experienced comparable or more dangerous situations).

Additionally, many veterans have received health care skills training (e.g., medics, nurses, doctors) while serving in the military and have gained experience providing emergency medical aid (e.g., advanced first aid, basic life support, combat lifesaver, etc.) within a team environment (Brock et al. 2013). Similar to many first responder groups, veterans often learn how to address a wide range of problems in a pressured, high-stakes environment. Indeed, these skills were recognized by the Federal Government through the Helping Veterans Become Physician Assistants Initiative (Brock et al. 2013), which was instituted in 2011 to facilitate veterans' entry into a career as a Physician Assistant (PA). The Health Resources and Services Administration (HRSA) developed work groups to focus on the recruitment and training of qualified veterans in PA careers (Brock et al. 2013). Veterans applying to PA programs were found to have greater health care experience than their non-veteran peers while demonstrating similar academic ability (Brock et al. 2013). Reciprocally, veterans may benefit when they can use their experience, knowledge, and skills to assist disaster-impacted communities.

Meaning Making and Connectedness in the Context of Disaster Work

Given that only a small fraction of the U.S. population serves in the U.S. military (approximately 0.4% active duty; Parker et al. 2017), many civilians rarely interface with servicemembers or veterans. This can lead to a disconnect wherein the majority of civilians have little understanding of military culture or their experiences, and it has led some to observe the existence of a civilian-veteran divide, or gap (Bankhead 2016; Zucchino and Cloud 2015). As noted earlier, the lack of civilian understanding or appreciation for veterans' experiences and acquired knowledge and skills, combined with the loss of a strong military social support network, can contribute to a sense of isolation following military separation.

Kranke et al. (2017b) examined qualitative narratives from nine veterans who described their personal experience of responding to disaster as part of a larger organization (Team Rubicon; see Table 5.1, which provides examples of veteran-focused volunteer and disaster response relevant organizations). Team Rubicon (TR) is a global disaster response non-profit organization founded by two U.S. Marine Corps veterans in 2010. TR is unique in that the majority (more than two-thirds) of their employees and volunteers are veterans (Team Rubicon 2017); others include first responders or civilians with specific skillsets (e.g., logistics, foreign language translation, communications). In this qualitative study, thematic analysis was used to elucidate major areas of importance across the nine narratives. Five key themes were derived from the interviews with veterans. Two themes related to the characteristics derived from their military service that prepared them for disaster work: (1) the ability to use skills acquired during military service, and (2) relative (to civilians) preparedness for difficult and potentially traumatic tasks (e.g., exposure to dead bodies, destruction of property and infrastructure) and the chaos that can accompany disaster work. A third theme highlighted the gratification veterans experienced that came from being of service to the community. Veterans also emphasized the importance of having post-disaster peer support from fellow veterans with whom they had responded to the disaster. The authors put forth that this type of peer support and camaraderie during and following disaster response may lessen the sense of isolation that many veterans experience following military separation. Finally, consistent with the military's emphasis on selfless service and dedication to the mission, veterans expressed that identification as a helper to those impacted by disaster was beneficial to their mental health and self-esteem

(Kranke et al. 2017b). In this way, deploying to serve in a disaster-response capacity aligns in many ways with war-time deployments – veterans use the skills they have gained in the military in altruistic ways that enhance their communities.

Opportunities to work alongside civilian disaster response volunteers during a disaster deployment may facilitate positive civilian/veteran connections and enhance veterans' perceptions of their own abilities to connect with civilians in the future, while also increasing civilians' understanding of the applicable skills which veterans often possess (Kranke et al. 2017b). Kranke and colleagues (2017b) suggested that, in this way, disaster work may be an avenue through which civilians can connect with veterans, decreasing negative beliefs or stigma related to veteran status, and increasing a sense of belongingness. In addition, many of the elements which bond individuals together in war-time deployments also help veterans and civilians transcend the civilian-military cultural divide during disaster-response deployments. Aligned with Sherif's earlier research (1958), the mutual interdependence created by engagement in a superordinate task (i.e., disaster response operations) can create a powerful affinity between veterans and civilians who serve side by side.

Upon reporting to the disaster response organization's lead team member at the main organization site, Cynthia found herself both excited and nervous as to what this new experience would bring. She was greeted by the leadership team, issued an official volunteer shirt and given her assignment. Given her military background, Cynthia was tasked with assisting the logistics team on her first day, where she would help obtain and transport food and materials essential to keeping the operation functioning smoothly. Because of her ability to speak Spanish, Cynthia was assigned to a response team where she supported the team's mission by translating between the response team's leadership and local people who spoke Spanish. For the remainder of the week, Cynthia would assist a strike team in clearing debris ("mucking out") from flooded homes. Of note, this is a task which can be both physically and emotionally exhausting.

The next day, Cynthia left the main site for the first time with her response team and was stunned by what she saw: the destruction of entire neighborhoods from flood waters. What Cynthia saw in this disaster brought back memories of the destroyed homes and neighborhoods that she witnessed overseas while in the Marines. Her teams' assignment for the day was to muck out a house; this involved the removal of anything and everything within the home that had been touched by flood waters. Drywall, carpeting, flooring, furniture, appliances… it all had to be removed and discarded since floodwaters are considered to be contaminated. Although the work was physically exhausting, as the hours rolled by Cynthia felt a sense of clear purpose, thinking of the impacted families for whom this support was critical, and she began developing friendships with fellow teammates.

The rest of the week consisted of mucking out homes, talking with affected locals, and developing closer bonds with her fellow volunteers. On her flight home, Cynthia reflected on the devastation from the event that she had witnessed, the people she had helped, and the new friends she had made. It was gratifying to feel that she and her teammates had contributed to the recovery of that community. For example, assisting uninsured families with the first steps of getting their homes rebuilt by saving them thousands of dollars in demolition labor. For her, the work was satisfying both physically and emotionally.

To her surprise, several days after returning home, Cynthia started to notice that she felt more down than she had in a while. She recalled the leadership team on her disaster response sharing that some volunteers might feel this way once they returned home. They had noted that because of the intensity of and focus on responding to the disasters' impact, and the close bonds that often develop between teammates, there may be a sense of loss once the response is over. They also warned that the intense work could leave one both physically and emotionally exhausted and emphasized the importance of self-care and rest when returning home. To Cynthia, the feelings were similar to those she had experienced shortly after separating from military service.

Risk for Deleterious Impact of Disaster Response Among Veterans

Exposure to disaster as well as combat exposure has been found to increase the likelihood of developing PTSD (e.g., Beaglehole et al. 2018; Jordan et al. 1991; Thomas et al. 2017) and depression (Bonde et al. 2016; for a review, see Quevillon et al. 2016). In comparison to professional disaster workers, volunteer workers have been found to experience more negative mental health impact (see Thormar et al. 2010, for a review). In a review of research focused on the mental health impact of disaster volunteering in the general population, a number of factors were highlighted as potential contributors to mental health concerns post-response (Thormar et al. 2010). These factors included identification with disaster victims (e.g., as a friend), level of exposure to disaster-related gruesome events, anxiety sensitivity, and paucity of social support following disaster response. However, it is largely unknown the extent to which these risk factors differ between veteran and civilian populations.

While much research has focused on the potentially deleterious impact of traumatic stress exposure on psychological health (e.g., development of PTSD and depression), there is less research focused on resilience among those who have experienced traumatic stressors. The results from current research are mixed with regards to whether previous combat exposure might place a veteran at higher risk of a psychological disorder following disaster exposure. Some studies have found no increased risk for the development of PTSD following witnessing or experiencing another traumatic event subsequent to combat exposure (Schnurr et al. 2004), whereas others have indicated post-combat service trauma exposure may be likely to exacerbate PTSD (Long et al. 1994; McCarroll et al. 1997; Solomon et al. 1987 in Jayasinghe et al. 2006). In an examination of utility workers deployed to the September 11, 2001, World Trade Center (WTC) attacks (9/11) and exposed to disaster-related stressors (e.g., working in conditions with potential for danger, witnessing destruction, and seeing human remains), it was shown that utility workers with a history of combat exposure were not more likely to develop PTSD than non-veteran colleagues (Jayasinghe et al. 2006). Based on their systematic review, Jenkinson et al. (2013) noted that the length or the demands of volunteer service might be important factors in how the service impacts psychological health. Specifically, maximum benefits may be achieved when there is enough volunteer service to gain the type of benefits described earlier but not so much that one becomes "burned out" or experiences negative impact related to the volunteer service becoming a burden.

These findings are consistent with those of another study of 2,136 older adults (ages 64–68) which demonstrated a non-linear relationship between the number of volunteer hours and psychological well-being (Windsor et al. 2008). Essentially, psychological well-being was lowest among those who either did not volunteer or volunteered at the highest levels, while a moderate amount of volunteer service appeared to be most strongly related to positive psychological well-being. Importantly, several studies have documented a similar curvilinear relationship between symptoms of PTSD and levels of posttraumatic growth, wherein moderate levels of symptoms were related to the highest levels of growth (e.g., Butler et al. 2005; McCaslin et al. 2009; Shakespeare-Finch and Lurie-Beck 2014). This body of research indicates that there may be an optimal level of disaster response work which could positively impact psychological well-being and meaning making.

Promoting Resilience During and Following Disaster Response

Disaster work can provide an opportunity for veterans to utilize specialized skills and develop new skills, access character strengths, engage in meaningful and purposeful service, and connect with other disaster responders and members of the community. Drawing from previous research, we posit that many veterans may be uniquely qualified for disaster response work and that such engagement can be a powerful facilitator of reintegration and emotional well-being, specifically increasing a personal sense of purpose and decreasing self-isolation. However, by their very nature, disaster settings may expose workers to varying levels of personal risk and indirect exposure to death and injury. Other characteristics, such as long hours and arduous and often emotionally taxing work, make it critical that factors related to self-care be addressed (Quevillon et al. 2016). Furthermore, veterans may be less likely than civilians to engage in self-care. One study of post-9/11 veterans found that veterans reported less self-compassion than their civilian counterparts (based on general population norms) (Dinh et al. 2014). Given that military training emphasizes that team members focus on the mission and de-emphasizes focus on oneself, ensuring that veterans engaged in disaster work are receiving support at both organizational and peer levels is critical (Quevillon et al. 2016). For those who are in a position to provide support to veterans engaged in disaster response, such as mental health providers or team leaders, understanding military culture can be an essential piece for providing effective interventions.

As noted above, the relative lack of emphasis on self-care and reluctance to seek help can prevent many veterans from receiving needed support. Teaching volunteers explicitly about the importance of self-care both during and after a disaster response operation can be essential, as prioritizing self-care over operational objectives may not come naturally to veterans. In other words, the individual comes first, and the mission comes second; a stark contrast to what servicemembers are taught during military service.

As an example of teaching self-care, TR acknowledges the existence of "Post-Deployment Blues" (https://teamrubiconusa.org/blog/getting-ahead-of-post-deployment-blues/). This term refers to an observed increase in levels of depression and other mental health symptoms following a volunteer's return home from a disaster response deployment. To fully understand the phenomenon of post-deployment blues, it is important to note that the experience of bonding with others and working toward a common goal is viewed in very positive ways by many, if not most, veterans. Veterans and civilians alike form strong affinities and become emotionally vulnerable with one another in ways that can be deeply meaningful, and even therapeutic, for both parties. Humor and storytelling are some of the consistently enjoyable parts of these shared deployments. Those who may have expended large amounts of time and resources during their disaster response deployment might experience more keenly the depletion of their physical and mental health as well as of their self-care abilities. Further, for volunteers who have experienced higher levels of traumatic exposure, morally injurious events or high levels of pre-disaster response mental health symptoms, the post-disaster response period may require them to access additional self-supportive services, whether it is increased social support from friends, family and other veterans, or access to formal mental health care services. Opportunities for healing and posttraumatic growth might be realized with appropriate focus on self-care and management of post-service health.

Educational and coping tools that are easy to access and use during and following disaster deployment can promote self-care and connection to resources should they be needed. Quevillon et al. (2016) reviewed strategies for self-care both during and after a disaster deployment. In addition to those methods discussed by Quevillon and colleagues, there are also a number of free, publicly available tools that have been developed by the Department of Veterans Affairs (VA) and Department of Defense (DoD) for use on one's computer or mobile device (i.e., web programs and mobile "apps"). The skills and strategies addressed by these types of programs or apps range from those that provide brief, on the spot, coping strategies (e.g., mindfulness, breathing exercises) to those that can help to address longer-standing concerns in the months following disaster work (e.g., symptoms of insomnia, posttraumatic stress, depression). While anyone could benefit from using these tools, they contain content and resources tailored specifically for servicemembers and veterans. We have provided a summary of some of these tools (see Table 5.2, which provides a summary of some of the available apps and online programs).

Table 5.2 Mobile application (apps) and online programs to promote self-care

Name of resource	Tool type	Description	For more information
AIMS for Anger Management	App (iOS, Android) Online program	Content includes psychoeducation about problematic anger and how to manage angry reactions, opportunities for finding support, the ability to create an anger management plan, anger tracking, and tools to help manage angry reactions.	App: https://www.ptsd.va.gov/appvid/mobile Online program:*www.veterantraining.va.gov/aims*
Mindfulness Coach	App (iOS, Android)	Designed to support independent mindfulness practice. The app also contains information about mindfulness and PTSD symptoms, increasing resilience and self-awareness, improving emotional balance, and building positive skills.	https://www.ptsd.va.gov/appvid/mobile/mindfulcoach_app.asp
Moving Forward	App (iOS) Online program	Designed to provide practical information and interactive tools for effective problem-solving and stress reduction.	App: https://www.ptsd.va.gov/appvid/mobile Online program:*www.veterantraining.va.gov/movingforward*
Provider Self-care Toolkit	Website	This toolkit contains assessment tools, strategies, and resources to help providers who are working with those who have experienced trauma practice self-care.	https://www.ptsd.va.gov/professional/treat/care/toolkits/provider/
PTSD Coach	App (iOS, Android)	Designed to provide psychoeducation about PTSD and tools for coping with the symptoms related to PTSD. The app includes a feature for screening and tracking symptoms, convenient, easy-to-use tools to help handle stress in the moment, and direct links to support and help.	https://www.ptsd.va.gov/appvid/mobile/ptsdcoach_app.asp
PTSD Coach Online	Website	Includes 17 different tools to help manage stress, as well as common issues following trauma, such as sleep difficulties, trauma reminders, and anger. The program is guided by video coaches.	https://www.ptsd.va.gov/apps/ptsdcoachonline

The products listed in the table were developed by the Department of Veterans Affairs (VA) and/or the Department of Defense (DoD). Visit www.ptsd.va.gov/appvid/mobile or www.veterantraining.va.gov for information about additional products and programs.

Before leaving the disaster response deployment, Cynthia and her teammates had exchanged numbers and encouraged each other to stay in touch. She reached out to one of her new friends, who also described that he had similar feelings. They talked and discussed what they were each doing to take care of themselves and agreed to keep closely in touch over the next couple of weeks. After talking, Cynthia felt better, and within weeks she felt like herself again. She continued to build time into her days for self-care, including walks outside and time to read before bed. Cynthia felt she had the social support she had been seeking since separating from the military. She appreciated the chance to put her abilities to work for those who needed help, providing her a greater sense of meaning. She was looking forward to the next opportunity to respond and to continue serving her community as she had in the military.

Summary

This chapter proposes that volunteerism, and in particular disaster response work, may offer an avenue for military veterans wishing to continue to serve their communities and to apply skills and abilities fostered during military service (e.g., leadership and organization skills, ability to work as an effective team member). Such service may promote meaning making (e.g., engagement in activities aligned with one's values), opportunities to utilize skills and character strengths, and social connectedness. Given the importance of social support in recovery from trauma (e.g., Steenkamp et al. 2017), ways in which social connectedness can be increased should garner additional attention. Moreover, volunteerism often provides an opportunity to connect with others, while sharing or working toward a common goal (not unlike military service). Finally, it is unknown whether service to disaster-impacted communities may have a healing effect for those coping with moral injuries related to their combat service. There is a need for a deeper understanding of the impact of disaster response involvement on the mental health of veterans and the factors related to these experiences that can lead to increased well-being, meaning making, and posttraumatic growth.

Acknowledgements This work was supported with resources and the use of facilities at the National Center for PTSD, Dissemination and Training Division, Menlo Park, CA. The contents of this manuscript do not represent the views of the Department of Veterans Affairs or the United States Government.

References

Adams, R. E., & Boscarino, J. A. (2015). Volunteerism and well-being in the context of the World Trade Center terrorist attacks. *International Journal of Emergency Mental Health, 17*, 274–282.

Ahern, J., Worthen, M., Masters, J., Lippman, S. A., Ozer, E. J., & Moos, R. (2015). The challenges of Afghanistan and Iraq veterans' transition from military to civilian life and approaches to reconnection. *PLoS One, 10*, e0128599. https://doi.org/10.1371/journal.pone.0128599.

Bankhead, C. (2016). *Resolving the civilian-military divide through an examination of select members of the United States Army profession* (Masters thesis). Retrieved from http://digitalcommons.liberty.edu/cgi/viewcontent.cgi?article=1435&context=masters.

Beaglehole, B., Mulder, R. T., Frampton, C. M., Boden, J. M., Newton-Howes, G., & Bell, C. J. (2018). Psychological distress and psychiatric disorder after natural disasters: Systemic review and meta-analysis. *British Journal of Psychiatry, 213*, 716–722. https://doi.org/10.1192/bjp.2018.210.

Bonde, J. P., Utzon-Frank, N., Bertelsen, M., Borritz, M., Eller, N. H., Nordentoft, M., et al. (2016). Risk of depressive disorder following disasters and military deployment: A systematic review with meta-analysis. *The British Journal of Psychiatry, 208*, 330–336. https://doi.org/10.1192/bjp.bp.114.157859.

Brock, D., Bolon, S., Wick, K., Harbert, K., Jacques, P., Evans, T., Abdullah, A., & Gianola, F. J. (2013). The military veteran to physician assistant pathway: Building the primary care workforce. *Academic Medicine, 88*, 1890–1894. https://doi.org/10.1097/ACM.0000000000000011.

Butler, L. D., Blasey, C. M., Garlan, R. W., McCaslin, S. E., Azarow, J., Chen, X., Desjardins, J. C., Dimiceli, S., Seagraves, D. A., Hastings, A., Kraemer, H. C., & Spiegel, D. (2005). Posttraumatic growth following the terrorist attacks of September 11, 2001: Cognitive, coping and trauma symptom predictors in an internet convenience sample. *Traumatology, 11*, 247–267. https://doi.org/10.1177/153476560501100405.

Currier, J. M., Holland, J. M., Drescher, K., & Foy, D. (2015). Initial psychometric evaluation of the moral injury questionnaire-military version. *Clinical Psychology & Psychotherapy, 22*, 54–63. https://doi.org/10.1002/cpp.1866.

Der-Martirosian, C., Strine, T., Atia, M., Chu, K., Mitchell, M. N., & Dobalian, A. (2014). General household emergency preparedness: A comparison between veterans and nonveterans. *Prehospital and Disaster Medicine, 29*, 134–140. https://doi.org/10.1017/S1049023X1400020X.

Dinh, J., Walser, R., Best, S., Cloitre, M., & McCaslin, S. (2014, March). *Self-compassion is associated with emotional stress and perceived health-related functioning in veterans*. Poster presented at the 72nd annual scientific meeting of the American Psychosomatic Society, San Francisco.

Drescher, K. D., & Foy, D. W. (2008). When they come home: Posttraumatic stress, moral injury, and spiritual consequences for veterans. *Reflective Practice: Formation and Supervision in Ministry, 28*, 85–102.

Drescher, K. D., Foy, D. W., Kelly, C., Leshner, A., Schutz, K., & Litz, B. (2011). An exploration of the viability and usefulness of the construct of moral injury in war veterans. *Traumatology, 17*, 8–13. https://doi.org/10.1177/1534765610395615.

Fulton, J. J., Calhoun, P. S., Wagner, H. R., Schry, A. R., Hair, L. P., Feeling, N., et al. (2015). The prevalence of posttraumatic stress disorder in Operation Enduring Freedom/Operation Iraqi Freedom (OEF/OIF) veterans: A meta-analysis. *Journal of Anxiety Disorders, 31*, 98–107. https://doi.org/10.1016/j.janxdis.2015.02.003.

Geiger, J. F. (2016). Emergency preparedness of veterans and nonveterans. *Journal of Emergency Management, 14*, 327–333. https://doi.org/10.5055/jem.2016.0297.

Goodwin, G. F., Blacksmith, N., & Coats, M. R. (2018). The science of teams in the military: Contributions from over 60 years of research. *American Psychologist, 73*, 322–333. https://doi.org/10.1037/amp0000259.

Hardison, C. M., Krueger, T. C., Shanley, M. G., Saavedra, A. R., Clague, A., Crowley, J. C., Martin, J., Wong, J. P., & Steinberg, P. S. (2017). *What veterans bring to civilian workplaces: A prototype toolkit for helping private-sector employers understand the nontechnical skills developed in the military*. Santa Monica: RAND Corporation. https://www.rand.org/pubs/tools/TL160-1.html.

Held, P., Klassen, B. J., Hall, J. M., Friese, T. R., Bertsch-Gout, M. M., Zalta, A. K., & Pollack, M. H. (2018). "I knew it was wrong the moment I got the order": A narrative thematic analysis of moral injury in combat veterans. *Psychological Trauma*, May 3 epub. https://doi.org/10.1037/tra0000364.

Hendin, H., & Haas, A. P. (1991). Suicide and guilt as manifestations of PTSD in Vietnam combat veterans. *American Journal of Psychiatry, 148*, 586–591. https://doi.org/10.1176/ajp.148.5.586.

Jayasinghe, N., Jedel, S., Leck, P., Difede, J., Klausner, E., & Spielman, L. (2006). Are male disaster workers with Vietnam military service at greater risk for PTSD than peers without combat history? *The Journal of Nervous and Mental Disease, 194*, 859–863. https://doi.org/10.1097/01.nmd.0000244831.73276.6c.

Jenkinson, C. E., Dickens, A. P., Jones, K., Thompson-Coon, J., Taylor, R. S., Rogers, M., et al. (2013). Is volunteering a public health intervention? A systematic review and meta-analysis of the health and survival of volunteers. *BMC Public Health, 13*, 773–782. https://doi.org/10.1186/1471-2458-13-773.

Jinkerson, J. D. (2016). Defining and assessing moral injury: A syndrome perspective. *Traumatology, 22*, 122–130. https://doi.org/10.1037/trm0000069.

Jordan, B. K., Schlenger, W. E., Hough, R., Kulka, R. A., Weiss, D., Fairbank, J. A., & Marmar, C. R. (1991). Lifetime and current prevalence of specific psychiatric disorders among Vietnam veterans and controls. *Archives of General Psychiatry, 48*, 207–215.

Kessler, R. C., Chiu, W. T., Demler, O., & Walters, W. E. (2005). Prevalence, severity, and comorbidity of 12-month DSM-IV disorders in the national comorbidity survey replication. *Archives of General Psychiatry, 62*, 617–627. https://doi.org/10.1001/archpsyc.62.6.617.

Kessler, R. C., Sonnega, A., Bromet, E., Hughes, M., & Nelson, C. B. (1995). Posttraumatic stress disorder in the national comorbidity survey. *Archives of General Psychiatry, 52*, 1048–1060. https://doi.org/10.1001/archpsyc.1995.03950240066012.

Koenig, C. J., Maguen, S., Monroy, J. D., Mayott, L., & Seal, K. H. (2014). Facilitating culture-centered communication between health care providers and veterans transitioning from military deployment to civilian life. *Patient Education and Counseling, 95*, 414–420. https://doi.org/10.1016/j.pec.2014.03.016.

Kok, B. C., Herrell, R. K., Thomas, J. L., & Hoge, C. W. (2012). Posttraumatic stress disorder. associated with combat service in Iraq or Afghanistan: Reconciling prevalence differences between studies. *The Journal of Nervous and Mental Disease, 200*, 444–450. https://doi.org/10.1097/NMD.0b013e3182532312.

Kranke, D., Gin, J., Saia, R., Schmitz, S., Weiss, E. L., & Dobalian, A. (2017a). Destigmatizing experiences of combat veterans engaged in civilian disaster relief: Implications for community transition. *Advances in Social Work, 18*(2), 630–644. https://doi.org/10.18060/21275

Kranke, D., Weiss, E. L., Heslin, K. C., & Dobalian, A. (2017b). "We are disaster response experts": A qualitative study on the mental health impact of volunteering in disaster settings among combat veterans. *Social Work in Public Health, 32*, 500–509. https://doi.org/10.1080/19371918.2017.1365033.

Kulka, R. A., Schlenger, W. E., Fairbank, J. A., Hough, R. L., Jordan, B. K., et al. (1990). *Trauma and the Vietnam War generation: Report of findings from the National Vietnam Veterans Readjustment Study*. New York: Brunner/Mazel.

Lawrence, K. A., Matthieu, M. M., & Robertson-Blackmore, E. (2017). Completion of a veteran-focused civic service program improves health and psychosocial outcomes in Iraq and Afghanistan veterans with a history of traumatic brain injury. *Military Medicine, 182*, e1763–e1770. https://doi.org/10.7205/MILMED-D-16-00150.

Length of basic training and your first paycheck. (2019). Retrieved from https://www.military.com/join-armed-forces/length-of-basic-training-and-your-first-paycheck.html.

Litz, B. T., Stein, N., Delaney, E., Lebotwitz, L., Nash, W. P., Silva, C., & Maguen, S. (2009). Moral injury and moral repair in war veterans: A preliminary model and intervention strategy. *Clinical Psychology Review, 29*, 695–706. https://doi.org/10.1016/j.cpr.2009.07.003.

Long, N., Chamberlain, K., & Vincent, C. (1994). Effect of the Gulf war on reactivation of adverse combat-related memories in Vietnam veterans. *Journal of Clinical Psychology, 50*, 138–144.

Lum, T. Y., & Lightfoot, E. (2005). The effects of volunteering on the physical and mental health of older people. *Research on Aging, 27*, 31–55.

Maguen, S., Metzler, T. J., Litz, B. T., Seal, K. H., Knight, S. J., & Marmar, C. R. (2009). The impact of killing in war on mental health symptoms and related functioning. *Journal of Traumatic Stress, 22*, 435–443. https://doi.org/10.1002/jts.20451.

Matthieu, M. M., Lawrence, K. A., & Robertson-Blackmore, E. (2017). The impact of a civic service program on biopsychosocial outcomes of post 9/11 US military veterans. *Psychiatry Research, 248*, 111–116. https://doi.org/10.1016/j.psychres.2016.12.028.

McCarroll, J. E., Ursano, R. J., & Fullerton, C. S. (1997). Exposure to traumatic death in disaster and war. In C. S. Fullerton & R. J. Ursano (Eds.), *Progress in psychiatry series, No. 51. Posttraumatic stress disorder: Acute and long-term responses to trauma and disaster* (pp. 37–58). Arlington: American Psychiatric Association.

McCaslin, S. E., de Zoysa, P., Butler, L. D., Hart, S., Marmar, C. R., Metzler, T. J., & Koopman, C. (2009). The relationship of posttraumatic growth to peritraumatic reactions and posttraumatic stress symptoms among Sri Lankan university students. *Journal of Traumatic Stress, 22*, 334–339. https://doi.org/10.1002/jts.20426.

McCaslin, S. E., Turchik, J. A., & Hatzfeld, J. J. (2015). Considerations in the treatment of veterans with posttraumatic stress disorder. In U. Schnyder & M. Cloitre (Eds.), *Evidence based treatments for trauma-related psychological disorders* (pp. 413–430). Cham: Springer. https://doi.org/10.1007/978-3-319-.

Morrow-Howell, N., Hinterlong, J., Rozario, P. A., & Tang, F. (2003). Effects of volunteering on the well-being of older adults. The *Journals of Gerontology Series B: Psychological Sciences and Social Sciences, 58*, S137–S145.

Musick, M. A., Herzog, A. R., & House, J. S. (1999). Volunteering and mortality among older adults: Findings from a national sample. *The Journals of Gerontology Series B: Psychological Sciences and Social Sciences, 54*, S173–S180.

National Center for Veterans Analysis and Statistics. (2018). Profile of veterans: 2016. Data from the American community survey. Accessed 9 May 2018 at https://www.va.gov/vetdata/docs/SpecialReports/Profile_of_Veterans_2016.pdf.

Niemiec, R. M. (2014). *Mindfulness and character strengths: A practical guide to flourishing*. Boston: Hogrefe.

Niemiec, R. M. (2018). *Character strengths interventions: A field guide for practitioners*. Boston: Hogrefe.

Niemiec, R. M., & McGrath, R. E. (2019). *The power of character strengths*. Cincinnati: VIA Institute on Character.

Owens, G. P., Steger, M. F., Whitesell, A. A., & Herrera, C. J. (2009). Posttraumatic stress disorder, guilt, depression, and meaning in life among military veterans. *Journal of Traumatic Stress, 22*, 654–657. https://doi.org/10.1002/jts.20460.

Park, C. L. (2016). Meaning making in the context of disasters. *Journal of Clinical Psychology, 72*, 1234–1246. https://doi.org/10.1002/jclp.22270.

Parker, K., Cilluffo, A., & Stepler, R. (2017). *Six facts about the U.S. military and its changing demographics*. Retrieved from http://www.pewresearch.org/fact-tank/2017/04/13/6-facts-about-the-u-s-military-and-its-changing-demographics/.

Peterson, C., & Seligman, M. E. P. (2004). *Character strengths and virtues: A handbook and classification*. Washington, DC: American Psychological Association; New York: Oxford University Press.

Quevillon, R. P., Gray, B. L., Erickson, S. E., Gonzalez, E. D., & Jacobs, G. A. (2016). Helping the helpers: Assisting staff and volunteer workers before, during, and after disaster relief operations. *Journal of Clinical Psychology, 72*, 1348–1363. https://doi.org/10.1002/jclp.22336.

Schnurr, P. P., Lunney, C. A., & Sengupta, A. (2004). Risk factors for the development versus maintenance of posttraumatic stress disorder. *Journal of Traumatic Stress, 17*, 85–95. https://doi.org/10.1023/B:JOTS.0000022614.21794.f4.

Schulenberg, S. E. (2016). Disaster mental health and positive psychology – Considering the context of natural and technological disasters: An introduction to the special issue. *Journal of Clinical Psychology, 72*, 1223–1233. https://doi.org/10.1002/jclp.22409.

Shakespeare-Finch, J., & Lurie-Beck, J. (2014). A meta-analytic clarification of the relationship between posttraumatic growth and symptoms of posttraumatic stress disorder. *Journal of Anxiety Disorders, 28*, 223–229. https://doi.org/10.1016/j.janxdis.2013.10.005.

Sherif, M. (1958). Superordinate goals in reduction of intergroup conflict. *American Journal of Sociology, 63*, 349–356.

Solomon, Z., Garb, R., Bleich, A., & Grupper, D. (1987). Reactivation of combat-related posttraumatic stress disorder. *American Journal of Psychiatry, 144*, 51–55.

Springer, S. (2018, April). *Veteran suicide, moral injury, and a theory-driven approach to effective treatment*. Workshop presented at the 51st annual meeting of the American Association of Suicidology, Washington.

Steenkamp, M. M., Schlenger, W. E., Corry, N., Henn-Haase, C., Qian, M., Li, M., et al. (2017). Predictors of PTSD 40 years after combat: Findings from the National Vietnam Veterans Longitudinal Study. *Depression and Anxiety, 34*, 711–722. https://doi.org/10.1002/da.22628.

Team Rubicon. (2017). Annual Report 2016. Los Angeles https://teamrubiconusa.org/app/uploads/2017/08/TR_2016_Annual-Report_web.pdf.

Thoits, P. A., & Hewitt, L. N. (2001). Volunteer work and well-being. *Journal of Health and Social Behavior, 42*, 115–131.

Thomas, M. M., Harpaz-Rotem, I., Tsai, J., Southwick, S. M., & Pietrzak, R. H. (2017). Mental and physical health conditions in U.S. combat veterans: Results from the National Health and Resilience in Veterans Study. *The Primary Care Companion for CNS Disorders, 19*(3), 17m02118. https://doi.org/10.4088/PCC.17m02118.

Thormar, S. B., Gersons, B. P. R., Juen, B., Marschang, A., Djakababa, M. N., & Olff, M. (2010). The mental health impact of volunteering in a disaster setting: A review. *The Journal of Nervous and Mental Disease, 198*, 529–538. https://doi.org/10.1097/NMD.0b013e3181ea1fa9.

Trivedi, R. B., Post, E. P., Sun, H., Pomerantz, A., Saxon, A. J., Piette, J. D., et al. (2015). Prevalence, comorbidity, and prognosis of mental health among U.S. veterans. *American Journal of Public Health, 105*, 2564–2569. https://doi.org/10.2105/AJPH.2015.302836.

Wilson, J. (2012). Volunteerism research: A review essay. *Nonprofit and Voluntary Sector Quarterly, 41*, 176–212.

Windsor, T. D., Anstey, K. J., & Rodgers, B. (2008). Volunteering and psychological well-being among young-old adults: How much is too much? *The Gerontologist, 48*, 59–70.

Wisco, B. E., Marx, B. P., May, C. L., Martini, B., Krystal, J. H., Southwick, S. M., & Pietrzak, R. H. (2017). Moral injury in U.S. combat veterans: Results from the National Health and Resilience in Veterans Study. *Depression and Anxiety, 34*, 340–347. https://doi.org/10.1002/da.22614.

Wolfe, J., Erickson, D. J., Sharkansky, E. J., King, D. W., & King, L. A. (1999). Course and predictors of posttraumatic stress disorder among Gulf War veterans: A prospective analysis. *Journal of Consulting and Clinical Psychology, 67*, 520–528.

Zucchino, D., & Cloud, D. S. (2015). U.S. military and civilians are increasingly divided. *The Los Angeles Times*. Retrieved from http://www.latimes.com/nation/la-na-warrior-main-20150524-story.html.

Chapter 6
The Hero's Journey to Resilience and Thriving in the Context of Disaster

Bruce W. Smith

During the fall of 1995, I was beginning to enter data and read through the questionnaires of people in Oklahoma City who were affected by the bombing of the Murrah Federal Building on the previous April 19. Ken Pargament, a mentor who had helped me design my first study of Midwest flood, had suggested that I include a new measure developed by Crystal Park and Larry Cohen on what they called "stress-related growth" (Park et al. 1996). It was a parallel measure to Rich Tedeschi and Larry Calhoun's now frequently used Posttraumatic Growth Inventory (Tedeschi and Calhoun 1996). As an afterthought, I included an open-ended question asking participants to describe any learning, growth, or benefits that they thought they had experienced since the bombing. What I saw in response to this question was not only a foreshadowing of positive psychology, but also an echo of something with deep resonance with our common human experience over thousands of years.

If you remember the Oklahoma City Bombing, you may also remember that the two people who were shown to be responsible were two American White men. At the time, there were frequent stories in the news about how these two men being from the same country where the bombing occurred may have made it that much harder for us to feel a bond and trust our neighbors. This was in stark contrast to the very consistent theme that I saw running through the responses to that simple open-ended question. Over and over, I read about how the sudden tragedy that took the lives of so many friends and family members gave the people of Oklahoma City a new sense of pride and appreciation for being part of such a wonderful community that they could count on. There was a common story that was clearly coming through in the response to the question that I very much do not think I would have seen in only examining the results of the multiple regression analyses (Pargament et al. 1998).

B. W. Smith (✉)
Department of Psychology, University of New Mexico, Albuquerque, NM, USA
e-mail: bwsmith@unm.edu

S. E. Schulenberg (ed.), *Positive Psychological Approaches to Disaster*,
https://doi.org/10.1007/978-3-030-32007-2_6

Since that fall in 1995, I have been to graduate school at Arizona State University, completed a functional neuroimaging postdoc at the National Institutes of Mental Health, and studied resilience in relation to an earthquake, first responder stress, avian flu and nuclear attack scenarios, chronic pain, cardiovascular disease, and cancer; and also came to learn about the chronic stress and daily hassles that affect college students and the general adult population. In 2008, our lab developed what has become a broadly used measure to assess resilience as the ability to bounce back from stress (Smith et al. 2008) and focused on identifying the kinds of psychosocial resources that are most important and targeted to foster and boost resilience and thriving (Smith et al. 2013). But there has been one thing that has never completely left the back of my mind, that has continued to come through in the words of so many that I have read about, and that I have found exceptionally hard to articulate in academic language.

In this chapter, I would like to take the extra flexibility and freedom that writing a chapter can sometimes afford to offer this to you as something to think about in what may be something of a more personal style. A clue to what I am going to say is of course in the title with the words "hero's journey" that may or may not already be familiar to you (Campbell 1949). But I want to ask for your patience and open mind in allowing me to come back to this phrase in a new way after I take you on the more familiar journey of academic writing. My plan is to begin by trying to clarify how at least I have come to define the words resilience and thriving, put these meanings in the context of positive psychology and the conventional things that we study to foster them, provide a foundation in some of the fresh and creative developments in enabling people to cope with stress, and then make a bridge back to what may be at the heart of what I was surprised by in the words of so many in Oklahoma City (Pargament et al. 1998).

What Are Resilience and Thriving in the Context of Disaster?

As with the words spirituality and mindfulness, I find myself frustrated with the broad, vague, and multiple meanings that people attach to the word resilience. That became a pet peeve of mine that I tried to do something about by creating what I called the "Brief Resilience Scale" back in 2008. I did my best to try to discover what the most original, basic, and conceptually clear meaning of the word was and settled on the familiar metaphor of bouncing back. This idea seems to be rooted in physics and engineering with what happens when a flexible material springs back to its original form after something pushes it off center (Merriam-Webster 2018). I have found it useful to distinguish between what I call resilience as bouncing back from stress, from resistance which is not being pushed off center in the first place, from thriving which I like to define as moving to a higher level of health or functioning (Smith et al. 2008) as have others such as Charles Carver (1998) and O'Leary and Ickovics (1995).

When a natural or technological disaster strikes, it is likely that there will be many who, either because they are on the periphery or because of some other combination of fortunate circumstances will resist and not be moved away from their normal equilibrium. George Bonanno (2004) and others have shown how often people who experience a trauma or loss are not pushed off balance enough to develop anxiety, depression, or PTSD. However, it is the very nature of a disaster to have broad and often devastating effects for many, at least for a period of weeks or months (Neria et al. 2008; Parker et al. 2016). It is the returning to their previous level of adaptation, health, and functioning that I would call resilience in the sense of bounce back or recovering. When an earthquake shatters the foundations of our home or the flood waters wash it away, resilience might involve recovering both our physical home and our previous sense of being at home.

In contrast, thriving would involve going above and beyond where we were before in learning, growing, or in finding or creating some kind of benefit. For me and for others who have used the Posttraumatic Growth Inventory (Tedeschi and Calhoun 1996), the subscales of relating to others, new possibilities, personal strength, appreciation of life, and spiritual change provide good examples of the range of ways that people may sometimes go above and beyond. For the family that loses their home, or sense of home, using the word thriving, in this sense, might mean rebuilding in a way that provides a more beautiful, warm, or welcoming house or at least one that is more greatly valued and appreciated. For an individual or a community on a psychological, spiritual, or existential level, it might mean coming to a greater sense of identity, belongingness, and/or appreciation of the interdependence and trustworthiness of the whole community as happened with Oklahoma City in the months after the bombing (Pargament et al. 1998).

What Has Positive Psychology Added to Our Understanding of Resilience and Thriving?

Of course, here we have to clearly define what we mean by positive psychology. The dangers of associating positive psychology with superficial pleasure, with what Martin Seligman refers to as "happiology" (Seligman 2011) or a naïve positive thinking, have been well-documented (Peterson 2008). What Paul Wong (Wong 2011) has called *Positive Psychology 2.0* and Itai Ivtzan *2nd Wave Positive Psychology* (Ivtzan et al. 2016) are placing more emphasis on meaning in contrast to pleasure, the value of negative as well as positive emotions, and challenged us to bring positive psychology to bear on the worst that can happen, such as when disaster strikes. In this sense, positive psychology has been defined by Chris Peterson's "the science of what makes life most worth living" (Peterson 2008). As I have clarified my own definition in writing a textbook (Smith 2018), I have settled on expressions like the science of what enables us to make the most of our lives and live them to the fullest.

So what has this kind of science added to our understanding of bouncing back and going beyond our previous level of health and functioning? The two things that have consistently come home to me are the role of positive emotions in building resources and to aiming for optimal functioning during stress. Barbara Fredrickson's focus on positive emotions and their potential for broadening and building our strengths (Fredrickson 2004) and the resources we need when disaster strikes is an obvious contribution (Tugade and Fredrickson 2004). Moreover, the movement beyond hedonism and self-focused pleasure to eudaimonia (Seligman 2011) and other-focused compassion (Keltner 2010) and elevation (Haidt 2003) allow us to begin to understand the community spirit that developed in Oklahoma City and that develops after so many disasters. What the fast acting fight-or-flight response did not explain, our new understanding of the slower and more subtle tend and befriend response has given us the chance to begin to see and appreciate (Taylor et al. 2000).

Beyond the necessary focus on our capacity for the positive emotions that contribute to individual and community resilience, what may be an easily overlooked contribution of positive psychology is what it may look like to function at our best in the context of trauma or disaster (Donaldson et al. 2015). If we judge ourselves from the bell curve of an average day for the average person in the top 20% of the world socioeconomic ladder, then how we look in the aftermath of a fire that destroys our town may not even approach the mean. But if we consider the context that disaster mental health researchers are providing about the way these events can shake the foundations of our lives, we have a completely new bell curve for comparison and a goal to aspire to. In the language of Laura King, who developed an elegant variation (King 2001) of the original Pennebaker writing paradigm (Pennebaker 1997), positive psychology dares us to ask what might be our "best possible self" in the context of disaster.

Despite the pitfall of avoiding or denying the dark side of our lives, the "better angels" of the nature of positive psychology have begun to show us how positive emotions and our strengths can make a difference in even the worst we can face – and that these occasions may be a prime test of our being at our best. Of course this notion of excelling at such times is not new to human experience, it just may be that tenure-track professors focusing on getting grants to study mental illnesses may have a hard time finding funding for them. As Stefan Schulenberg brought out in his introduction to the special issue of the *Journal of Clinical Psychology* that was the impetus for this volume (Schulenberg 2016), Viktor Frankl (1963) had already begun to show us what is possible in the worst of circumstances in a way that the most sophisticated growth-curve model from a multisite RCT never could. No wonder *Man's Search for Meaning* was voted the best positive psychology book even though it predated positive psychology (Frankl 1963).

What Do We Know About What Enables Us to Be Resilient and Thrive in Response to Disasters?

In my own mind, there are a couple of ways to approach this question. First, there is what we have learned about the variables that contribute to resilience and thriving (Blanc et al. 2016). Second, there are the interventions that we have found empirical support for in helping those who have been faced with disasters and other traumas (Brown et al. 2017). Because of my own interest in resilience (defined as the ability to bounce back) and in identifying good targets in interventions for individuals, I have tried to add to what we know about the constellations of attitudes and behaviors associated with things like personal mastery, self-efficacy, optimism, hope, and the many forms and strategies of adaptive coping that we have identified (Smith et al. 2013). Of course, what I and many in psychology have neglected are the social and contextual factors that are harder to study or influence in the kind of interventions we design (Davidson 2010; Paton and Johnston 2017).

One of the large shifts in our models of the factors that may make a difference for those affected by disaster has been a move toward the value of accepting reality versus controlling it. In studying urban firefighters who are frequently exposed to traumatic stress, I was initially surprised to find that it was mindfulness more than a sense of personal mastery that was related to lower levels of anxiety, depression, and PTSD symptoms (Smith et al. 2011). But now it completely makes sense to me how a mindful acceptance of what is may enable us to come to terms with something that may be so large and overwhelming and that we cannot change. Likewise, the work of Kristin Neff (Neff 2003), in bringing the idea of self-compassion to Western psychology, has also given us a way to be kind to ourselves when things do not go our way. In the aftermath of a disaster, for example, this might mean not being hard on ourselves for not being able to prevent or change what happened.

The individual qualities or characteristics that have consistently come up as valuable for many when disaster strikes are the sense of meaning and purpose that Frankl highlighted in both secular forms and those that are often associated with religion or spirituality (Frankl 1963). Having someone or something else to live for after our home is destroyed or losing a loved one may be a powerful motivation for doing what it takes to bounce back or eventually find benefits in the aftermath of a life shattering event. In my own work with Ken Pargament, we found that what we called "positive religious coping" was generally related to better psychological and spiritual outcomes in the aftermath of a large Midwest flood (Smith et al. 2000). As I have come to understand it, though they certainly affect some people in harmful ways at times, religion and spirituality may often be beneficial as they foster optimism, a sense of meaning and purpose, posttraumatic growth, and an extended network of social support (Jang and LaMendola 2007; Park 2016; Salsman et al. 2005).

When it comes to social relationships and the broader context of the community, there is much that we are just beginning to learn about how they may affect resilience and thriving. But it is clear that how well we adapt following major stressors and traumas is much of an interactive process among individuals and the broader context. If there is any time that we discover that we need other people, it is when disaster strikes and we are most vulnerable. The value of social support has been a consistent finding in multiple studies of disasters and other traumatic events (Cook and Bickman 1990; Simeon et al. 2005). From a positive psychology perspective we might add to that the value of cultivating the positive relationships that are a part of Carol Ryff's model of psychological well-being (Ryff 1989). Just as positive emotions may enable us to broaden and build our strengths for coping with disasters, so our positive relationships may be the very context needed to manifest themselves.

What Can We Learn From Interventions That May Help Us After We Experience Trauma?

Rather than trying to identify the variables that are the strongest predictors of better outcomes for those affected by disasters and trauma, we might also try to identify the specific techniques that may foster resilience and thriving in these contexts. They will undoubtedly involve and overlap with these variables, but they may also give us a better idea of how change happens and how to make it happen. The first technique is exposure, which is a primary focus of most successful treatments for anxiety and post-traumatic stress. Both prolonged exposure therapy (PE) and cognitive processing therapy (CPT) involve exposure and have been effective for trauma victims (Asmundson et al. 2019; Powers et al. 2010). They work by exposing the individual to the most upsetting aspects of what happened until it is no longer so distressing. This can break the cycle of avoidance and re-experiencing that can keep a person constantly aroused.

The second technique that is also at the foundation of cognitive-behavioral approaches is cognitive reappraisal (Beck et al. 1979). Of course, this is our ability to change the way that we think about things. While PE might primarily focus on having someone expose themselves to what was most upsetting about an earthquake or a flood, for example, CPT would directly focus on getting them to change the way that they think about themselves or their environment (Hembree et al. 2003; Resick et al. 2016). For example, if you and your family are victims of a sudden and unexpected earthquake, then you may question your judgment about where you built your house and doubt your ability to protect yourself in the future. Not only would CPT involve exposing yourself to the disaster by thinking and writing about it, it would also directly address your cognitions and challenge you to regain some of your trust in the environment and in your ability to be safe and take care of those around you.

The third technique has been shown to be a primary factor in cognitive-behavior therapies but not directly addressed in interventions such as prolonged exposure or cognitive processing therapy (Jacobson et al. 1996). Behavioral activation is the name for the technique that involves getting people to identify and do behaviors and activities that they find most reinforcing and rewarding (Lewinsohn 1975; Martell et al. 2001). The result can be to get a depressed person to begin to again experience pleasure or to increase the motivation of an anxious person exposing themselves to what they are afraid of rather than avoiding it. Behavioral activation may work hand-in-hand with interventions that may also foster a sense of meaning and purpose. For example, if a mother loses a spouse who is a firefighter to a wildfire, a meaning-focused approach might help her build on her sense that her children are a primary source of meaning by enabling her to identify activities that foster her relationship with them and encourage her to engage in them more frequently.

Together, exposure, cognitive reappraisal, and behavioral activation may complement one another to increase both resilience and thriving in the midst or the aftermath of a disaster. Despite the chaos and loss that a person may experience, behavioral activation can help build the motivation that may be necessary to do everything it takes to bounce back and rebuild one's life (Lewinsohn 1975; Martell et al. 2001). For those with PTSD symptoms, it can provide the motivation to do the hard work of exposing oneself to the most upsetting memories and reality of what has happened (Hembree et al. 2003) while reducing the avoidance that hinders proactive coping. Behavioral activation may also contribute to thriving and post-traumatic growth by helping us to identify new sources of pleasure and happiness. Finally, cognitive reappraisal may be most important for thriving because it enables us to think about and look for new ways to see what happened and to learn, grow, and benefit from it.

What Have We Been Missing in the Variables and Techniques That We Have Been Focusing on?

Although I am not yet going to come back to that "hero's journey" idea in the title of this chapter, I am ready to take a major step in that direction. When I was in graduate school, I remember first reading about the early studies of James Pennebaker focusing on expressive writing (e.g., Pennebaker and Beall 1986). As you may know, he had university students write for 15–20 minutes for 3–4 days about the most traumatic or stressful experiences they had. As he and others continued to use a similar research paradigm, there were generally consistent findings that writing freely about a stressful experience versus writing about trivial things had various kinds of health benefits (Baikie and Wilhelm 2005; Konig et al. 2013). If these results were consistent for people who have experienced major stressful events, this could have important implications for resilience. I began to wonder if the writing those people in Oklahoma City did in response to that open-ended question could have had a similar effect.

As much as this kind of writing might have health benefits and help someone to recover from the adverse effects of stress, might this kind of writing also have implications for thriving as I have defined it? Before long there were people like Annette

Stanton who changed the instructions from simply writing about the most stressful experiences to actually writing about the positive aspects of the experiences and the benefits that they had found (Stanton et al. 2002). She did this with women who had breast cancer and found that those that wrote about benefits and the positive aspects of their cancer experience had fewer cancer-related medical visits in the future. What would it be like to use a similar benefit finding exercise with those affected by disasters? Would this facilitate the search for meaning and posttraumatic growth that may be important in their aftermath (Dursun et al. 2016).

One of the biggest questions for Pennebaker and for others who were using these writing interventions had to do with why they worked (Pennebaker 1989). At first, many looked back to the old ideas about emotional catharsis and thought it might have to do with the expression of negative emotions. But the analyses of the words used by those who benefitted the most soon led to the idea that it was more about how the writing evolved across the writing sessions into a coherent story or narrative (Pennebaker and Seagal 1999). This idea received support when Joshua Smyth asked one group of students to write a narrative involving a clear beginning, middle, and end and making their writing "story-like" and another group of students to write in the format of a bullet list that followed no particular temporal order (Smyth et al. 2001). Smyth found that the only group showing signs of improvement relative to the trivial writing control group was the one that used the narrative format and that the bullet list group showed no difference between it and a neutral control group.

At the same time, this idea of narrative coherence had come to the forefront for another researcher who primarily focused on personality and human development rather than coping with stressful or traumatic events. Dan McAdams has long been an articulate proponent of the value of a narrative approach to understanding human beings (McAdams 1993). He has used both quantitative and qualitative methods to understand personality and how we come to see and understand our "self." He has developed a three-level model of personality that includes: (1) the kind of broad personality characteristics studied in quantitative research such as the "Big Five" personality characteristics, including neuroticism, extraversion, openness to experience, agreeableness, and conscientiousness, (2) the characteristic ways that we adapt to our lives, including our coping mechanisms, desires, and beliefs, and (3) the life stories that give us a unique sense of meaning and purpose, or what he calls our "narrative identity."

McAdams developed a way to study this narrative identity and has written about how it may be important for each of us as individuals and even for communities in forming a collective identity (McAdams 2006). In examining the personal stories provided by research participants, he has tried to identify any differences in structure and content that may be related to psychological well-being. He has argued that one of the most important aspects of a story is "narrative coherence," or how well the story fits together into a unified whole. He contends that the most important aspects of content have to do with how much a person is able to "make meaning" from their story, whether there is a coherent positive resolution, and whether the narrator transitions from a negative to a positive state which he identifies as a "redemption" narrative (McAdams 2001). Is it possible that the ability to construct a narrative that is not only coherent but also involves a movement to a positive resolution may foster resilience and thriving in the context of disaster?

The final part of the story regarding the value of writing and developing a narrative goes back to the work of Laura King. She adapted the writing technique that Pennebaker developed in a way that fits particularly well with positive psychology. Rather than ask people to write about their most traumatic or stressful experiences, she has asked them to write about the "best possible self" that they could imagine for themselves in the future (King 2001). She found that people experience many of the same benefits as writing about stressful experiences but without experiencing as many negative emotions and distress while writing. Could this kind of an intervention be adapted as a way to bring positive psychology to people who have experienced a disaster? Rather than just generally imagining what the best possible self would be in the future, the instruction could be to imagine the best possible outcome from the disaster and what it would look like for the best possible self to come to life and use its strengths in making it happen.

What About the Use of Writing and Stories in Interventions for Traumatic Events?

Alright, I am almost ready to really focus on the hero's journey, but I provide a little more context in terms of some relevant empirically-supported interventions. First of all, there has been cross-pollination between Pennebaker's work and the thinking about and implementation of prolonged exposure and cognitive processing therapy (Konig et al. 2013; Sloan and Marx 2006). As people are recalling and telling what happened to them, they are not only emotionally exposing themselves to it and thinking about it in a new and different way, they are also probably making more sense of what happened and developing a more coherent story about it. Moreover, one of the great challenges of coming to terms with a trauma involves integrating the normal everyday events that characterized our lives before the trauma with those out of the ordinary and earth-shattering memories and experiences we may have during a disaster. Being able to develop a more coherent narrative about both may help to make this possible.

Thus, the one other part of the plot that cannot be neglected includes recently developed interventions that are more directly tied to the verbal and written expression of a traumatic or stressful experience. These two interventions have very similar names and even acronyms that rhyme. Closest to the original Pennebaker paradigm is what was developed by Denise Sloan and colleagues and has been called Written Exposure Therapy (WET; Sloan et al. 2013). WET was designed to be a brief therapy for PTSD and involves similar writing instructions to those used in the Pennebaker paradigm (Pennebaker 1997). That is, people are asked to write about an event as they look back on it. As with exposure therapies, WET appears to work by helping to extinguish the fear associated with a traumatic stress and also to help the person establish a sense of distance from the event. There is also some evidence that WET may be effective without being as aversive as PE or CPT (Sloan et al. 2018).

The other intervention with empirical support that involves building a coherent narrative is called Narrative Exposure Therapy (NET; Schauer et al. 2011). With NET, a person who has experienced trauma is asked to create a chronological narrative of his or her whole life. Although this narrative involves focusing the most on traumatic experiences, it also involves incorporating positive events. By expressing the narrative, the cognitive, affective, and sensory memories of the trauma are contextualized into a coherent autobiographical story. There is growing evidence that this method may be effective for refugees and even for children (Gwozdziewycz and Mehl-Madrona 2013; Pfefferbaum et al. 2017). The key differences between NET and WET are that NET involves the presence of another person and focusing on the person's life as a whole. In addition, although the NET facilitator may not have to be a trained therapist, the emphasis is on their using empathy, active listening, and unconditional positive regard (Schauer et al. 2011).

Where Does the Idea of a Hero's Journey Come Into Resilience and Thriving in Disaster?

The first time that I heard about the Harry Potter books was from a fellow graduate student who was over 30 years old. I wondered if he really was over 30. For years, I rebelled against the Harry Potter hype and when I forced myself to attend the first movie (e.g., *Harry Potter and the Sorcerer's Stone*; Rowling 1997) to see what I might be missing, I left before the Quidditch match was over. That changed as I began to hear more and more of the students that I taught about how Harry or Hermione helped them get through their childhood. And then there is the colleague I admire at another university who has taken inspiration for his teaching from Yoda in the Star Wars series (Lucas 1977), and the famous neuroscientist I once worked with who was motivated and inspired by the idea of being like a Jedi Knight. There seems to be something about certain stories that speaks to us and affects us in a way that is difficult to reduce to one variable, the results of a statistical analysis, or a technique for trying to bring about change.

In trying to get a handle on this I came across the old Bill Moyers interviews on T.V. with Joseph Campbell (Campbell 1988) which led me back to Campbell's seminal work called *The Hero with a Thousand Faces* (Campbell 1949). As you may know, he became so fascinated with the stories that arose in different languages and cultures around the world and began to see similarities and patterns among them. He borrowed the phrase "monomyth" from James Joyce's novel *Ulysses* (Joyce 1922) and began to apply it to what became known as the "hero's journey" to refer to the progression of events that often recur in some of our most cherished and life-giving stories. This progression often includes a call to a new adventure, meeting a mentor, going through various trials, preparing for big challenges, experiencing a life-threatening challenge, surviving the challenges in a way that brings about a reward or a transformation, and returning to the ordinary world with a gift to share with others (Campbell 1949).

As I thought of the people I saw in my clinical work, the students I taught in my classes, and about the story of my own life, I began to see more aspects of this pattern and progression, especially in relation to great challenges and stress. I remembered the ideas of James Pennebaker (Pennebaker and Seagal 1999) and studies of people like Joshua Smyth (Smyth et al. 2001) about how a coherent narrative or story seemed to be a key feature of those who benefitted from writing about their stress or trauma. Moreover, I went back to the work of Dan McAdams and his discovery that it was the stories with a positive resolution and those with a redemptive theme that were expressed by those who seemed to have the greatest well-being (McAdams 2006). I also discovered Michael Steger's take on meaning and the distinction he and a co-author made between a security-oriented narrative which involves maintenance and protection and a growth-oriented narrative which involves growing and giving back (Shin and Steger 2014).

In our search for the strongest predictors and most effective techniques for our treatment manuals, I wondered if there was something more basic, organic, and human that we had been overlooking. I was thinking about the words of a broad-minded developmental psychology colleague who emphasizes the need to consider the interaction of the whole system across time. Just as Western psychology has benefited from the rediscovery of mindfulness which has roots in ancient meditative practices, I wondered if there was something to be gained in taking a fresh look at the stories that have and continue to sustain us. In our desire to put our faith in numbers and be perceived as a hard science, I wondered if we had missed something that is much more often studied in the humanities. If, as Pennebaker and McAdams have surmised (McAdams 1993; Pennebaker and Seagal 1999), creating a coherent narrative may be a key to well-being in the context of our stresses and traumas, then perhaps this process could add something to our ability to bounce back and experience growth in the context of the challenges we face.

It is difficult to imagine a kind of event where the common human hero's journey that Campbell highlighted may be more relevant than what happens when we are confronted with a disaster (Campbell 1949, 1988). First, it is certainly a call to adventure, although one that we may first respond to with a "refusal of the call" (also a frequent part of these stories). Second, while there may not often be a long period of trials and preparation when disaster strikes, this preparation may actually involve much of what this kind of book is about and what happens during much of our previous lives as positive experiences enable us to broaden and build the strengths and resources we need when the time comes. Finally, the clearest parallels between the progression of the classic hero's journey and the disaster experience may not just be the abyss of the disaster itself, but the challenge of bouncing back and the opportunity to learn and grow in a way we have something to offer to others when we return to our ordinary world.

There is one other point that may be critical in understanding the potential value of the hero's journey for those experiencing disasters. This involves the distinction between the general idea of a common hero's journey and the specific expressions of it for different people in different places and times (Campbell 2004). That is, the basic progression is the same and may be a template for human resilience and thriving in the context of disasters and a whole range of human stressors and traumas. But I suspect that just as we have learned in observing how social modeling can increase self-efficacy (Bandura 1997), it probably matters how similar the people and the challenges are to us. So for the progression of a hero's journey story to be most valuable to someone in the throes of a disaster, the devil may be in the details of the story and how easy they are to relate to and how much they speak to key aspects of our experiences. I remember the first time that I did a study of the natural disaster that was the 1993 Midwest flood. Those who were religious found particular hope in the story of Noah in the Bible (Smith et al. 2000).

What Can the Hero's Journey Add in Increasing Resilience and Thriving in Disasters?

As I have continued to reflect on it, there may be several ways that the idea of a common human hero's journey and its specific expressions may add to how we can better help people who have experienced disasters. First, we may be able to find new ways to use stories as guides to enable people to develop the kind of coherent narratives that people like McAdams and Pennebaker have highlighted (McAdams 1993; Pennebaker and Seagal 1999). Just as mentors like Yoda, Dumbledore, and Gandalf are mentors in some of our favorite stories, so we may be able to do a better job of using stories as guides for finding the way through disaster (Lucas 1977; Rowling 1997; Tolkien 1954). What if we did research to develop better stories of people who have survived and thrived after disasters? What if we identified the elements of these stories that were more universally beneficial and those that we might need to vary for different people? We might then use them as examples and starting points for people coping with disasters.

Second, the idea of a common human hero's journey provides a way to put our predictor variables and therapeutic techniques into a broader human context that we may be able to more easily relate to. These stories often include memorable and moving examples of mastery, mindfulness, self-efficacy, self-compassion, and optimism, with hope expressed through the very idea that it is possible to come through the abyss to a better place. The stories might also be used to provide better examples and increased motivation and support for the processes and techniques at the heart of empirically-supported treatments such as PE and CPT (Hembree et al. 2003; Resick et al. 2016). Cognitive reappraisal may be an inherent part of imagining ourselves in a larger story with a meaningful and rewarding ending. Going through the abyss to get to a better place could be a metaphor for undergoing exposure therapy and the possibility of a reward or transformation can aid the behavioral activation necessary to achieve it.

Third, the idea of a hero's journey may be an excellent way to really bring positive psychology to life in the context of a disaster. Not only may it provide prime examples of how to bring our strengths to bear on some of our greatest challenges, it may also give us primary visions for what it might look like for us to be our "best possible self" (King 2001) in the context of some of the worst possible circumstances. The subtitle of the book *Second Wave Positive Psychology* is *Embracing the Dark Side of Life* (Ivtzan et al. 2016) and the last chapter is aptly titled "The Hero's Journey." In it Piers Worth walks us through the stages of the hero's journey as outlined by Campbell (1949) and gives examples from stories we have already alluded to: *Harry Potter* (Rowling 1997), *Star Wars* (Lucas 1977), and *Lord of the Rings* (Tolkien 1954). These kinds of stories may be part of what has been missing in showing how positive psychology can embrace the dark side and what will enable psychology to come full circle to a more holistic psychology that better integrates both the light and the darkness.

Fourth, the idea of the hero's journey is inherent socially and community-oriented in a way that fits the context of disasters and the human condition as a whole. The most memorable and lasting hero's journey stories arose out of the greatest challenges that we have faced as a species and they end with something to offer back to the community. They have stayed with us for so long not just because they have inspired and motivated individuals, but because they have helped to build and sustain whole communities. Just as the people of Israel took comfort in the story of their being freed from slavery in Egypt in the story of the Torah of the Jewish faith and the Old Testament of the Christian Bible, so the African American slave community in the nineteenth century U.S. drew on this story to hold them together and give them hope for a better future (Raboteau 1995). The communal value of the general idea and specific expressions of the hero's journey are a challenge to us to make our work extend beyond individuals to the community.

Where Do We Go From Here in Using the Hero's Journey to Foster Resilience and Thriving?

Finally, I would like to say more about how we might begin to bring some of the value of the hero's journey to those who have experienced disasters. An initial step might be to try to identify hero's journey stories that might speak to people who have experienced different kinds of disasters. This could begin with focus groups with people who have done well even after experiencing the worst of a disaster. Then, the idea of a hero's journey could be presented with relevant examples, and they could be asked to identify stories that have spoken to them or reflect what it means to be resilient. In addition, they could be encouraged to cultivate their own stories in a way that best reflects the particularities of their own experiences. The goal would be to develop a clear idea of the kind of hero's journey story that would be most beneficial for someone who has experienced a disaster with variations that allow for individual differences.

Next, the idea of a hero's journey and some of the examples that may be most beneficial for people who have experienced disasters could be offered as resources for others coping with disaster. These could be in the form of verbal, written, or video testimonies of previous survivors about their own story and experiences or of them talking about how they found the motivation or inspiration from a well-known story. These stories could be offered as examples to draw from in one of the interventions or treatment approaches that more directly allow for the construction of a coherent narrative such as Written Exposure Therapy (WET; Sloan et al. 2013) or Narrative Exposure Therapy (NET; Schauer et al. 2011). They could also be offered to supplement other empirically-supported treatments for trauma such as PE (Hembree et al. 2003) or CPT (Resick et al. 2016) as examples of exposure or cognitive reappraisal. In any approach, both disaster survivor and familiar hero's journey stories could be used to illustrate intervention targets such as mastery, self-efficacy, optimism, and hope, providing examples of resilience and thriving.

In addition, after introducing the idea of a hero's journey (Campbell 1949, 1988, 2004) and giving relevant examples, the stages of the hero's journey could be used as a focus for questions that target challenges at each phase of coping with a disaster. Some examples might be: Who are those who can guide us and help us in the process of recovery? What are the strengths and assets that we can draw on? What are the worst things we have experienced and the toughest challenges we have faced? What can we learn in the process? What do we have to offer others who might benefit from our own experience? Although these questions may be difficult to answer, they may be addressed with greater confidence and hope when asked in the context of a common human story where others have faced similar challenges. Rather than just looking back to create a narrative about a past trauma, this process could be a proactive challenge for individuals or communities to live the successful completion of their own hero's journey.

Last, the idea of a hero's journey could be used as a template for identifying stories that speak to the larger social network in building community resilience (Engle 2017; Gil-Rivas and Kilmer 2016). As it has been expressed in the seminal stories of world religions and cultures, the progression of the hero's journey may help us identify parallels that people can draw on for strength during disasters. For example, the story of the Buddha banishing his tempter Mara by simply touching the ground on the way to enlightenment might be used to inspire determination and resilience during a disaster (Trainor 2004). Likewise, the story of the phoenix bird has been used as a common expression of resilience across cultures (Blake 1964). Rather than taking a hands-off approach, psychologists and other mental health workers could be more proactive in learning about the stories that may be most likely to inspire and motivate those affected by disasters. Those who intervene with individuals or communities could talk about the potential value of stories in coping and be ready to point to and share culturally-appropriate examples.

Conclusion

As I have tried to take a more narrative approach in writing this chapter, I would like to return to the original story with which I began. As you may remember, in going through the responses to the open-ended question I asked people affected by the Oklahoma City bombing, I was surprised to find that so many reported that they had benefited by coming to a greater appreciation of their community for how they supported and took care of each other (Pargament et al. 1998). In having now learned more about the hero's journey (Campbell 1949), I see this as an example of the kind of transformation and reward that stories often point to and that can occur following disasters. As I have followed the aftermath of other disasters through the years, I have seen how often those affected by one will travel hundreds or even thousands of miles to help those affected by another. In this way, their own hero's journey shows how often resilience (as bouncing back) and thriving (as growing beyond) can be joined in the aftermath of disasters.

Whether or not we even use the phrase "hero's journey" or talk about any of the stages, it may be important to remember that there are stories that have evolved out of the fiery furnace of the great trials that we have faced and experienced as a species. Many of these stories have been passed down because they have continued to provide meaning, motivation, inspiration, and hope and – as with Viktor Frankl's story – often in the context of the very worst (Frankl 1963). For as much hard work as we have done in identifying the predictors of resilience and thriving and the intervention techniques that target them, there may be something essential that is lost if we do not listen to our most hard won stories. Although disasters may often be sudden and unexpected, resilience and thriving are things that unfold over time. Moreover, it may be in the progression of the human stories of how we have survived and learned from our greater challenges where we find that which is most important to offer those who are facing them anew.

References

Asmundson, G. J. G., Thorisdottir, A. S., Roden-Foreman, J. W., Baird, S. O., Witcraft, S. M., Stein, A. T., et al. (2019). A meta-analytic review of cognitive processing therapy for adults with posttraumatic stress disorder. *Cognitive Behaviour Therapy, 48*(1), 1–14.

Baikie, K., & Wilhelm, K. (2005). Emotional and physical health benefits of expressive writing. *Advances in Psychiatric Treatment, 11*, 338–346.

Bandura, A. (1997). *Self-efficacy: The exercise of control*. New York: W. H. Freeman and Company.

Beck, A. T., Rush, A. J., Shaw, B. F., & Emery, G. (1979). *Cognitive therapy of depression*. New York: The Guilford Press.

Blake, N. F. (1964). *The phoenix*. Manchester: Manchester University Press.

Blanc, J., Rahill, G. J., Laconi, S., & Mouchenik, Y. (2016). Religious beliefs, PTSD, depression and resilience in survivors of the 2010 Haiti earthquake. *Journal of Affective Disorders, 190*, 697–703.

Bonanno, G. (2004). Loss, trauma, and human resilience: Have we underestimated the human capacity to thrive after extremely aversive events? *American Psychologist, 59*, 20–28.

Brown, R. C., Witt, A., Fegert, J. M., Keller, F., Rassenhofer, M., & Plener, P. L. (2017). Psychosocial interventions for children and adolescents after man-made and natural disasters: A meta-analysis and systematic review. *Psychological Medicine, 47*, 1893–1905.

Campbell, J. (1949). *The hero with a thousand faces*. Princeton: Princeton University Press.

Campbell, J. (1988, June 21). *Joseph Campbell and the power of myth.* Interview by Bill Moyers. Episode1: The hero's adventure.

Campbell, J. (2004). *Pathways to bliss: Mythology and personal transformation*. Novato: New World Press.

Carver, C. S. (1998). Resilience and thriving: Issues, models, and linkages. *Journal of Social Issues, 54*, 245–266.

Cook, J. D., & Bickman, L. (1990). Social support and psychological symptomatology following a natural disaster. *Journal of Traumatic Stress, 3*, 541–556.

Davidson, D. J. (2010). The applicability of the concept of resilience to social systems: Some sources of optimism and nagging doubts. *Journal of Society and Natural Resources, 12*, 1135–1149.

Donaldson, S. I., Dollwet, M., & Meghana, A. R. (2015). Happiness, excellence, and optimal human functioning revisited: Examining the peer-reviewed literature linked to positive psychology. *Journal of Positive Psychology, 10*(3), 185–195.

Dursun, P., Steger, M. F., Bentele, C., & Schulenberg, S. E. (2016). Meaning and posttraumatic growth among survivors of the September 2013 Colorado floods. *Journal of Clinical Psychology, 72*, 1247–1263.

Engle, J. (2017). Stories of tragedy, trust and transformation? A case study of education-centered community development in post-earthquake Haiti. *Process in Planning, 124*, 1–34.

Frankl, V. E. (1963). *Man's search for meaning*. New York: Pocket Books.

Fredrickson, B. L. (2004). The broaden-and-build theory of positive emotions. *Philosophical Transactions of the Royal Society B: Biological Sciences, 359*, 1367–1378.

Gil-Rivas, V., & Kilmer, R. P. (2016). Building community capacity and fostering disaster resilience. *Journal of Clinical Psychology, 72*, 1318–1332.

Gwozdziewycz, N., & Mehl-Madrona, L. (2013). Meta-analysis of the use of narrative exposure therapy for the effects of trauma among refugee populations. *The Permanente Journal, 17*(1), 70–76.

Haidt, J. (2003). Elevation and the positive psychology of morality. In C. L. M. Keyes & J. Haidt (Eds.), *Flourishing: Positive psychology and the life well-lived* (pp. 275–289). Washington, DC: American Psychological Association.

Hembree, E. A., Rauch, S. A., & Foa, E. B. (2003). Beyond the manual: The insider's guide to prolonged exposure therapy for PTSD. *Cognitive and Behavioral Practice, 10*, 22–30.

Ivtzan, I., Lomas, T., Hefferon, K., & Worth, P. (2016). *Second wave positive psychology: Embracing the dark side of life*. New York: Routledge.

Jacobson, N. S., Dobson, K. S., Truax, P. A., Addis, M. E., Koerner, K., Gollan, J. K., Gortner, E., & Prince, S. E. (1996). A component analysis of cognitive-behavioral treatment for depression. *Journal of Consulting and Clinical Psychology, 64*, 295–304.

Jang, L., & LaMendola, W. F. (2007). Social work in natural disasters: The case of spirituality and post-traumatic growth. *Advances in Social Work, 8*, 305–316.

Joyce, J. (1922). *Ulysses*. London: Egoist Press.

Keltner, D. (2010). The compassionate instinct. In D. Keltner, J. Marsh, & J. A. Smith (Eds.), *The compassionate instinct* (pp. 8–15). New York: W. W. Norton.

King, L. A. (2001). The health benefits of writing about goals. *Personality and Social Psychology Bulletin, 27*, 798–807.

Konig, A., Eonta, A., Dyal, S. R., & Vrana, S. R. (2013). Enhancing the benefits of written emotional disclosure through response training. *Behavior Therapy, 45*, 344–357.

Lewinsohn, P. M. (1975). The behavioral study and treatment of depression. In M. Hersen, R. M. Eisler, & P. M. Miller (Eds.), *Progress in behavioral modification* (Vol. 1, pp. 19–65). New York: Academic.

Lucas, G. (1977). *Star wars episode IV: A new hope.* Twentieth Century Fox, 1977. Film.

Martell, C. R., Addis, M. E., & Jacobson, N. S. (2001). *Depression in context: Strategies for guided action*. New York: W. W. Norton.
McAdams, D. (1993). *The stories we live by: Personal myths and the making of the self*. New York: Guilford Press.
McAdams, D. (2001). When bad things turn good and good things turn bad: Sequences of redemption and contamination in life narrative and their relation to psychosocial adaptation in midlife adults and in students. *Personality and Social Psychology Bulletin, 27*, 474–485.
McAdams, D. (2006). *The redemptive self: Stories Americans live by*. New York: Oxford University Press.
Merriam-Webster. Retrieved from the following on December 28, 2018: https://www.merriam-webster.com/dictionary/resilience.
Neff, K. D. (2003). The development and validation of a scale to measure self-compassion. *Self and Identity, 2*, 223–250.
Neria, Y., Nandi, A., & Galea, S. (2008). Post-traumatic stress disorder following disasters: A systematic review. *Psychological Medicine, 38*, 467–480.
O'Leary, V. E., & Ickovics, J. R. (1995). Resilience and thriving in response to challenge: An opportunity for a paradigm shift in women's health. *Women's Health, 1*, 121–142.
Pargament, K. I., Smith, B. W., Koenig, H. G., & Perez, L. (1998). Patterns of positive and negative religious coping with major life stressors. *Journal for the Scientific Study of Religion, 37*, 710–724.
Park, C. L. (2016). Meaning making in the context of disasters. *Journal of Clinical Psychology, 72*, 1234–1246.
Park, C. L., Cohen, L. H., & Murch, R. L. (1996). Assessment and prediction of stress-related growth. *Journal of Personality, 61*, 71–105.
Parker, G., Lie, D., Siskind, D. J., Martin-Khan, M., Raphael, B., Crompton, D., & Kisely, S. (2016). Mental health implications for older adults after natural disasters—A systematic review and meta-analysis. *International Psychogeriatrics, 28*, 11–20.
Paton, D., & Johnston, D. (2017). *Disaster resilience: An integrated approach* (2nd ed.). Springfield: Charles C. Thomas.
Pennebaker, J. W. (1989). Confession, inhibition, and disease. In L. Berkowitz (Ed.), *Advances in experimental social psychology* (Vol. 22, pp. 211–244). New York: Academic.
Pennebaker, J. W. (1997). Writing about emotional experiences as a therapeutic process. *Psychological Science, 8*, 162–166.
Pennebaker, J. W., & Beall, S. K. (1986). Confronting a traumatic event: Toward an understanding of inhibition and disease. *Journal of Abnormal Psychology, 95*, 274–281.
Pennebaker, J. W., & Seagal, J. D. (1999). Forming a story: The health benefits of narrative. *Journal of Clinical Psychology, 55*, 1243–1254.
Peterson, C. (2008, May 16). What is positive psychology, and what is it not? *Psychology Today*. Retrieved from https://www.psychologytoday.com/us/blog/the-good- life/200805/what-is-positive-psychology-and-what-is-it-not.
Pfefferbaum, B., Nitiéma, P., Tucker, P., & Newman, E. (2017). Early child disaster mental health interventions: A review of the empirical evidence. *Child & Youth Care Forum, 46*, 621–642.
Powers, M. B., Halpern, J. M., Ferenschak, M. P., Gillihan, S. J., & Foa, E. B. (2010). A meta-analytic review of prolonged exposure for posttraumatic stress disorder. *Clinical Psychology Review, 30*, 635–641.
Raboteau, A. J. (1995). *A fire in the bones: Reflections on African-American religious history*. Boston: Beacon Press.
Resick, P. A., Monson, C. M., & Chard, K. M. (2016). *Cognitive processing therapy for PTSD: A comprehensive manual*. New York: Guilford Press.
Rowling, J. K. (1997). *Harry Potter and the sorcerer's stone*. New York: Arthur A. Levine.
Ryff, C. (1989). Happiness is everything, or is it? Explorations on the meaning of psychological well-being. *Journal of Personality and Social Psychology, 57*, 1069–1081.
Salsman, J. M., Brown, T. L., & Brechting, E. H. (2005). The link between religion and spirituality and psychological adjustment: The mediating role of optimism and social support. *Personality and Social Psychology Bulletin, 31*, 522–535.

Schauer, M., Neuner, F., & Elbert, T. (2011). *Narrative exposure therapy: A short term treatment for traumatic stress disorders* (2nd ed.). Cambridge, MA: Hogrefe Publishing.

Schulenberg, S. E. (2016). Disaster mental health and positive psychology – Considering the context of natural and technological disasters: An introduction to the special issue. *Journal of Clinical Psychology, 72*, 1223–1233.

Seligman, M. E. P. (2011). *Flourish: A visionary new understanding of happiness and well-being*. New York: Free Press.

Shin, J. Y., & Steger, M. F. (2014). Promoting meaning and purpose in life. In A. C. Parks & S. M. Schueller (Eds.), *The Wiley Blackwell handbook of positive psychological interventions* (pp. 90–110). West Sussex: Wiley.

Simeon, D., Greenberg, J., Nelson, D., Schmeidler, J., & Hollander, E. (2005). Dissociation and posttraumatic stress 1 year after the World Trade Center disaster: Follow-up of a longitudinal survey. *The Journal of Clinical Psychiatry, 66*, 231–237.

Sloan, D. M., Lee, D. J., Litwack, S. D., Sawyer, A. T., & Marx, B. P. (2013). Written exposure therapy for veterans diagnosed with PTSD: A pilot study. *Journal of Traumatic Stress, 26*, 776–779.

Sloan, D. M., & Marx, B. P. (2006). Exposure through written emotional disclosure: Two case examples. *Cognitive and Behavioral Practice, 13*, 227–234.

Sloan, D. M., Marx, B. P., Lee, D. J., & Resick, P. A. (2018). A brief exposure-based treatment vs cognitive processing therapy for posttraumatic stress disorder: A randomized noninferiority clinical trial. *JAMA Psychiatry, 75*, 233–239.

Smith, B. W. (2018). *Positive psychology for your hero's journey*. New York: Kindle Direct Publishing.

Smith, B. W., Dalen, J., Wiggins, K., Tooley, E., Christopher, P., & Bernard, J. (2008). The Brief Resilience Scale: Assessing the ability to bounce back. *International Journal of Behavioral Medicine, 15*, 194–200.

Smith, B. W., Epstein, E. M., Ortiz, J. A., Christopher, P. J., & Tooley, E. M. (2013). The foundations of resilience: What are the critical resources for bouncing back from stress? In S. Prince-Embury (Ed.), *Resilience in children, adolescents, and adults* (167–188). New York: Oxford.

Smith, B. W., Ortiz, J. A., Steffen, L. E., Tooley, E. M., Wiggins, K. T., Yeater, E. A., Montoya, J. D., & Bernard, M. L. (2011). Mindfulness is associated with fewer PTSD symptoms, depressive symptoms, physical symptoms, and alcohol problems in urban firefighters. *Journal of Consulting and Clinical Psychology, 79*, 613–617.

Smith, B. W., Pargament, K. I., Brant, C., & Oliver, J. M. (2000). Noah revisited: Religious coping and the impact of a flood. *Journal of Community Psychology, 28*, 169–186.

Smyth, J. M., True, N., & Souto, J. (2001). Effects of writing about traumatic experiences: The necessity for narrative structure. *Journal of Social and Clinical Psychology, 20*, 161–172.

Stanton, A. L., Danoff-Burg, S., Sworowski, L. A., Collins, C. A., Branstetter, A. D., Rodriguez-Hanley, A., Kirk, S. B., & Austenfeld, J. L. (2002). Randomized, controlled trial of written emotional expression and benefit finding in breast cancer patients. *Journal of Clinical Oncology, 20*, 4160–4168.

Taylor, S. E., Klein, L. C., Lewis, B. P., Gruenewald, T. L., Gurung, R. A. R., & Updegraff, J. A. (2000). Biobehavioral responses to stress in females: Tend-and-befriend, not fight-or-flight. *Psychological Review, 107*, 411–429.

Tedeschi, R. G., & Calhoun, L. G. (1996). The Posttraumatic Growth Inventory: Measuring the positive legacy of trauma. *Journal of Traumatic Stress, 9*, 455–471.

Tolkien, J. R. R. (1954). *Lord of the rings* (Vol. 1–3). London: Allen & Unwin.

Trainor, K. (2004). *Buddhism: The illustrated guide*. New York: Oxford University Press.

Tugade, M. M., & Fredrickson, B. L. (2004). Resilient individuals use positive emotions to bounce back from negative emotional experiences. *Journal of Personality and Social Psychology, 86*, 320–333.

Wong, P. T. P. (2011). Positive psychology 2.0: Towards a balanced interactive model of the good life. *Canadian Psychology, 52*, 69–81.

Chapter 7
Firefighters: An Occupational Case Study of Resilience

Victoria Alicia Torres and Suzy Bird Gulliver

The phoenix is a mythological bird that is burned and reborn from the ashes. Often alluded to in literature, the phoenix represents the concept of renewal subsequent to adversity. Much like the phoenix that has its plight to thank for new life, firefighters are revered because of the many difficulties they face in service of others' tragedy (Bush 2002). The process of becoming a firefighter is fraught with challenges including exposure to potentially traumatic events, grueling physical training, sleep interruption and deprivation, and shifting social norms and contexts (Beaton et al. 1998; Vargas de Barros et al. 2013). Cumulatively, these stress exposures likely harden or prepare a recruit or probationary ("probie") firefighter to face disastrous situations. The process of rebirth and growth following adversity has many intertwining facets involved in the phoenix-like reconstruction and renewal.

To date, the main thrust of the relatively small scientific literature on firefighters and disaster rescue workers is toward identification of rates and incidence of psychopathology and negative aspects of the human condition (Mao et al. 2018). Research conducted by investigators at the Warriors Research Institute (WRI) of Baylor Scott & White in Central Texas demonstrates that those who enter fire service with no current psychopathology and very limited history of lifetime mental health diagnoses evidence very low rates of psychopathology over the first 3 years of fire service, with less than 2% developing posttraumatic stress disorder (PTSD), about 2% reporting major depression, and less than 1% endorsing any anxiety disorder. In general, those with a negative emotionality personality profile tend to display more negative symptoms over the early course of fire service (Gulliver et al. 2018b; Gulliver et al. under review; Meyer et al. under review). Earlier reviews of

V. A. Torres
Department of Psychology, University of Mississippi, Oxford, MS, USA

S. B. Gulliver (✉)
Warriors Research Institute, Baylor Scott & White Health, Waco, TX, USA

Texas A&M College of Medicine Health Science Center, Temple, TX, USA
e-mail: Suzy.gulliver@bswhealth.org

S. E. Schulenberg (ed.), *Positive Psychological Approaches to Disaster*,
https://doi.org/10.1007/978-3-030-32007-2_7

the literature by WRI personnel suggested that the established cross-sectional rates for Axis I psychopathology were in keeping with veteran samples (cf., Meyer et al. 2012), but the WRI's first assessment study of seasoned firefighters revealed a rate of only 4.2% with PTSD (Meyer et al. 2012). While the focus on firefighter psychopathology opened treatment doors for the meaningful minority that suffer mental health consequences of their occupational stress, and has likely reduced stigma across the firefighting profession, the many positive aspects of the human condition such as resilience, meaning-making, spirituality, and posttraumatic growth (PTG) remain grossly understudied (Gillham and Seligman 1999). This area represents an exciting new avenue of research as it appears likely that the average firefighter may serve as an exemplar of many of the strengths put forth by the VIA Institute on Character (particularly the virtues of courage and justice; VIA Institute on Character 2019).

Fire service is often considered a "calling" or vocation rather than a job. This passion is evident when considering a firefighter's ability to press on despite odds that appear extremely grim. Firefighters habitually choose duty to their communities over fear or even regard for personal health, safety, or well-being. Needless to say, firefighters are individuals who are dedicated to service. Yet, their extrinsic gains pale in comparison to the work that they accomplish as they are routinely exposed to horrific scenes in the course of their work (Corneil et al. 1999). Despite their very dangerous, unpredictable job, firefighters are motivated to respond when disasters strike. What pushes them to surmount these challenges? How do they fair in the wake of disaster? How do firefighters go from experiencing terrible situations in their work life to responding appropriately in their home lives? The literature on professional firefighters shows that the majority of firefighters complete full 20-plus year careers and fire service has consistently high job satisfaction ratings (Schorr and Boudreaux 2005). Early retirements are relatively rare and are usually linked to line-of-duty injuries (other than behavioral health injuries).

At any moment, a company may be called to respond to anything from a false alarm to a serious, widespread disaster. For this reason, firefighters remain vigilant. This facet of their work perfectly positions them as a model for trauma and resilience in disaster situations along with studies of the impact of prolonged stress on health. Prior to disaster situations, firefighters tend to be highly attentive to preparedness. In times of disaster, they are the first line of defense. It appears that we have much to learn from these "real-life phoenixes." Positive psychology research literature helps to address many of our disaster-related questions and lends valuable insight into what are thought to be "protective factors," or facets that may help a person to bounce back after adversity. For example, a study of firefighters' electronic diary entries demonstrated that firefighters who had positive perceptions of their work competence and positive reflections after work experienced delayed emotional benefits at home (Sonnentag and Grant 2012). Findings like these are vital for understanding how to live a fulfilling life. This chapter reviews protective factors that are characteristic of firefighters, explores how and why these strategies might be adaptive, and considers what questions are worthy of future study.

Protective Psychological Factors of Firefighters

Though there is quite a bit of interplay between positive psychological concepts, it is useful to begin our discussion of these constructs separately to gain a broader view of how each area contributes to the dynamic processes that occur subsequent to disaster.

Resilience

When adversity strikes, it often seems as though life will never return to normal again. In our most difficult times, we hope for the strength to adapt and overcome. The study of this process of returning to pre-crisis levels of functioning after an event evoking significant life threat has been deemed "resilience." A recent review of 54 studies in the nature and prevalence of trajectories following exposure to traumatic stressors shows that the more frequent response to trauma is resilience, defined as a stable trajectory of healthy functioning after a highly adverse event (Galatzer-Levy et al. 2018). According to a study by Blaney and Brunsden (2015), firefighters from the UK and Canada defined resilience as "an 'ability' to cope, recover, carry on, bounce back, protect, function, move on, or otherwise deal with stressors, and an 'immunity' or capacity to withstand challenges utilizing innate capacities such as mental toughness, focused, positive outlook, reframing events, etc." (p. 3). Disaster healthcare rescuers from China viewed, "having personality strengths, utilizing appropriate coping strategies, having social support, and making adequate preparations for rescue work" as pivotal features for resilience (Mao et al. 2019, p. 1). Thus, there is a small literature that demonstrates that firefighters think about their own resilience, and have made contributions to the definition of the term.

Firefighters represent a useful model for resilience since they witness potentially traumatic situations so routinely. Overall, investigators have noted that firefighters appear to be a resilient group; however, the mechanisms underlying their resilience still remain worthy of study. As noted above, elevated risk of trauma-related psychopathology was originally postulated in the literature on firefighters, with rates of PTSD in cross-sectional survey studies ranging from 12% to 56% (cf., Meyer et al. 2012). One rigorous diagnostic assessment study of career firefighters in an urban department countered these data; however, Meyer et al. (2012) found that out of 142 firefighters, the rate of PTSD was only 4.2% when using a standardized clinical interview and self-report measures, which is lower than the estimated incidence rate for US citizens. Further, there was no relationship between the frequency of encounters with potentially traumatic events firefighters were exposed to and the number of psychological symptoms endorsed, which suggests that firefighters were highly resilient. Researchers have found that there are individual, situational, and organizational features that contribute to resilience. Below, we briefly review the literature specific to firefighters.

Individual Factors and Resilience

Religiousness and Spirituality

Religiousness and spirituality are concepts that are deeply embedded in culture and as such, have been difficult to study broadly due to the high amount of diversity in belief systems. Accordingly, these concepts have been defined in a number of ways throughout empirical literature. However, fairly universally, religiousness is thought of as an external tool for accessing the divine. Spirituality is considered to be central to a person's identity and is often defined by a person's unique experience with God, a higher power, or the greater world (Gall et al. 2011). Religiousness and spirituality have been defined as separate yet distinct multidimensional constructs that both involve "a personal or group search for the sacred" (Zinnbauer and Pargament 2005, p. 35). In spite of the challenges of studying religiousness and spirituality, the study of the intersection of psychology and religiousness and spirituality continues to grow. As one can imagine, when a disaster occurs, ideals concerning religiousness and spirituality become more complex as people's conceptualization of their world can become completely upended by these emotionally taxing events (Park et al. 2012).

It appears that religiousness and spirituality are embedded in the "warrior culture" of emergency responders as observationally, most fire departments have a fire Chaplain (Malmin 2013). Frequently, this chaplain is of the same faith organization as many of the firefighters themselves. An early survey conducted by our research group demonstrates that firefighters are moderately likely to seek counseling or support from departmental Chaplains; however, they were more likely to rely on family and co-workers than on a Chaplain (Gulliver et al. 2018a).

Among firefighters, very few religion and spirituality studies have been conducted. Our literature search in this area yielded only one peer-reviewed manuscript directly addressing spirituality, religiousness, and resilience in this population. Ogińska-Bulik and Zadworna-Cieślak (2015) recruited 200 emergency service workers (37.1% firefighters, 25.8% paramedics, 37.1% police officers) from the Podkarpacie, Lodz, and Warsaw regions. Using the Self-Description Questionnaire to measure spirituality, participants were asked questions concerning religiousness, ethical sensitivity, and harmony in relation to a traumatic experience as measured by the Impact of Event Scale. Researchers found that there was no relationship between spirituality and posttraumatic stress symptoms; however, there was a relationship between spirituality and PTG as measured by the Posttraumatic Growth Inventory (PTGI; Tedeschi and Calhoun 1996). Those who were more spiritual tended to experience more PTG as compared to those who were less spiritual ($r = 0.40$, $p < 0.001$). More specifically, those who scored higher on the "harmony" and "religiousness" aspects of the scale tended to experience more PTG after the traumatic event than those who scored lower on these subscales. While harmony was captured in this study as "expressing a sense of belonging to the world, seeing the world as friendly, feeling internal peace and happiness," religiousness was measured by "the level of religious practices in everyday life" (Ogińska-Bulik and Zadworna-Cieślak 2015, p. 6).

Meaning-Making

Meaning-making is a complex and multifaceted cognitive process (Wong 2013). Empirically, meaning in life has been studied both quantitatively and qualitatively and several common broad and subjective themes have been noted across the meaning literature (Florez et al. 2016). Overall, meaning refers to the degree to which individuals perceive that their lives have significance and purpose (Shrira et al. 2015). It has also been found to drive motivation and to occur dynamically across the lifespan (Wong 2013).

In the context of fire service, studies regarding meaning are sparse with only four publications unearthed in our search. Two of these are opinion pieces and two are survey studies. Following the terrorist attacks of September 11, 2001, several international investigators developed an integrative treatment approach with a meaning-based component specifically tailored to first responders (Haugen et al. 2013). Meaning-making is postulated to be an active mechanism of change whereby people exposed to trauma have their perceptions of the safety of their world threatened, and may suffer from attendant insecurity regarding the most balanced interpretation of the meaning of the event to them individually, to their community, and to their community's position in the world (Haugen et al. 2013). Coaching firefighters on meaning-making was put forth as a means of helping return to baseline and/or respond resiliently to trauma. As these authors suggest, additional exploration of how well firefighters respond to stress with psychological flexibility and solid meaning-making techniques will aid us in understanding the mechanisms of action that account for the resilience of the professional group. The second opinion piece is written by a firefighter and sociologist (Woodall 1997) and suggests that the meaning and associations a firefighter makes to a traumatic event is a double-edged sword: when firefighters empathize too much, they suffer, but if they distance too much, their performance suffers.

An exploratory study of three dimensions of meaning in life (personal meaning, presence of meaning, search for meaning) and burnout among Polish firefighters indicated that firefighters who endorsed higher levels of personal meaning and presence of meaning reported more personal accomplishment and less emotional exhaustion and de-personalization than those who had a detached style (Krok 2016). In this study, personal meaning, "an individually constructed cognitive system which endows life with personal significance" was measured using the Personal Meaning Profile (Krok 2016, p. 34). Presence of meaning and search for meaning were measured using the Meaning in Life Questionnaire which captures how meaningful a respondent perceives their life to be and the extent to which the participant is seeking meaning or purpose in life (Krok 2016). Similarly, among Israeli firefighters who extinguished the 2010 Mount Carmel forest fire, investigators found that positive affect and meaning in life differentially related to PTSD symptoms depending on the function of the other construct in a high stress situation (Shrira et al. 2015). Specifically, for firefighters with high positive affect (thought to be a personality construct rather than a reactive mood state) meaning in life was not related to either PTSD or coping self-efficacy. However, for firefighters with low positive affect, meaning in life predicted lower PTSD scores and higher coping self-efficacy. Of course, this study is exploratory as well, given that it was cross-sectional.

Posttraumatic Growth

While resilience is considered a return to normal, investigators have noted that PTG, defined as "the experience of positive changes that occur as a result of the struggle with major life crises," goes above and beyond the ability to bounce back and is thought to occur separately from resilience since it requires a complete reconstruction of pre-disaster assumptions (Tedeschi et al. 2015, p. 504; Westphal and Bonanno 2007). As noted by Schulenberg (2016), while the study of positive psychology is a fairly new area of research cultivated in the late 1990's, growth in the face of adversity has been of interest to humans from time eternal. Early authors drew on their personal experience of growth through periods of extraordinary trauma such as the Holocaust (c.f., Frankl 1963). Over the past few decades, several investigators have studied PTG among a variety of emergency service personnel including both volunteer and full-time Austrian and Australian ambulance personnel (Ragger et al. 2019; Shakespeare-Finch et al. 2003), police officers (Paton 2005), and firefighters (Armstrong et al. 2014; Kehl et al. 2015; Sattler et al. 2014). These investigators raised three questions, "What is the prevalence rate of PTG among emergency service personnel?" "Is it possible to increase the likelihood that first responders will experience PTG?" "Clinically, how can we bolster more PTG?"

Addressing the first question, Shakespeare-Finch et al. (2003) found that more than half of their sample of 526 seasoned Australian ambulance officers reported moderate levels of PTG and that those who endorsed experiencing a traumatic event in their personal lives and a work-related traumatic event around the same time experienced more PTG than those who denied experiencing both a personal and a work-related trauma in the same time frame. Armstrong et al. (2014) replicated these findings in a second sample of firefighters. In the context of disaster, these PTG prevalence rates lend potentially useful conjecture especially in regard to methods of measuring this construct among this group and people in other high-risk professions.

In response to the second and third questions ("Is it possible to increase the likelihood that first responders will experience PTG?"; "Clinically, how can we bolster more PTG?"), Paton (2005) conducted a thorough review of literature which highlights key influences on PTG among protective service professionals including police officers, firefighters, and emergency medical technicians (EMTs). Several of these key points correspond to selection and training of personnel. First, based on work by Fredrickson and colleagues (2003, as cited in Paton 2005) and Shakespeare-Finch et al. (2003), factors associated with increased PTG include older age at entry to duty and higher levels of emotional support, expression, and positive reframing.

Paton (2005) reported Linley and Joseph (2004) and Paton and Jackson's (2002) finding that self-efficacy appears to be predictive of PTG. Paton suggests that involvement in a cohesive team during and after a crisis appears to be a facilitative factor of PTG (Lyons et al. 1998; Park 1998; Paton and Stephens 1996, as cited in Paton 2005). Finally, at an organizational level Paton (2005) made several recommendations which are consistent with literature in this area, including planning for future situations and bolstering cognitive and procedural flexibility, to support PTG (Tuckey and Hayward 2011, as cited in Paton 2005). (For further reading on PTG interventions please see Calhoun and Tedeschi (1999) and Roepke (2015)). In keeping with Paton's (2005) findings, Armstrong et al. (2014) reported that increased self-care coping was predictive of PTG among 218 Australian firefighters who had experienced work-related traumatic events.

A study of 1,916 European firefighters revealed several associations between PTG and firefighter work-related traumatic events (Kehl et al. 2015). Those who had a lower education level (i.e., lowest formal education vs. higher secondary/university) and did not know people who died in the event were more likely to experience higher levels of PTG. Additionally, those who experienced more emotional distress and who perceived that their own life was in danger were more likely to experience PTG. Interestingly, the country the firefighter served in also had an impact on PTG. For example, Czech and Turkish firefighters experienced more PTG compared to the average amount of growth endorsed by the total sample of participants. Finally, and perhaps most pertinent to our conversation, firefighters reported experiencing or witnessing natural disasters including floods, earthquakes, and landslides and these experiences were positively associated with growth. Authors speculated that the lack of blame and cohesive community aspects inherent in natural disasters may promote more growth as compared with other types of disasters.

Investigation into reports from Israeli firefighters one month after a massive fire lends more insight into these associations. Among this sample of 65 firefighters, PTG was evident to a small degree. Specifically, firefighters endorsed changes in personal strength and appreciation for life (Leykin et al. 2013).

Personality

There is a paucity of research on personality, a person's collective pattern of characteristic responses, among firefighters, particularly as it relates to resilience. Our literature search revealed two studies associated with negative outcomes, and our group has one manuscript under review on personality and symptoms in firefighters. The first study is cross-sectional, and found that neuroticism was associated with PTSD following exposure to wildfires. The second study demonstrated that neuroticism was associated with occupational burnout in French firefighters. To our knowledge, no other study has prospectively examined the influence of personality on the development of PTSD and other negative outcomes. In our longitudinal assessment study of firefighter recruits, higher negative emotionality (NEM) measured during fire academy prospectively predicted greater PTSD symptom severity over 3 years using the PTSD Checklist – Civilian version (PCL-C; Meyer et al. under review). High NEM interacted with high levels of trauma exposure to predict greater PTSD symptom severity. PCL-C scores were about 18 points higher than those reporting average NEM scores by 3 year follow-up. (A difference of 10 points or greater is considered a clinically significant difference on the PCL-C.) The interaction was significant on both the firefighter-specific trauma exposure measure developed by our team (FFWE) and a general trauma exposure measure (THQ). Thus, NEM, which is roughly normally distributed in the general population, is important to consider in relation to understanding long-term health risks associated with entry into an occupation with high levels of trauma exposure. What remains to be seen is whether more "adaptive" personality structures are related to measures of resiliency. Our study was focused primarily on the development of vulnerability trajectories, and so our measures of resilience were less than adequate. However, we have new studies under review that should begin to fill this gap in the literature.

Self-Forgiveness

Self-forgiveness refers to a person's ability to regulate their own self-directed adverse reactions to perceptions of their failures or shortcomings. Empirical literature has demonstrated that those who are able to forgive themselves for perceived wrongdoing tend to be healthier both mentally and physically (Hirsch et al. 2011; Wilson et al. 2008). To our knowledge, only one study published thus far has investigated the role of self-forgiveness and resiliency factors among firefighters (Carpenter et al. 2019). This study assessed a community sample of 72 firefighters from the United States and Canada on variables including self-forgiveness, stigma regarding mental health or internal stigma, and symptoms of mental health conditions. As predicted, firefighters with greater self-forgiveness reported less internalized stigma concerning a mental health problem, as well as less depressive symptoms, lower suicidal ideation, and fewer PTSD symptoms. Although this study did not directly assess resilience, given that the sample was career fire service, the relationships suggest that self-forgiveness, a modifiable individual difference, may be one of the constructs related to the overarching wellness in firefighters.

Heart Rate Variability

From a psychobiological lens to the study of resilience, Schwerdtfeger and Dick (2018) used ecological momentary assessment and heart rate variability to capture snippets of a workday in the life of 38 German firefighters. Heart rate variability (HRV) is thought to be a non-modifiable variable, although increasingly findings are exploring whether this variable is in fact malleable. Nonetheless, HRV is thought to be an individual difference variable. The goal was to explore the relationship between self-report measures of resilience, real-time momentary resilience measured via an app with four questions scored on a 7-point Likert-type scale, and heart rate variability. They found that questionnaire responses of resilience and aggregated momentary assessment, a brief repeated measure of resilience during the day, were related. Additionally, when firefighters faced stressful operations and reported momentary feelings of resilience via aggregated momentary assessment, they were more likely to have stronger reductions in HRV and less negative affect. This response appears to be a protective mechanism as the body prepared itself to react in a given context. These findings demonstrate that there are differences in psychobiological responses to stress among firefighters, and that those with high feelings of resilience are more likely to cope well with the stress of the work.

Psychological Flexibility

Psychological flexibility is "about being aware of thoughts and feelings that unfold in the present moment without needless defense, and depending on what the situation affords, persisting or changing behavior to pursue central interests and goals" (Kashdan and Rottenberg 2010, p. 6). In a series of papers with war veterans, colleagues demonstrated that psychological flexibility predicted PTSD-related resilience and PTSD symptom severity over time, after accounting for NEM and other established risk factors (Meyer et al. 2013, 2018, 2019). In one prospective study, people with higher psychological flexibility prior to exposure to a mass shooting reported lower PTSD symptom severity over time (Orcutt et al. 2014). Taken together, these findings indicate that low psychological flexibility is not merely a correlate of mental health symptoms; it can be distinguished from NEM. However, to our knowledge, no one has examined psychological flexibility in firefighters.

Situational Factors and Resilience

Social Support and Work Group Coherence

Social support is the perception that one is part of a nurturing social network and has access to instrumental assistance from others. Anecdotally, it appears that the emphasis on social support among firefighters is a large part of the overall culture of the occupation as evidenced by the language firefighters use. Specifically, firefighters refer to their companies as a "brotherhood" and endorse the idea of "having each other's backs." In an early firefighter study, our group found that lower perceived social support directly predicted mental health and substance use symptoms and that lower social support interacted with self-blame to further predict these negative outcomes (Meyer et al. 2012). In another firefighter study, declining social support interacted with increasing PTSD symptom scores to predict higher levels of suicidal ideation (Carpenter et al. 2015). In addition, numerous older studies of firefighters corroborate the association between decreased social support and PTSD symptomatology (Beaton et al. 1999; Dudek and Koniarek 2000; Regehr et al. 2000, 2001), and Murphy et al. (1999) documented a "dramatic decline in perceived social support at home between the baseline and two-year follow-up assessments" (p. 191) in a prospective, longitudinal analysis of professional firefighters. Beaton et al. (1999) demonstrated that when perceived workplace coherence declines, symptoms increase. As mentioned in previous paragraphs, the focus of most work to date has been on predicting illness, as opposed to predicting resilience, so additional assessment of healthy social support and the relationship to resilience is warranted. Further, it may be of interest to assess firefighters' baseline social support level to see how it compares with other occupations. If it is higher than that of other professions, lowered social support could have a more detrimental impact on this group than what is found in other groups.

External Stigma

To the authors' knowledge, no one outside the WRI has examined the role of stigma and resilience in fire service specifically. However, in the general population studies have noted the detrimental impact of stigma both to help-seeking behavior and to the health of those with mental health problems (Clement et al. 2015; Corrigan 2004). An early survey of firefighters and behavioral health (Gulliver et al. 2018a) showed that perceptions of stigma were thought to be a major barrier to behavioral health, both in terms of seeking treatment, and recognizing when people in the profession were under duress. Interestingly, Carpenter et al. (2019) did not demonstrate a meaningful relationship between externalized stigma and self-forgiveness. Thus, the role of perceived external stigma in relation to resilience is as yet insufficiently explored.

Organizational Factors and Resilience

Next to nothing has been empirically examined regarding organizational factors in fire service and resilience. Gist (2007) drafted a chapter that describes some organizational facets that he postulates promote resilience. He pinpoints the importance of re-examining former assumptions about addressing trauma and emphasizes the importance of the organization's role in fostering resilience among emergency service personnel given that occupational stress has been presented as an important consideration in firefighter well-being (Gist 2007). Gist (2007) highlights a number of organizational strategies and protective facets including the importance of effective communication along the chain of command, support from human resources for adequate training, and a well-practiced incident management system. That said, there is a marked absence of studies looking at organizational factors in fire service.

Adaptive Facets of Protective Factors

Self-care practices for disaster relief operations personnel before, during, and after response have been outlined based on existing empirical literature (Quevillon et al. 2016). At present, efforts have also been made to provide tools and information to firefighters facing behavioral health issues via trained peer support specialists. As fire service culture has focused more consistently on health and wellness over the entire career, an emphasis on Peer Support and training spread across the United States and Canada. The fact that so many professional firefighters have participated in peer support training underscores the level of resilience endemic to the population. To date, over 3,400 North American firefighters have completed the International Association for Fire Fighters (IAFF) Peer Support training program (Dobani et al. in press).

Traditionally, the Union has supported the deployment of skilled fire personnel from the United States and Canada to disaster situations ranging from the suicide of a member, to scenes of mass violence, to natural disasters. In the expanding push to ensure high quality, evidence-based peer support services, especially at disaster scenes, the IAFF is building a disaster relief training for peer support specialists that rests heavily on the workgroup that reviewed disaster response. See the following website for further details: http://client.prod.iaff.org/#page=disasterRelief

This training will be available online for firefighters that have been trained as peer supporters, and emphasizes skill acquisition wherein peer support specialists are given skills to help fellow firefighters with safety, calmness, self-efficacy, connectedness, and hope. The content areas are drawn from the suggestions put forth by Hobfoll and colleagues (2007). The online training program teaches through information dissemination, video clips of firefighters demonstrating the skills, and knowledge checks. Following slides defining the construct (e.g., "Promoting Safety") and explaining the importance of the concept, a video clip demonstrates a Peer performing the skill (e.g., a safety check-in). The videoclip is followed by knowledge check questions. Per Hobfoll et al. (2007), the online training includes the practice of calming techniques, instruction on how to shape and reward self-efficacious statements, training in effective means of checking in on social and familial support networks, and assisting with the development of a future-orientation.

Future Studies

In general, the limited literature on resilience in firefighters means that the breadth and scope of the research still needed far exceeds the space allotted here. Our exploration of the literature suggests that posttraumatic growth, psychological flexibility, personality, and social support are all areas worthy of additional investigation. Beyond the individual difference variables reported here, the core virtues and character strengths put forth by Peterson and Seligman (2004) represent a useful framework for considering the future of research related to firefighters' individual difference variables and positive psychology. Assessing the frequency and degree with which these state and trait variables occur among firefighters may be useful in providing a more representative picture of how resilient an individual firefighter may be. In addition, the paucity of research on the impact of situational variables as well as organizational variables will certainly contribute to a more complete picture of the resilient nature of fire service as a whole—that is, a picture that incorporates our view of illness alongside healthy outcomes and protective factors.

Additionally, as previously alluded to, many firefighters view fire service as a lifestyle rather than solely as a source of income. An emerging agenda for research will assess purpose and meaning in the context of a person's occupation, and may be particularly well explored within firefighters. Numerous questions abound including, "Is it protective for firefighters to consider their work a 'calling' rather than a 'job'?" and "How can firefighters cultivate more meaning from such challenging circumstances?". These facets are highlighted and expounded upon in Dik et al.'s (2013) book entitled, *Purpose and Meaning in the Workplace*.

Micro-questions, such as how recurrent trauma load impacts posttraumatic growth and whether the tendency for posttraumatic growth is driven by other personality variables such as self-forgiveness, are also of interest. In addition, cultural factors may impact differences in resilience across countries as alluded to in Kehl et al.'s (2015) investigation or even within and between departments in a specific region. Notably, authors reported several cultural differences across their UK and Canadian samples including differing responsibilities (Blaney and Brunsden 2015). Clearly, the road ahead for understanding this interesting professional group is wide open.

Conclusions

In sum, the men and women drawn to careers as modern phoenixes are strong models for the study of resilience in the face of disaster. The young literature on this unique professional group yields modest suggestions that firefighters with greater positive affectivity, stronger meaning-making skills and high levels of psychological flexibility (all conducive to posttraumatic growth) combined with positive HRV, strong social support, cohesive working groups and Union and city leadership that is supportive of their service are more likely to demonstrate positive adjustment and adaptation in the face of disaster. Additional research will likely have benefits for the professional group, the families of that group, and the communities they serve. Moreover, additional study of firefighters across their lifespan will broaden our understanding of the mechanisms of action for adaptive change in humans influenced by disaster.

References

Armstrong, D., Shakespeare-Finch, J., & Shochet, I. (2014). Predicting post-traumatic growth and post-traumatic stress in firefighters. *Australian Journal of Psychology, 66*(1), 38–46.

Beaton, R., Murphy, S., Johnson, C., Pike, K., & Corneil, W. (1998). Exposure to duty-related incident stressors in urban professional firefighters and paramedics. *Journal of Traumatic Stress, 11*(4), 821–828. https://doi.org/10.1023/A:1024461920456.

Beaton, R., Murphy, S., Johnson, C., Pike, K., & Corneil, W. (1999). Coping responses and posttraumatic stress symptomatology in urban fire-service personnel. *Journal of Traumatic Stress, 12*(2), 293–308. https://doi.org/10.1023/A:1024776509667.

Blaney, L., & Brunsden, V. (2015). Resilience and health promotion in high-risk professions: A pilot study of firefighters in Canada and the United Kingdom. *The International Journal of Interdisciplinary Organizational Studies, 10*(2), 23–32.

Bush, N. E. (2002). Afterward: Making meaning after a frightening near-death experience. *Journal of Near-Death Studies, 21*(2), 99–133.

Calhoun, L. G., & Tedeschi, R. G. (1999). *Facilitating posttraumatic growth: A clinician's guide*. Mahwah: Lawrence Erlbaum Associates.

Carpenter, G. S. J., Carpenter, T. P., Kimbrel, N. A., Flynn, E. J., Pennington, M. L., Cammarata, C., et al. (2015). Social support, stress, and suicidal ideation in professional firefighters. *American Journal of Health Behavior, 39*(2), 191–196.

Carpenter, T., Pennington, M. L., Seebeck, J., Gomez, D. R., Denman, T. C., Kimbrel, N. A., et al. (2019). Dispositional self-forgiveness in firefighters predicts less help-seeking stigma and fewer mental health challenges. *Stigma and Health*. https://doi.org/10.1037/sah0000172.

Clement, S., Schauman, O., Graham, T., Maggioni, F., Evans-Lacko, S., Bezborodovs, N., et al. (2015). What is the impact of mental health-related stigma on help-seeking? A systematic review of quantitative and qualitative studies. *Psychological Medicine, 45*(1), 11–27. https://doi.org/10.1017/S0033291714000129.

Corneil, W., Beaton, R., Murphy, S., Johnson, C., & Pike, K. (1999). Exposure to traumatic incidents and prevalence of posttraumatic stress symptomatology in urban firefighters in two countries. *Journal of Occupational Health Psychology, 4*(2), 131–141.

Corrigan, P. (2004). How stigma interferes with mental health care. *American Psychologist, 59*(7), 614–625. https://doi.org/10.1037/0003-066X.59.7.614.

Dik, B. J., Byrne, Z. S., & Steger, M. F. (Eds.). (2013). *Purpose and meaning in the workplace*. Washington, DC: American Psychological Association.

Dobani, F., Pennington, M. L., Coe, E., Morrison, P., & Gulliver, S. B. (in press). Bridging the gaps: Toward effective collaboration between peer supporters and behavioral health professionals. In C. A. Bowers, D. C. Beidel, & M. R. Marks (Eds.), *Mental health intervention and treatment of first responders and emergency workers*. Hershey: IGI Global.

Dudek, B., & Koniarek, J. (2000). Relationship between sense of coherence and post-traumatic stress disorder symptoms among firefighters. *International Journal of Occupational Medicine and Environmental Health, 13*(4), 299–305.

Florez, I. A., Schulenberg, S. E., & Stewart, T. L. (2016). Meaning and automatic stereotyping: Advancing an agenda for research. In A. Batthyany (Ed.), *Logotherapy and existential analysis: Proceedings of the Viktor Frankl Institute, Vienna* (Vol. 1, pp. 107–124). Cham: Springer International Publishing. https://doi.org/10.1007/978-3-319-29424-7_11.

Frankl, V. E. (1963). *Man's search for meaning*. New York: Pocket Books.

Galatzer-Levy, I. R., Huang, S. H., & Bonanno, G. A. (2018). Trajectories of resilience and dysfunction following potential trauma: A review and statistical evaluation. *Clinical Psychology Review, 63*, 41–55.

Gall, T. L., Malette, J., & Guirguis-Younger, M. (2011). Spirituality and religiousness: A diversity of definitions. *Journal of Spirituality and Mental Health, 13*(3), 158–181. https://doi.org/10.1080/19349537.2011.593404.

Gillham, J. E., & Seligman, M. E. (1999). Footsteps on the road to a positive psychology. *Behaviour Research and Therapy, 37*(1), S163–S173.

Gist, R. (2007). Promoting resilience and recovery in first responders. In B. Bongar, L. M. Brown, L. E. Beutler, J. N. Breckenridge, & P. G. Zimbardo (Eds.), *Psychology of terrorism* (pp. 418–433). New York: Oxford University Press.

Gulliver, S. B., Pennington, M. L., Torres, V. A., Steffen, L. E., Mardikar, A., Leto, F., et al. (2018a). Behavioral health programs in fire service: Surveying access and preferences. *Psychological Services, 16*(2), 340–345. https://doi.org/10.1037/ser0000222.

Gulliver, S. B., Zimering, R., Knight, J., Morissette, S., Kamholz, B., Meyer, E., et al. (2018b). Tobacco and alcohol use among firefighters during their first 3 years of service. *Psychology of Addictive Behaviors, 32*(3), 255–263.

Gulliver, S. B., Zimering, R. T., Knight, J., Morissette, S. B., Kamholz, B. W., Pennington, M. L.,… Meyer, E. C. (under review). A prospective study of the relationship between trauma exposure and development of PTSD and depression symptoms in fire fighters during their first three years of service.

Haugen, P. T., Splaun, A. K., Evces, M. R., & Weiss, D. S. (2013). Integrative approach for the treatment of posttraumatic stress disorder in 9/11 first responders: Three core techniques. *Psychotherapy, 50*(3), 336–340.

Hirsch, J. K., Webb, J. R., & Jeglic, E. L. (2011). Forgiveness, depression, and suicidal behavior among a diverse sample of college students. *Journal of Clinical Psychology, 67*(9), 896–906. https://doi.org/10.1002/jclp.20812.

Hobfoll, S. E., Watson, P., Bell, C. C., Bryant, R. A., Brymer, M. J., Friedman, M. J., et al. (2007). Five essential elements of immediate and mid–term mass trauma intervention: Empirical evidence. *Psychiatry: Interpersonal and Biological Processes, 70*(4), 283–315.

Kashdan, T., & Rottenberg, J. (2010). Psychological flexibility as a fundamental aspect of health. *Clinical Psychology Review, 30*(7), 865–878. https://doi.org/10.1016/j.cpr.2010.03.001.

Kehl, D., Knuth, D., Hulse, L., & Schmidt, S. (2015). Predictors of post event distress and growth among firefighters after work-related emergencies—A cross-national study. *Psychological Trauma: Theory, Research, Practice and Policy, 7*(3), 203–211. https://doi.org/10.1037/a0037954.

Krok, D. (2016). Can meaning buffer work pressure? An exploratory study on styles of meaning in life and burnout in firefighters. *Archives of Psychiatry and Psychotherapy, 18*(1), 31–42.

Leykin, D., Lahad, M., & Bonneh, N. (2013). Posttraumatic symptoms and posttraumatic growth of Israeli firefighters, at one month following the Carmel fire disaster. *Psychiatry Journal*, 1–5. https://doi.org/10.1155/2013/274121.

Malmin, M. (2013). Warrior culture, spirituality, and prayer. *Journal of Religion and Health, 52*(3), 740–758.

Mao, X., Fung, O. W. M., Hu, X., & Loke, A. Y. (2018). Psychological impacts of disaster on rescue workers: A review of the literature. *International Journal of Disaster Risk Reduction, 27*, 602–617.

Mao, X., Loke, A. Y., Fung, O. W. M., & Hu, X. (2019). What it takes to be resilient: The views of disaster healthcare rescuers. *International Journal of Disaster Risk Reduction, 36*, 1–8. https://doi.org/10.1016/j.ijdrr.2019.101112.

Meyer, E. C., Kotte, A., Kimbrel, N. A., DeBeer, B. B., Elliott, T. R., Gulliver, S. B., & Morissette, S. B. (2019). Predictors of lower-than-expected posttraumatic symptom severity in war veterans: The influence of personality, self-reported trait resilience, and psychological flexibility. *Behaviour Research and Therapy, 113*, 1–8. https://doi.org/10.1016/j.brat.2018.12.005.

Meyer, E. C., La Bash, H., DeBeer, B. B., Kimbrel, N. A., Gulliver, S. B., & Morissette, S. B. (2018). Psychological inflexibility predicts PTSD symptom severity in war veterans after accounting for established PTSD risk factors and personality. *Psychological Trauma: Theory, Research, Practice, and Policy, 11*(4), 383–390. https://doi.org/10.1037/tra0000358.

Meyer, E. C., Morissette, S. B., Kimbrel, N. A., Kruse, M. I., & Gulliver, S. B. (2013). Acceptance and action Questionnaire – II scores as a predictor of posttraumatic stress disorder symptoms among war veterans. *Psychological Trauma: Theory, Research, Practice, and Policy, 5*(6), 521–528. https://doi.org/10.1037/a0030178.

Meyer, E. C., Zimering, R., Daly, E., Knight, J., Kamholz, B. W., & Gulliver, S. B. (2012). Predictors of posttraumatic stress disorder and other psychological symptoms in trauma-exposed firefighters. *Psychological Services, 9*(1), 1–15.

Meyer, E. C., Zimering, R. T., Knight, J., Morissette, S. B., Kamholz, B. W., Pennington, M. L.,... Gulliver, S. B. (under review). Negative emotionality interacts with trauma exposure to prospectively predict greater PTSD symptom severity during the first three years of fire service.

Murphy, S. A., Beaton, R. D., Pike, K. C., & Johnson, L. C. (1999). Occupational stressors, stress responses, and alcohol consumption among professional firefighters: A prospective, longitudinal analysis. *International Journal of Stress Management, 6*(3), 180–196.

Ogińska-Bulik, N., & Zadworna-Cieślak, M. (2015). Spirituality and the negative and positive effects of traumatic experiences in a group of emergency service workers. *Polish Journal of Applied Psychology, 13*(2), 9–24.

Orcutt, H. K., Bonanno, G. A., Hannan, S. M., & Miron, L. R. (2014). Prospective trajectories of posttraumatic stress in college women following a campus mass shooting. *Journal of Traumatic Stress, 27*(3), 249–256.

Park, C. L., Mills, M. A., & Edmondson, D. (2012). PTSD as meaning violation: Testing a cognitive worldview perspective. *Psychological Trauma: Theory, Research, Practice and Policy, 4*(1), 66–73. https://doi.org/10.1037/a0018792.

Paton, D. (2005). Posttraumatic growth in protective services professionals: Individual, cognitive and organizational influences. *Traumatology, 11*(4), 335–346.

Peterson, C., & Seligman, M. E. P. (2004). *Character strengths and virtues: A handbook and classification*. New York: Oxford University Press.

Quevillon, R. P., Gray, B. L., Erickson, S. E., Gonzalez, E. D., & Jacobs, G. A. (2016). Helping the helpers: Assisting staff and volunteer workers before, during, and after disaster relief operations. *Journal of Clinical Psychology, 72*(12), 1348–1363. https://doi.org/10.1002/jclp.22336.

Ragger, K., Hiebler-Ragger, M., Herzog, G., Kapfhammer, H., & Unterrainer, H. F. (2019). Sense of coherence is linked to post-traumatic growth after critical incidents in Austrian ambulance personnel. *BMC Psychiatry, 19*(1), 89. https://doi.org/10.1186/s12888-019-2065-z.

Regehr, C., Hemsworth, D., & Hill, J. (2001). Individual predictors of posttraumatic distress: A structural equation model. *The Canadian Journal of Psychiatry, 46*(2), 156–161.

Regehr, C., Hill, J., & Glancy, G. D. (2000). Individual predictors of traumatic reactions in firefighters. *The Journal of Nervous and Mental Disease, 188*(6), 333–339.

Roepke, A. M. (2015). Psychosocial interventions and posttraumatic growth: A meta-analysis. *Journal of Consulting and Clinical Psychology, 83*(1), 129–142.

Sattler, D. N., Boyd, B., & Kirsch, J. (2014). Trauma-exposed firefighters: Relationships among posttraumatic growth, posttraumatic stress, resource availability, coping and critical incident stress debriefing experience. *Stress and Health, 30*(5), 356–365.

Schorr, J. K., & Boudreaux, A. S. (2005). Responding to terrorism in the USA: Firefighters share experiences in their own words. *Journal of Aggression, Maltreatment & Trauma, 10*(1–2), 577–589.

Schulenberg, S. E. (2016). Disaster mental health and positive psychology – Considering the context of natural and technological disasters: An introduction to the special issue. *Journal of Clinical Psychology, 72*(12), 1223–1233.

Shakespeare-Finch, J. E., Smith, S. G., Gow, K. M., Embelton, G., & Baird, L. (2003). The prevalence of post-traumatic growth in emergency ambulance personnel. *Traumatology, 9*(1), 58–71.

Shrira, A., Shmotkin, D., Palgi, Y., Soffer, Y., Hamama, Y. R., Tal-Katz, P., et al. (2015). How do meaning in life and positive affect relate to adaptation to stress? The case of firefighters following the Mount Carmel forest fire. *The Israel Journal of Psychiatry and Related Sciences, 52*(3), 68–70.

Sonnentag, S., & Grant, A. M. (2012). Doing good at work feels good at home, but not right away: When and why perceived prosocial impact predicts positive affect. *Personnel Psychology, 65*(3), 495–530.

Tedeschi, R. G., & Calhoun, L. G. (1996). The Posttraumatic Growth Inventory: Measuring the positive legacy of trauma. *Journal of Traumatic Stress, 9*(3), 455–471.

Tedeschi, R. G., Calhoun, L. G., & Groleau, J. M. (2015). Clinical applications of posttraumatic growth. In S. Joseph (Ed.), *Positive psychology in practice: Promoting human flourishing in work, health, education, and everyday life* (pp. 503–518). Hoboken: Wiley.

Vargas de Barros, V., Martins, L. F., Saitz, R., Bastos, R. R., & Ronzani, T. M. (2013). Mental health conditions, individual and job characteristics and sleep disturbances among firefighters. *Journal of Health Psychology, 18*(3), 350–358.

VIA Institute on Character. (2019). The 24 character strengths. Retrieved from https://www.viacharacter.org/character-strengths

Westphal, M., & Bonanno, G. A. (2007). Posttraumatic growth and resilience to trauma: Different sides of the same coin or different coins? *Applied Psychology, 56*(3), 417–427.

Wilson, T., Milosevic, A., Carroll, M., Hart, K., & Hibbard, S. (2008). Physical health status in relation to self-forgiveness and other-forgiveness in healthy college students. *Journal of Health Psychology, 13*(6), 798–803. https://doi.org/10.1177/1359105308093863.

Wong, P. T. P. (Ed.). (2013). *The human quest for meaning: Theories, research, and applications* (2nd ed.). Retrieved from https://ebookcentral.proquest.com.

Woodall, S. J. (1997). Hearts on fire: An exploration of the emotional world of firefighters. *Clinical Sociology Review, 15*(1), 153–162.

Zinnbauer, B. J., & Pargament, K. I. (2005). Religiousness and spirituality. In R. F. Paloutzian & C. L. Park (Eds.), *Handbook of the psychology of religion and spirituality* (pp. 21–42). New York: The Guilford Press.

Chapter 8
Responding to Adolescents Following Natural and Technological Disasters: The Essential Nature of Hope

Alexis K. Liberto, Emily Thomas Johnson, and Stefan E. Schulenberg

According to the U.S. Census Bureau (2014), there are approximately 42 million adolescents (ages 10–19) residing in the United States. With specific regard for natural disasters, early estimates from the U.S. National Survey of Adolescents indicated that approximately 25% of these youth have experienced a natural disaster in their lifetimes (Kilpatrick and Saunders 1995). More than 4% of adolescents have experienced a natural disaster (e.g., hurricane, tornado, earthquake) in the past year (Becker-Blease et al. 2010). Thus, whether one considers the broad range of experiences throughout an adolescent's development or a given time period in the adolescent's life, it is apparent that natural disasters are common occurrences with potentially traumatic consequences. Despite the apparent problematic nature of natural disasters, little published information addresses the short-term mental health care needs of adolescents specifically (Cohen et al. 2016). This may be due to the common utilization of broad terms such as *children*, *youth*, and *childhood*, which may refer to adolescence (12–18 years of age) selectively in some contexts and/or younger children in other contexts. Our assertion in this paper is that greater attention needs to be paid to age and developmental level in the extant literature. The developmental focus of this chapter is on adolescence.

Understanding the developmental time period or "sensitive period" of an individual's exposure to trauma is essential to understanding the etiology of various

A. K. Liberto (✉) · S. E. Schulenberg
Department of Psychology, Clinical-Disaster Research Center, University of Mississippi, Oxford, MS, USA
e-mail: aklibert@go.olemiss.edu

E. T. Johnson
Behavior, Attention, and Developmental Disabilities Consultants, Sardis, MS, USA

S. E. Schulenberg (ed.), *Positive Psychological Approaches to Disaster*,
https://doi.org/10.1007/978-3-030-32007-2_8

physical and mental health concerns that may develop over time (e.g., Bernstein and Pfefferbaum 2018; Cohen et al. 2006; Cohen et al. 2016; Dunn et al. 2017; Knudsen 2004; Speier 2000). This particular developmental time period is crucial to highlight due to the unique vulnerabilities adolescents experience. For example, neurological research into adolescent brain development seeks to explore how adolescents understand and contextualize their experienced trauma, in this case, a disaster event (Crane and Clements 2005). Such research assists in understanding not only the behaviors exhibited by adolescents that have experienced trauma, but also the neural pathways elicited when adolescents attempt to conceptualize the trauma itself (Knudsen 2004). Another reason adolescence is an important developmental period to explore in this context is the opportunity to gather first-hand narratives and perspectives on how adolescents conceptualize trauma and its impact. The research literature has relied significantly on parental input after trauma exposure, neglecting the perspectives of the adolescents themselves (Shemesh et al. 2005). For this reason there is an insufficient understanding of the needs of this population in this circumstance.

The lack of adolescence-specific research involving interventions post-disaster may be attributed to the common practice of treating adolescents as being more similar to adults in terms of mindset in their response (as opposed to the mindset of children). Thus, often there is a reliance on adult-related research with respect to working with adolescents (Dogan-Ates 2010). This is not necessarily an erroneous assumption as similarities do exist in the physiological brain structure and cognitive appraisals exhibited by adolescents and adults in the experience of disaster-related events (Eth and Pynoos 1985; Knudsen 2004). Indeed, the National Child Traumatic Stress Network and National Center for PTSD (2006) recommend that mental health practitioners working as disaster mental health (DMH) responders communicate with adolescents "adult-to-adult" in an effort to convey an understanding that their experiences and concerns regarding the event are more advanced than that of a young child. However, even with such a recommendation, it remains key that mental health professionals working with adolescents post-disaster consider the developmental context. For example, setting up age-appropriate discussion groups creates opportunities for adolescents to communicate their struggles, share with peers, as well as engage in behavioral activities in efforts to enhance adaptive processing of the event (Brymer et al. 2006). A growing number of recommendations have been produced for mental health and school-based professionals for working with youth following a disaster, though only a small portion of them are dedicated to adolescents specifically (Brymer, Reyes, and Steinberg 2012; Brymer, Taylor, et al. 2012). Further, there remains a lack of empirically-driven research studies utilizing these particular strategies with adolescents and examining their efficacy in the disaster-related context (Cohen et al. 2006). There are research-supported recommendations for working with adolescents post-disaster that are congruent with recommendations for aiding younger children (e.g., Vernberg et al. 2016). However, it is unclear when and in what ways adolescents should be considered more like adults or more like older children. Thus, in this chapter we aim to focus on adolescents (ages 12–18) in particular with this thought in mind. Prior to further discussion of disaster-related impacts and recommendations for assisting adolescents following disaster, as well as outlining the importance and essential nature of hope theory in this context, we take a moment to clarify the term, *disaster*, with particular consideration for natural and technological events.

Natural and Technological Disasters

Defining *disaster* can be an exercise in and of itself, as there are many characteristics that are encompassed by the word itself. The Federal Emergency Management Agency (FEMA) notes the importance of defining disaster in an effort to know how to respond accordingly. As such, FEMA defines disaster as "an occurrence of a natural catastrophe, technological accident, or human-caused event that has resulted in severe property damage, deaths, and/or multiple injuries" ("FEMA – Glossary" n.d.). The Center for Disease Control's (CDC) definition circumscribes a disaster as "a serious disruption of the functioning of society, causing widespread human, material or environmental losses, that exceeds the local capacity to respond, and calls for external assistance" ("Health Studies – Disaster Training and Response | CDC" 2018). Natural disasters and severe weather, as described by such organizations as the CDC and the American Red Cross, include earthquakes, landslides and mudslides, volcano eruptions, extreme heat, lightning, wildfire, floods, tornadoes, winter weather, hurricanes, and tsunamis ("Natural Disasters and Severe Weather | CDC" 2019; "Types of Emergencies" 2019). Technological incidents, alternatively, may include chemical/oil spills, contaminated food and water, inhalation of chemical vapors, etc., as well as explosions and fires ("Types of Emergencies" 2019). The Water Crisis in Flint, Michigan serves as an example, with adolescents exhibiting significant behavioral health concerns leading to reductions in quality of life.

No two disasters are alike (Dursun et al. 2016). Each disaster occurs in its own socio-political-cultural-economic context (Raley, Weber, Lemon, and Schulenberg, this volume). Such disasters can have tremendous adverse effects on physical and mental well-being. These adverse effects can last for prolonged periods of time, affecting not only the individual, but the family and community as well (Winter and Sampson 2017).

While there are other forms or classes of disasters that may impact individuals, families, and communities, such as incidents of terrorism (e.g., a mass shooting) and pandemics ("Types of Emergencies" 2019), they exist outside the scope of this chapter. Here we retain a specific focus on natural and technological disasters. As such, for the remainder of this chapter, the term *disaster* refers explicitly to natural and technological events. Thus, collectively the scope of this chapter considers the adolescent developmental period in the immediate context of a natural or technological disaster. Prior to a discussion of various interventions for disaster-affected youth, with specific attention paid to the essential nature of hope, we summarize some of the psychological effects that adolescents may experience in response to a disaster.

Psychological Effects of Disaster: The Immediate Context

A number of emotional consequences to the experience of disaster have been identified, with particular regard for youth (American Red Cross 2017; Berkowitz et al. 2010; Szente 2016; United Nations Children's Fund (UNICEF) 2000; Vernberg et al. 2016). Initial responses displayed by youth following an event include failure to recognize or confusion related to what has occurred; concern related to the experience; separation from, or loss of, immediate family; lack of appetite; increased thirst; nightmares; mourning/sadness/grief; hopelessness and uncertainty about the future (Doostgharin 2009; see also Table 8.1 for a summary). When looking at adolescents specifically, initial concerns relate to having a sense of a foreshortened future, pessimistic attitudes, as well as changes in their thoughts about career and family planning (Dogan-Ates 2010). Additionally, adolescents struggle with self-identity post-disaster (Speier 2000). This struggle can include the pull between wanting to be independent and wanting to rely on established relationships for guidance and support (Speier 2000; Vernberg et al. 2016). Because of the unique needs of this particular age group, there is a continuous need for mental health professionals to serve in disaster response, who are trained in disasters and mental health care, as well as knowledgeable and competent in providing immediate developmentally-appropriate support (Berkowitz et al. 2010; Doostgharin 2009; Vernberg et al. 2016).

Table. 8.1 Summary of psychological, behavioral, and physical concerns exhibited by adolescents post-disaster

Study	Psychological or behavioral responses
Brymer et al. (2006); Owens et al. (2012); Speier (2000)	Alcohol and other drug use
Balaban (2006); Brymer et al. (2006); Speier (2000)	Antisocial behaviors (e.g., stealing, aggressive behavior, acting out)
Balaban (2006); Dyregrov et al. (2018); Kar and Bastia (2006)	Anxiety (e.g., panic, phobias, obsessive-compulsive behaviors)
Balaban (2006); Brymer, Reyes, and Steinberg (2012); Brymer, Taylor, et al. (2012); Speier (2000)	Avoidance of developmentally-appropriate separations (e.g., going to camp or college)
Balaban (2006); Kar and Bastia (2006); Speier (2000)	Depression and sadness
Speier (2000)	Physical complaints (e.g., headaches or stomach pains)
American Red Cross (2017); Brymer et al. (2006); Kar and Bastia (2006)	Preoccupation with death and suicidal ideation
Brymer et al. (2006); Speier (2000); World Health Organization (WHO) (2011)	Risk-taking behaviors (e.g., sexual promiscuity, seeking revenge)
Brymer et al. (2006); Speier (2000)	School problems (e.g., disruptive behavior or avoidance, decline in academic performance)
Speier (2000)	Sleep disturbances (e.g., heavy sleep, sleep terrors, sleeplessness)
Brymer et al. (2006); Speier (2000); WHO (2011)	Withdrawal and isolation (e.g., shame, guilt, disbelief)

Unlike the limited literature on intervention efforts specifically geared to adolescents, extensive research has been undertaken as to adolescents' mental health and developmental risks following a disaster (Dogan-Ates 2010). In other words, we know more about the psychological impact of disasters on adolescents as opposed to what we know about disaster-related interventions for adolescents in the short term. For example, more research into addressing issues of trauma exposure and the risk of developing symptoms of depression, anxiety, and posttraumatic stress disorder (PTSD) following a disaster has become increasingly prominent, demonstrating that such symptoms can persist into adulthood (e.g., Cohen et al. 2006; Dogan-Ates 2010; Dunn et al. 2017; Dyregrov et al. 2018; Kar and Bastia 2006). Additionally, erratic behavioral changes are also commonly exhibited by adolescents following a disaster, including the presence of maladaptive cognitions that contribute to increases in risk taking (Gaffney 2006; Jacobs 2016; Owens et al. 2012; Speier 2000). Understanding the psychological and behavioral impacts disasters have on this developmental age group are an important foundation to establishing appropriate response and recovery efforts.

Adolescents and Disaster-Related Interventions: The Immediate Context

The need to identify potential psychological impacts adolescents are at risk of developing post-disaster highlights the importance of expanding short-term interventions available to disaster mental health personnel. Because adolescents are typically seen as being more similar to adults than to younger school-aged children from a cognitive perspective, the literature appears mixed on how best to go about implementing such interventions. Common psychological impacts may be minimized through developmentally-appropriate and immediately-administered interventions reviewed and documented in various reports and manuals. Examples of such interventions utilized by disaster mental health workers in the immediate, short-term context are discussed in greater detail below. While there are various empirically-supported treatments for adolescents within the first three months following a disaster event (see, for example, Pfefferbaum et al. 2017), an in-depth review of such interventions is beyond the scope of this chapter given our emphasis on immediate response and recovery efforts.

In reviewing the disaster mental health literature, there are a number of strategies applicable to various settings that demonstrate promise for facilitating resilience in adolescents adversely affected by disasters in the short term. Relief efforts primarily focus on identifying and meeting the basic physical and medical needs of those directly affected by the event. Restoration of previous relationships (e.g., reuniting with family) are often prioritized (Szente 2016; World Health Organization, or WHO 2011). Mental health professionals may work with a number of adolescents in a shelter setting post-disaster. At such times, it is beneficial to provide social support through means that these youths can relate to, as well as ease discomfort. It is important that mental health professionals use age-appropriate concepts (e.g., encouraging honesty about emotions, expectations, fears, and facts about the disaster), communicating to these youths that they are active members of their respective communities, empowering them and highlighting their independence as key players in their recovery (Speier 2000; Vernberg et al. 2016; WHO 2011). Interventions may include the utilization of developmentally-appropriate education and activities with peers, with a consideration of language and questions that may be asked (e.g., speaking to adolescents in a more mature manner than one would adopt with a younger, school-aged child; Berson and Baggerly 2009; Brymer et al. 2006; Johnson and Ronan 2014; Masten and Narayan 2012; Vernberg et al. 2016). Language tailored for younger children, but used with adolescents, may leave these older youth feeling as though they are "incompetent to manage the current crisis," or mental health professionals may come across as "childish and condescending" (Vernberg et al. 2016, pp. 1334–1335). Shared activities with same-age peers often assist with adaptive coping as well (Speier 2000; Vernberg et al. 2016).

Disaster mental health providers can also assist in speaking with adolescents related to available support options in terms of what is available and how best to access these resources. This process serves as a catalyst for developing goals, which is an important aspect of Psychological First Aid (PFA) and hope theory, both of which are discussed in greater depth in subsequent sections of this chapter. Additionally, mental health professionals may facilitate the normalization of adaptive help-seeking behaviors, such as how best to speak with available personnel as to whether and how the adolescent may be of assistance, as well as demonstrate appreciation for the help that the adolescent receives (Vernberg et al. 2016). Such opportunities often function as a means to increase self-efficacy and instill empowerment (Brymer et al. 2006). Increases in such aspects of self-agency are associated with the development of hope (Arata et al. 2000). In other words, assisting with short-term goal setting and problem-solving routes to attainment at this step promotes hope building during these interactions (via concepts termed *agency* and *pathways* in hope theory, discussed shortly).

With further regard for intervention, it is important to pass on accurate information related to family members and disaster response activities (Brymer, Reyes, and Steinberg 2012; Brymer, Taylor, et al. 2012). This may also include addressing media and social networking safety concerns, in an effort to minimize the impact the disaster may have on adolescents and their families, as well as protecting their privacy (Speier 2000; WHO 2011). Accurate information allows for realistic goal setting and pathways development. To the extent possible, adolescents should be put in touch with family in an effort to utilize any pre-existing social support that is already in place (Masten and Osofsky 2010). For adolescents, this may also include connecting them with similar-age friendships and informal peer networks. Social support is key to promoting better personal adjustment, overall well-being, and resilience, in general and with specific regard for disasters (Bokszczanin 2012; Bonanno et al. 2008; Brymer et al. 2006; Peek 2008; Southwick and Charney 2018; Speier 2000). Peer groups often help in the development of feelings of connectedness. Throughout these intervention efforts, it is essential to consider culture, economic resources, and family dynamics (Berkowitz et al. 2010; Domenech Rodríguez and Bernal 2012; Rabalais et al. 2002).

During interactions, mental health professionals should actively listen as they aim to assist these youth in developing self-efficacy in terms of their ability to adaptively respond and recover from the disaster, that is, empowering them to be active agents in their growth as they begin to move forward (Doostgharin 2009; Jacobs 2016). Encouraging and creating opportunities for adolescents to express their emotions is vital to their adaptive processing of the disaster and making meaning out of the event (*meaning making*), a concept discussed later in this chapter (Brymer et al. 2006; Brymer, Reyes, and Steinberg 2012; Brymer, Taylor, et al. 2012; Crane and Clements 2005; Speier 2000), as well as throughout this volume. Adolescents who participate in opportunities to process the disaster will often experience strong emotions. Supportive intervention from adults is a method of promoting calming, as is an emphasis on their developing and utilizing adaptive coping skills independently (Speier 2000). Calming, adolescent-friendly areas should be designated in disaster recovery spaces (such as a shelter). These areas should be well away from heavy traffic locations (Brymer et al. 2006; Crane and Clements 2005). Methods of calming and coping take a variety of forms, including age-appropriate play-related activities, relaxation exercises, affording proximity to adults seen as "safe," and providing direct and factual information in response to expressed concerns (Speier 2000).

Psychoeducation related to common stress reactions may also serve adolescents in gaining realistic expectations about the process of recovery (Brymer et al. 2006; Kilmer and Gil-Rivas 2010). Hearing stories of other adolescents succeeding or overcoming adversity is a documented means to improving their sense of agency (Pedrotti et al. 2008). Moreover, sharing stories of others that have faced and overcome similar events may serve to increase their sense of determination to do so as well. As with any approach, interventions should be administered judiciously by those trained and in full consideration of the situational and cultural context (see other chapters, this volume).

Following disasters, to the extent feasible, it is important to normalize routines, activities, and contexts (Masten and Osofsky 2010). Resuming normal activities and shifting focus from distress to daily tasks can assist in building hope in the present and toward the future. Disaster mental health professionals can assist by supporting adolescents when they are allowed to return to the incident area, once it is deemed safe (Aghabakhshi and Gregor 2007; Vernberg 2002). Disaster mental health providers may need to work with caregivers, families, and schools to provide resources for disaster-related interventions as well as to build on strengths already present in the community (Brymer et al. 2006; Clettenberg et al. 2011; Jacobs 2016; Reyes 2006). In this manner, collective hope may be fostered, empowering these youth in the present. A comprehensive framework for such strategies is encapsulated by what is termed, *Psychological First Aid*, or PFA. PFA is a "gold standard" of care in the immediate disaster context.

Psychological First Aid

Psychological First Aid (PFA) involves many practical steps, such as building rapport with individuals, meeting basic needs, listening, providing realistic reassurance, helping people connect, and giving age-appropriate information about the extent of the disaster along with the encouragement of adaptive coping. Multiple organizations including the National Child Traumatic Stress Network and the National Center for PTSD have developed PFA guidelines for disaster mental health workers that are guided by evidence-informed psychosocial interventions geared toward assisting individuals in the acute aftermath of a disaster (Brymer et al. 2006). Organizations, such as the American Red Cross (2017), have designed courses to facilitate PFA and its post-disaster utility. In addition, Community-Based Psychological First Aid (CBPFA) offers adaptive coping skills useful in the immediate disaster response, or for stressful circumstances that may occur on a more frequent basis (Jacobs 2016). More specifically, CBPFA is a particular model of PFA originally developed in Denmark to help individuals cope with distress from a disaster, building off the strengths available in the community (Jacobs 2016). It is useful with mental health professionals and non-mental health professionals alike. CBPFA acknowledges the unique cultural nuances that exist within each community and highlights the importance of taking care of oneself in difficult situations (Jacobs 2016). The availability of community and peer social support often play pivotal roles in helping adolescents cope, facilitating the development of resilience (Crane and Clements 2005).

Although the aforementioned PFA models offer help across many different age groups, there is some concern when working with children and adolescents with respect to exposing these youth to peers who may be experiencing significantly greater distress (Cohen et al. 2006; Cohen et al. 2016). Additionally, the risk of assigning more "catastrophic meaning" to the disaster than adolescents would have concluded on their own accord is an area of debate when assessing risks and benefits (Cohen et al. 2016, p. 235). However, in a study completed in Australia looking at a similar version of PFA, referred to as teen Mental Health First Aid (tMHFA), researchers found that discussing mental health issues following a disaster was helpful (Hart et al. 2018). After tMHFA training, adolescents were able to accurately identify acute mental health concerns with respect to their peers and provide an appropriate level of support (Hart et al. 2018). Additionally, stigma surrounding mental health concerns decreased from baseline findings. Education from adolescents' tMHFA training was associated with a decreased motivation to distance themselves from peers experiencing concerns, as well as significant increases in the adolescents' willingness to help (Hart et al. 2018). Because adolescents have entered a developmental period where increased existential cognitive processing begins to occur, their need to have an opportunity to learn about and discuss their emotional distress appears to be pivotal. Having an *opportunity to participate* is the emphasis, as opposed to their feeling pressured or otherwise compelled to participate. While adolescence can be a complicated, sensitive developmental period, peer discussion can stimulate understanding, just as it often does with adults.

Considering that there is little research looking specifically at adolescents' response and recovery efforts immediately following a disaster, there are a multitude of theories that illuminate effective ways to address the gap in the literature. One of these theories is Snyder's (1994) hope theory, which has utility in helping adolescents to understand, process, and recover from their disaster-related experiences. Snyder (1994) described hope as encompassing positive thoughts or cognitions that relate to an individual's meaningful life goals. When working to instill hope in others, one must teach a set of skills that build on what adolescents tend to do naturally, but often struggle to do following a disaster, that is, think about the future. The development of hopeful thinking is valuable for adaptive coping in the present moment, with an eye toward future recovery. Within this chapter, we focus on the promotion of hope when responding to adolescents immediately following a disaster event. It is our literature-guided assertion that hope is an essential aspect of positive coping post-disaster.

Hope Theory

Snyder's (1994) model of hope involves three interrelated components of "successful agency (goal-directed determination), pathways (planning to meet goals)" (Snyder et al. 1991, p. 571), and goals, specifying that the building and integrating of goal setting plays a major role in hope theory acting as anchor points. Hope theory and its components have worthwhile utility in assisting adolescents in terms of effective coping (see for instance, Gallagher et al. 2019). As previously discussed, adolescence is considered a sensitive period from a developmental standpoint in which existential concepts become increasingly salient. Such concepts potentially include consideration of death and suffering, as well as career aspirations and family planning (Dogan-Ates 2010). These concepts fit well within the framework of hope theory and will be expanded upon in greater depth.

Individuals must have internal determination, a belief that one can begin and sustain movement along an envisioned route toward a given goal(s). Within hope theory, goal-directed determination is referred to as *agency* (Snyder et al. 1991). When barriers appear and disrupt goal attainment, successful agentic thinking is hypothesized to allow people to channel positive motivations towards alternative, attainable pathways (Snyder 1994). Following agency, attainable goals with some degree of uncertainty regarding their realization have been found to be capable of motivating behavior (Snyder et al. 1991). These goals can either be short term or long term in scope. To perform behavior, individuals must believe they are capable of generating workable routes to their goals (Snyder et al. 2000). This mental capacity to plan plausible goal routes is described as *pathways* thinking (Snyder 1994). High hope people perceive themselves as being capable of producing alternate routes to their goals despite original routes being blocked (Snyder 1994).

The applicability of hope theory among adolescents has shown to be beneficial in a wide range of contexts. Hope acts as an effective protective factor relating to how adolescents respond to various situations. Some areas of applicability include academic achievement (Chang and DeSimone 2001; Gallagher et al. 2017), the experience of uncomfortable psychological symptoms such as depression and anxiety (Arnau et al. 2007; Gilman et al. 2006), and psychological flexibility and sense of well-being (Ciarrochi et al. 2007). Much of the hope-related research having to do with adolescence also includes aspects of modern conceptualizations of positive psychology such as optimism, courage, perseverance, character strengths, resilience, and purpose (e.g., Bronk et al. 2009; Peek 2008; Seligman and Csikszentmihalyi 2000). Many of these concepts have overlapping aspects, though hope theory itself has lone implications quite useful for facilitating adolescents' adaptive coping following a disaster (e.g., Gallagher et al. 2019).

It is difficult to discuss hope theory without mentioning its influence on the field of positive psychology (Norrish and Vella-Brodrick 2009). Simply stated, hope is an essential aspect of positive psychology. However, regarding the current subject matter, a review of disaster-related studies has shown little attention paid to the role of positive psychology in disasters when considering response and recovery efforts (i.e., interventions in the immediate disaster context), in general and with regard for adolescents specifically, despite the established role of hope in positive psychology (Samonei et al. 2014). Positive psychology strives as a movement towards understanding human happiness and optimal functioning through a focus on human strengths, cognitions, and behaviors that encourage personal growth (Gable and Haidt 2005; Linley et al. 2006). The role positive psychology plays among the adolescent population is vital. Keyes (2006) found that among 1,234 adolescents (ages 12–18), 55% were only moderately healthy from a mental health standpoint, reporting average emotional, psychological, and social well-being. In this same sample, 6% of these youth were mentally unhealthy. The negative trend of mental health status declined with age, suggesting that human flourishing decreases as cognitive processes and responsibilities increase (Keyes 2006). Thus, intervening with positive psychology interventions, such as the application of hope theory, is necessary and can work as preventative mental health support. Its utilization may be useful not only in a general sense as stressful events occur, but, in our perspective, it possesses special functionality following events that are potentially traumatic, such as a disaster.

Miller and Harvey (2001) presented a review of how the experience of loss, a part of every human life, can be a platform for highlighting human strengths and potential. Additionally, loss can cause the evaluation of life goals and priorities. As such, identifying positive aspects of the disaster experience, a process that occurs over time, can have longer-term benefits that can assist in moving towards an individual's life goals. The discovery of meaning in a disaster event is associated with adaptation and growth (Park 2010; Schulenberg 2016; Schulenberg et al. 2014; Tedeschi et al. 2018; Thompson and Pitts 1994). Therefore, applications of hope theory, such as agentic and pathways thinking, seem to be well suited for response and recovery efforts post-disaster, in general and also with specific regard for adolescents.

Hope Building and Psychological First Aid Post-disaster

The majority of American youth typically describe their thinking as hope filled (Lopez et al. 2009). Adolescents endorsing low levels of hope are able to develop higher levels of hope with support. Mental health providers can assist in building hope in adolescents given its specific relevance to the disaster-related context. As noted previously, goal-directed determination is known as *agency*, while *pathways* involves the generation of plausible goal routes (Snyder 1994; Snyder et al. 1991). Hope theory is highly compatible with PFA models. Both are proactive, empowering approaches. PFA aids adolescents by facilitating agency and pathways thinking. Both involve the designation of goals and how to meet them given realistic, logistical considerations (Snyder 1994; Snyder et al. 1991). Agentic thinking affords opportunities to develop new pathways when existing pathways are blocked. Moreover, it is essential that people believe in their ability to generate workable routes to their goals (Snyder et al. 2000), necessitating a sense of self-efficacy (Bandura 1982; Bernardo 2015; Jovanović 2013; Marques et al. 2009). Self-efficacy is another link between hope theory and models of PFA. Goal setting and planning cultivate self-efficacy, and thus, potentially empowers adolescents to engage in behaviors that move them towards their set goals, even under the aversive conditions that may exist post-disaster. Goals may involve the short term or the long term. With regard to the short term, agentic and pathways thinking have utility in ensuring that one is safe, that one receives medical attention (as necessary), that one has access to food, water, and shelter, and that one is able to reconnect with loved ones. These steps are necessary to ensure one's well-being in the short term. In other words, it helps them to navigate their circumstances with greater effectiveness, with implications for adaptive recovery in the long term.

The availability of PFA post-disaster is essential for resilience and recovery. Many organizations have developed PFA guidelines and related recommendations for attending to individuals post-disaster. Hope theory research and applications can do much with respect to informing and complementing PFA efforts. The encouragement of hopeful thinking in adolescents post-disaster is highly important, and, we would argue, essential to resilience and overall good psychological adjustment post-disaster. The conceptualization of agency and pathways is consistent with the positive psychology literature, as well as congruent with Frankl's argument of the essential nature of meaning and purpose to the human condition (Frankl 1959; Schulenberg 2016; Schulenberg et al. 2008). Further, some adolescents have described perceived meaning and purpose in life that stem from feelings of hopefulness. Development of purpose is largely related to Erikson's stage theory (1968; 1980 as cited in Bronk and Mangan 2016) that incorporates identity formation, and the process of meaning making derived from Park's (2010) and Steger's (2012) research with respect to the importance of people's ability to make sense of their lives. Both meaning and purpose are often discussed throughout the positive psychology literature, and are considered core concepts (Russo-Netzer et al. 2016; Schulenberg 2016).

Among adolescents, it is difficult to distinguish between meaning and purpose (Bronk and Mangan 2016). In decades past, the terms were often used synonymously. In contemporary positive psychological thinking and research, meaning often has to do with one's perceived significance, that one's life matters (Martela and Steger 2016). Meaning is related to both resilience and posttraumatic growth (Weber et al. 2019). Alternatively, purpose has to do with values-oriented, goal-directed behavior (Bronk and Mangan 2016; Kosine et al. 2008). The distinction between these two terms seems to become increasingly important during late adolescence and into emerging adulthood (Bronk and Mangan 2016; Rockenbach et al. 2014), though more research is warranted as to the salience of meaning and purpose considering the developmental context.

How does one make meaning in the context of experiencing a stressful event? Park's (2010) review of the meaning-making literature found that meaning making occurs when an individual engages in behaviors to reduce the distress that arises from a discrepancy between a person's appraised meaning of the situation and their global beliefs. Such behaviors include automatic and deliberate processes that can serve as effective coping skills (Park 2010; Park and George 2013). When looking at the meaning-making literature among adolescents considering the context of disasters, the identification of specific processes involved is limited. In adults, research has established a relationship between an individual's religiousness and spirituality and their assigned meaning to both situational and global beliefs (Park 2007). Additionally, a relationship between religiousness and spirituality, and effective coping skills has been established (Park 2007; Steger and Frazier 2005). Krok (2015) replicated these findings among late adolescents (ages 16–20), although the researcher further demonstrated that spirituality was more strongly associated with "task-oriented coping" (p. 201). Other studies have demonstrated how spirituality provides adolescents with awareness as well as agency factors in engaging in effective coping behaviors (King and Benson 2006). Together, these studies help to exemplify how spirituality may serve as one factor that can help adolescents build hope and also meaning in the wake of a disaster, motivating these youth to engage in goal setting and planning not only for the present, but also in terms of orientation toward the future.

Meaning and purpose are important positive psychological concepts with relevance to disaster mental health and models of Psychological First Aid (PFA). Meaningful and purpose-oriented thinking is consistent with hope theory, specifically agency and pathways thinking. Hope theory, as we have asserted, is also of relevance to disaster mental health and models of PFA. Given the relationship between these concepts and adaptive functioning across a range of domains (Melton and Schulenberg 2008), it seems apparent that there is much potential utility in considering hope theory in the context of short-term and long-term recovery post-disaster. Consistent with models of PFA, adolescents have the capacity to become active agents in self-change and the facilitation of positive outcomes. Or, in positive psychology terms, responding to adversity with the capability to derive meaning from their circumstances, responding to hardship in resilient fashion. Once individuals become aware of hope theory and have established a firm grasp on its concepts and utility, they can become responsible for implementation of the components in their unique life experiences (Lopez et al. 2009). While hope theory predates the fields of positive psychology and disaster mental health, its emphasis on agency and pathways fits with both, having the capacity to aid adolescents in their post-disaster response in both the short term and the long term.

Hope Theory and Interventions

Mental health professionals should consider hope theory in working with adolescents post-disaster. Helping adolescents to identify their values, interests, and abilities creates a foundation for hopeful thinking, that is, agency and pathways thinking, further facilitating self-efficacy and purpose. As goals and directions are identified hopeful thinking is highlighted and ultimately facilitated. Mental health professionals can work with adolescents to identify workable goals that are positive, realistic, obtainable, and specific, establishing anchors for growth in hopeful thinking (Brymer et al. 2006; Pedrotti et al. 2008). Goals should be calibrated to the adolescents' age, circumstance, and obtainability, as recommended in both PFA and CBPFA models (Brymer et al. 2006; Jacobs 2016; Lopez et al. 2009). Mental health professionals may need to provide direct instruction and assistance in helping these youth to prioritize goals, as they will have better knowledge of goal applicability and resources available to the adolescent at the given time.

Moreover, mental health professionals can assist adolescents in visualizing and verbalizing the steps to reach identified goals (Lopez et al. 2009). A collaboration with adolescents may be cultivated with the development of agency and the identification of effective pathways. That is, breaking down goals into smaller, more manageable aspects. This is a frequent method of enhancing pathways thinking and one that can empower adolescents in their ability to achieve them (Brymer et al. 2006). The identification and completion of smaller, manageable goals is a means of enhancing their self-efficacy, demonstrating that they have the means to succeed (Bronk and Mangan 2016; Brymer et al. 2006).

While family social support is an essential aspect of PFA models and affirming to youth, peers also may play a role in facilitating effective coping (Brymer et al. 2006; Jacobs 2016). Connecting peer support to goal setting and prioritizing, adolescents can utilize the help of their peers to figure out which goals to prioritize based on a common understanding of distinct needs and emotions often experienced during adolescence. Peer support post-disaster decreases the likelihood of maladaptive coping skills, such as emotional avoidance and isolation, as well as lessens the risk for symptoms of anxiety and depression (Banks and Weems 2014; See Table 8.1 for other common symptoms experienced by adolecents post-disaster). Encouraging adolescents to interact with peers allows them opportunities to share their stories with others who understand their viewpoint and perspective of the situation. Engaging in such behaviors can foster not only hope and purpose, but also resilience surrounding the disaster event (Peek 2008). Adolescents themselves are part of multiple communities, families, peer groups, cultural neighborhoods, schools, etc. where being resilient can be generalized and useful. Through such connections, hopeful thinking is cultivated with manifold benefits in multiple areas including meaning making, purpose, and self-efficacy.

In addition to developing effective coping skills through family and peer social support, adolescents' hopeful thinking may benefit through encouragement to engage in journaling and the monitoring of self-talk, which allows them to become more aware of their agency (Pedrotti et al. 2008). Adolescents often have negative self-scripts that need to be addressed to promote positive motivation. Mental health professionals, as well as family and peers, can offer examples, modeling, and practice opportunities related to positive self-scripting. As such, normalizing such thoughts post-disaster can help adolescents to engage in more adaptive coping skills, including indoor and outdoor activities that facilitate conversation where positive self-talk can be generated (Berkowitz et al. 2010). Engagement in positive activities may also facilitate an agency toward growth post-disaster.

Borrowing from the work of Bronk and Mangan (2016) and their efforts to develop purpose among adolescents, it could be useful to encourage adolescents to reflect on who and what they are grateful for, despite the horrific circumstance, as such reflection can aid in the development of hope. Having motivation to contribute to others in a way that gives back the good an individual has received is not an easy concept to grasp, especially with adolescents. However, some adolescents will excel in the character strength of gratitude, consistent with the literature in positive psychology. Engaging in behaviors, such as the expression of gratitude, can also help to emphasize to adolescents that reflection and hopeful thinking are processes that occur and fluctuate over time. Moreover, reflection on such topics, including discussion of something "beyond-the-self," may help adolescents consider the positive despite undesirable conditions (Bronk and Mangan 2016; see also Frankl 1959 with regard to self-transcendence).

Mental health professionals, family, and peers may also be of help in terms of shaping adolescents' capacity to problem solve. Pathways sometimes do not work. Strengthening the ability to identify barriers and potential solutions when they occur is important in teaching the flexibility needed for effective pathways thinking. By teaching individuals to identify several routes to their desired goals, they can pursue alternative pathways when obstacles become insurmountable (i.e., teaching youth how to overcome obstacles when they occur, when possible, but also developing the judgment and perspective to recognize when an alternative pathway may be more feasible). Such thinking and skill development is consistent with PFA models and also what we know about both self-efficacy and hope theory.

Once goals have been set, a next step would be to assist adolescents in how to set clear markers for selected goals. Markers provide a method for progress monitoring and allow for ongoing feedback from family, peers, and mental health specialists. By measuring progress, adolescents can experience a sense of success and optimism, fueling motivation to follow selected pathways they have set for themselves. This is important, as some adolescents commonly have reported not wanting to plan too far ahead in the future for fear of experiencing another tragedy or even, a shortened lifespan (Barnard et al. 1999; Dogan-Ates 2010). Again, by having disaster mental health workers as well as peers aid in coping through goal setting, the chances of increasing self-efficacy among adolescents is increased. Furthermore, increases in self-efficacy have the potential to foster a sense of empowerment that can develop within adolescents in an effort to highlight their ability to monitor their own set goals and set new goals once smaller ones have been accomplished. This process can also assist in helping adolescents deal with the struggle often experienced between wanting to be more independent and still receiving some guidance following a disaster (Brymer et al. 2006; Cohen et al. 2006; Speier 2000). It is important to note that empowerment theory is a separate entity in and of itself and thus, yields an abundance of information beyond the scope of this chapter. Nevertheless, empowerment theory is noteworthy as it builds off similar qualities of both hope theory and positive psychology (Perkins and Zimmerman 1995).

When responding to disasters, disaster mental health personnel often have availability that is significantly limited. As a result, they may not have extended intervention time to give to adolescents that have been adversely impacted by the event. Nonetheless, there are multiple methods that disaster mental health professionals can integrate while responding to a disaster that may assist in building hope in adolescents during these critical and stressful times. In initial response following a disaster, it is recommended that core actions, as outlined in PFA and CBPFA interventions, be implemented as the first line of response (e.g., Brymer et al. 2006; Jacobs 2016), and as with any approach, judiciously so (see other chapters, this volume). As such, these specific interventions are typically linked to methods of instilling and promoting hope. For example, Vernberg et al. (2016) asserted that disaster mental health providers should purposefully integrate hope promotion into all post-disaster social interactions and interventions. Along these lines, the initial experience of powerlessness and loss of belief is not unusual when faced with significant, unexpected adversity. Disaster mental health responders should take extra precaution and effort to not invalidate, or otherwise undermine, an individual's thoughts and feelings. However, they could potentially make a difference by modeling alternative ways of thinking and feeling about the event in the moment, including consideration of the aforementioned PFA and CBPFA interventions that highlight community strengths and assistance as well as utilization of social support.

Such methods will go a long way in helping adolescents to access their internal resources, facilitating resilience and self-efficacy, as well as empowerment and hopeful thinking, in the present moment with implications toward their respective futures.

Summary

Adolescents naturally think about the future as part of their developmental trajectory and transition into emerging adulthood. However, in the immediate aftermath of a disaster, adolescents may have difficulty processing the present and even contemplating their future. Adolescents may experience decreases in hopeful thinking, with hopeful thinking being a process that enhances present moment awareness, goal-setting and problem-solving, and therefore, future-oriented thinking. Hopeful thinking is related to an optimistic mindset. When adolescents exhibit higher levels of hope, they report better overall well-being (Snyder et al. 1991; 1997; 2000). Hope theory facilitates self-efficacy, and serves as a protective factor against forms of psychopathology, such as anxiety and depression (Banks and Weems 2014). Given what we know thus far, purposefully integrating hope theory (e.g., agentic and pathways thinking) into post-disaster interactions and interventions with adolescents gives disaster mental health professionals the capability to help this unique population and facilitate better adjustment moving forward. While few research studies have been conducted as to specific interventions for adolescents who have experienced a disaster, there remains a documented need for disaster mental health professionals to provide immediate, developmentally-appropriate support to these youth (Cohen et al. 2006; Doostgharin 2009).

This chapter reviewed multiple types of interventions for adolescents following a disaster, such as various PFA models. We offered a rationale and discussed ways disaster mental health responders could integrate hope into their work with adolescents. Suggestions are based on the existing literature. However, there remains a need for more research on adolescent-specific interventions in the disaster context. Adolescence is a unique developmental period that would benefit from consideration of hope theory and research post-disaster.

References

Aghabakhshi, H., & Gregor, C. (2007). Learning the lessons of Bam: The role of social capital. *International Social Work, 50*(3), 347–356. https://doi.org/10.1177/0020872807076048.

American Red Cross. (2017). *Psychological first aid: Helping others in times of stress – Instructor manual*. Washington, DC: American Red Cross Disaster Mental Health.

Arata, C. M., Picou, J. S., Johnson, G. D., & McNally, T. S. (2000). Coping with technological disaster: An application of the conservation of resources model to the *Exxon Valdez* oil spill. *Journal of Traumatic Stress, 13*(1), 23–39. https://doi.org/10.1023/A:1007764729337.

Arnau, R. C., Rosen, D. H., Finch, J. F., Rhudy, J. L., & Fortunato, V. J. (2007). Longitudinal effects of hope on depression and anxiety: A latent variable analysis. *Journal of Personality, 75*(1), 43–64. https://doi.org/10.1111/j.1467-6494.2006.00432.x.

Balaban, V. (2006). Psychological assessment of children in disasters and emergencies. *Disasters, 30*(2), 178–198. https://doi.org/10.1111/j.0361-3666.2006.00314.x.

Bandura, A. (1982). Self-efficacy mechanism in human agency. *American Psychologist, 37*(2), 122–147. https://doi.org/10.1037/0003-066X.37.2.122.

Banks, D. M., & Weems, C. F. (2014). Family and peer social support and their links to psychological distress among hurricane-exposed minority youth. *American Journal of Orthopsychiatry, 84*(4), 341–352. https://doi.org/10.1037/ort0000006.

Barnard, P., Nagy, J., & Morland, I. (1999). *Children, bereavement and trauma: Nurturing resilience*. London, England; Philadelphia: Jessica Kingsley Publishers.

Becker-Blease, K. A., Turner, H. A., & Finkelhor, D. (2010). Disasters, victimization, and children's mental health. *Child Development, 81*, 1040–1052. https://doi.org/10.1111/j.1467-8624.2010.01453.x.

Berkowitz, S., Bryant, R., Brymer, M., Hamblen, J., Jacobs, A., Layne, C., et al. (2010). *Skills for psychological recovery: Field operations guide*. Los Angeles: National Child Traumatic Stress Network & National Center for PTSD.

Bernardo, A. B. I. (2015). Hope in early adolescence: Measuring internal and external locus-of-hope. *Child Indicators Research, 8*(3), 699–715. https://doi.org/10.1007/s12187-014-9254-6.

Bernstein, M., & Pfefferbaum, B. (2018). Posttraumatic growth as a response to natural disasters in children and adolescents. *Current Psychiatry Reports, 20*(5), 20–37. https://doi.org/10.1007/s11920-018-0900-4.

Berson, I. R., & Baggerly, J. (2009). Building resilience to trauma: Creating a safe and supportive early childhood classroom. *Childhood Education, 85*(6), 375–379. https://doi.org/10.1080/00094056.2009.10521404.

Bokszczanin, A. (2012). Social support provided by adolescents following a disaster and perceived social support, sense of community at school, and proactive coping. *Anxiety, Stress, and Coping, 25*(5), 575–592. https://doi.org/10.1080/10615806.2011.622374.

Bonanno, G. A., Ho, S. M. Y., Chan, J. C. K., Kwong, R. S. Y., Cheung, C. K. Y., Wong, C. P. Y., & Wong, V. C. W. (2008). Psychological resilience and dysfunction among hospitalized survivors of the SARS epidemic in Hong Kong: A latent class approach. *Health Psychology, 27*(5), 659–667. https://doi.org/10.1037/0278-6133.27.5.659.

Bronk, K. C., Hill, P. L., Lapsley, D. K., Talib, T. L., & Finch, H. (2009). Purpose, hope, and life satisfaction in three age groups. *The Journal of Positive Psychology, 4*(6), 500–510. https://doi.org/10.1080/17439760903271439.

Bronk, K. C., & Mangan, S. (2016). Strategies for cultivating purpose among adolescents in clinical settings. In P. Russo-Netzer, S. E. Schulenberg, & A. Batthyany (Eds.), *Clinical perspectives on meaning: Positive and existential psychotherapy* (pp. 407–422). Cham: Springer International.

Brymer, M., Layne, C., Jacobs, A., Pynoos, R., Ruzek, J., Seinberg, A.… Watson, P. (2006). *Psychological first aid: Field operations guide* (2nd ed.). Retrieved from The National Child Traumatic Stress Network website: https://www.nctsn.org/sites/default/files/resources//pfa_field_operations_guide.pdf.

Brymer, M. J., Reyes, G., & Steinberg, A. M. (2012). Disaster behavioral health for children and adolescents: Best practices for preparedness, response, and recovery. In J. L. Framingham & M. L. Teasley (Eds.), *Behavioral health response to disasters* (pp. 143–158). Boca Raton: Taylor & Francis Group.

Brymer, M. J., Taylor, M., Escudero, P., Jacobs, A., Kronenberg, M., Macy, R., … Vogel, J. (2012). *Psychological first aid for the schools: Field operations manual* (2nd ed.). Retrieved from The National Child Traumatic Stress Network website: https://www.nctsn.org/sites/default/files/resources//pfa_schools.pdf.

Chang, E. C., & DeSimone, S. L. (2001). The influence of hope on appraisals, coping, and dysphoria: A test of hope theory. *Journal of Social and Clinical Psychology, 20*(2), 117–129. https://doi.org/10.1521/jscp.20.2.117.22262.

Ciarrochi, J., Heaven, P. C. L., & Davies, F. (2007). The impact of hope, self-esteem, and attributional style on adolescents' school grades and emotional well-being: A longitudinal study. *Journal of Research in Personality, 41*(6), 1161–1178. https://doi.org/10.1016/j.jrp.2007.02.001.

Clettenberg, S., Gentry, J., Held, M., & Mock, L. A. (2011). Traumatic loss and natural disaster: A case study of a school-based response to Hurricanes Katrina and Rita. *School Psychology International, 32*(5), 553–566. https://doi.org/10.1177/0143034311402928.

Cohen, J. A., Mannarino, A. P., Gibson, L. E., Cozza, S. J., Brymer, M. J., & Murrary, L. (2006). Interventions for children and adolescents following disasters. In E. C. Ritchie, P. J. Watson, & M. J. Friedman (Eds.), *Following mass violence and disasters: Strategies for mental health practice* (pp. 227–256). New York: The Guilford Press.

Cohen, J. R., Danielson, C. K., Adams, Z. W., & Ruggiero, K. J. (2016). Distress tolerance and social support in adolescence: Predicting risk for internalizing and externalizing symptoms following a natural disaster. *Journal of Psychopathology and Behavioral Assessment, 38*(4), 538–546. https://doi.org/10.1007/s10862-016-9545-y.

Crane, P. A., & Clements, P. T. (2005). Psychological response to disasters: Focus on adolescents. *Journal of Psychosocial Nursing and Mental Health Services, 43*(8), 31–38. https://doi.org/10.3928/02793695-20050801-11.

Dogan-Ates, A. (2010). Developmental differences in children's and adolescents' post-disaster reactions. *Issues in Mental Health Nursing, 31*(7), 470–476. https://doi.org/10.3109/01612840903582528.

Domenech Rodríguez, M. M., & Bernal, G. (2012). Frameworks, models, and guidelines for cultural adaptation. In G. Bernal & M. M. Domenech Rodríguez (Eds.), *Cultural adaptations: Tools for evidence-based practice with diverse populations* (pp. 23–44). Washington, DC: American Psychological Association. https://doi.org/10.1037/13752-002.

Doostgharin, T. (2009). Children affected by earthquakes and their immediate emotional needs. *International Social Work, 52*(1), 96–106. https://doi.org/10.1177/0020872808093346.

Dursun, P., Steger, M. F., Bentele, C., & Schulenberg, S. E. (2016). Meaning and posttraumatic growth among survivors of the September 2013 Colorado floods. *Journal of Clinical Psychology, 72*(12), 1247–1263. https://doi.org/10.1002/jclp.22344

Dunn, E. C., Nishimi, K., Powers, A., & Bradley, B. (2017). Is developmental timing of trauma exposure associated with depressive and post-traumatic stress disorder symptoms in adulthood? *Journal of Psychiatric Research, 84*, 119–127. https://doi.org/10.1016/j.jpsychires.2016.09.004.

Dyregrov, A., Yule, W., & Olff, M. (2018). Children and natural disasters. *European Journal of Psychotraumatology, 9*(Suppl 2), 1–3. https://doi.org/10.1080/20008198.2018.1500823.

Eth, S., & Pynoos, R. S. (Eds.). (1985). *Post-traumatic stress disorder in children*. Washington, DC: American Psychiatric Press.

FEMA – Glossary. (n.d.). Retrieved from https://training.fema.gov/programs/emischool/el361toolkit/glossary.htm#D.

Frankl, V. (1959). *Man's search for meaning*. New York, NY: Washington Square Press.

Gable, S. L., & Haidt, J. (2005). What (and why) is positive psychology? *Review of General Psychology, 9*(2), 103–110. https://doi.org/10.1037/1089-2680.9.2.103.

Gaffney, D. A. (2006). The aftermath of disaster: Children in crisis. *Journal of Clinical Psychology, 62*(8), 1001–1016. https://doi.org/10.1002/jclp.20285.

Gallagher, M. W., Marques, S. C., & Lopez, S. J. (2017). Hope and the academic trajectory of college students. *Journal of Happiness Studies, 18*(2), 341–352. https://doi.org/10.1007/s10902-016-9727-z.

Gallagher, M. W., Pedrotti, J. T., Lopez, S. J., & Snyder, C. R. (2019). Hope. In M. W. Gallagher & S. J. Lopez (Eds.), *Positive psychological assessment: A handbook of models and measures* (2nd ed., pp. 77–95). Washington, DC: American Psychological Association.

Gilman, R., Dooley, J., & Florell, D. (2006). Relative levels of hope and their relationship with academic and psychological indicators among adolescents. *Journal of Social and Clinical Psychology, 25*(2), 166–178. https://doi.org/10.1521/jscp.2006.25.2.166.

Hart, L. M., Morgan, A. J., Rossetto, A., Kelly, C. M., Mackinnon, A., & Jorm, A. F. (2018). Helping adolescents to better support their peers with a mental health problem: A cluster-randomised crossover trial of teen mental health first aid. *Australian & New Zealand Journal of Psychiatry, 52*(7), 638–651. https://doi.org/10.1177/0004867417753552.

Health Studies – Disaster Training and Response | CDC. (2018, May). Retrieved from https://www.cdc.gov/nceh/hsb/disaster/training.htm.

Jacobs, G. A. (2016). *Community-based psychological first aid: A practical guide to helping individuals and communities during difficult times*. Oxford: Butterworth-Heinemann.

Johnson, V. A., & Ronan, K. R. (2014). Classroom responses of New Zealand school teachers following the 2011 Christchurch earthquake. *Natural Hazards, 72*(2), 1075–1092. https://doi.org/10.1007/s11069-014-1053-3.

Jovanović, V. (2013). Evaluation of the Children's Hope Scale in Serbian adolescents: Dimensionality, measurement invariance across gender, convergent and incremental validity. *Child Indicators Research, 6*(4), 797–811. https://doi.org/10.1007/s12187-013-9195-5.

Kar, N., & Bastia, B. K. (2006). Post-traumatic stress disorder, depression and generalised anxiety disorder in adolescents after a natural disaster: A study of comorbidity. *Clinical Practice and Epidemiology in Mental Health, 2*(1), 17. https://doi.org/10.1186/1745-0179-2-17.

Keyes, C. L. M. (2006). Mental health in adolescence: Is America's youth flourishing? *American Journal of Orthopsychiatry, 76*(3), 395–402. https://doi.org/10.1037/0002-9432.76.3.395.

Kilmer, R. P., & Gil-Rivas, V. (2010). Exploring posttraumatic growth in children impacted by Hurricane Katrina: Correlates of the phenomenon and developmental considerations. *Child Development, 81*(4), 1211–1227. https://doi.org/10.1111/j.1467-8624.2010.01463.x.

Kilpatrick D. G., & Saunders B. E. (1995). *National survey of adolescents in the United States*, 1995 (ICPSR 2833) [Data file].

King, P. E., & Benson, P. L. (2006). Spiritual development and adolescent well-being and thriving. In E. C. Roehlkepartain, P. E. King, L. M. Wagener, & P. L. Benson (Eds.), *The handbook of spiritual development in childhood and adolescence* (pp. 384–398). Newbury Park: Sage.

Knudsen, E. I. (2004). Sensitive periods in the development of the brain and behavior. *Journal of Cognitive Neuroscience, 16*(8), 1412–1425. https://doi.org/10.1162/0898929042304796.

Kosine, N. R., Steger, M. F., & Duncan, S. (2008). Purpose-centered career development: A strengths-based approach to finding meaning and purpose in careers. *Professional School Counseling, 12*(2), 133–136. https://doi.org/10.5330/PSC.n.2010-12.133.

Krok, D. (2015). Religiousness, spirituality, and coping with stress among late adolescents: A meaning-making perspective. *Journal of Adolescence, 45*, 196–203. https://doi.org/10.1016/j.adolescence.2015.10.004.

Linley, P. A., Joseph, S., Harrington, S., & Wood, A. M. (2006). Positive psychology: Past, present, and (possible) future. *The Journal of Positive Psychology, 1*(1), 3–16. https://doi.org/10.1080/17439760500372796.

Lopez, S. J., Rose, S., Robinson, C., Marques, S. C., & Pais-Ribeiro, J. (2009). Measuring and promoting hope in school children. In R. Gilman, E. S. Huebner, & M. J. Furlong (Eds.), *Handbook of positive psychology in the schools* (pp. 37–51). Mahwah: Lawrence Erlbaum.

Marques, S. C., Pais-Ribeiro, J. L., & Lopez, S. J. (2009). Validation of a Portuguese version of the Children's Hope Scale. *School Psychology International, 30*(5), 538–551. https://doi.org/10.1177/0143034309107069.

Martela, F., & Steger, M. F. (2016). The three meanings of meaning in life: Distinguishing coherence, purpose, and significance. *The Journal of Positive Psychology, 11*, 531–545. https://doi.org/10.1080/17439760.2015.1137623.

Masten, A. S., & Narayan, A. J. (2012). Child development in the context of disaster, war, and terrorism: Pathways of risk and resilience. *Annual Review of Psychology, 63*(1), 227–257. https://doi.org/10.1146/annurev-psych-120710-100356.

Masten, A. S., & Osofsky, J. D. (2010). Disasters and their impact on child development: Introduction to the special section. *Child Development, 81*(4), 1029–1039. https://doi.org/10.1111/j.1467-8624.2010.01452.x.

Miller, E. D., & Harvey, J. H. (2001). The interface of positive psychology with a psychology of loss: A brave new world? *American Journal of Psychotherapy, 55*(3), 313–322. https://doi.org/10.1176/appi.psychotherapy.2001.55.3.313.

Melton, A. M. A., & Schulenberg, S. E. (2008). On the measurement of meaning: Logotherapy's empirical contributions to humanistic psychology. *The Humanistic Psychologist, 36*(1), 31–44. https://doi.org/10.1080/08873260701828870.

Natural Disasters and Severe Weather | CDC. (2019, January 29). Retrieved May 12, 2019, from https://www.cdc.gov/disasters/index.html.

Norrish, J. M., & Vella-Brodrick, D. A. (2009). Positive psychology and adolescents: Where are we now? Where to from here? *Australian Psychologist, 44*(4), 270–278. https://doi.org/10.1080/00050060902914103.

Owens, D. S., McKernan, B., & Framingham, J. L. (2012). Disaster and substance abuse services. In J. L. Framingham & M. L. Teasley (Eds.), *Behavioral health response to disasters* (pp. 319–336). Boca Raton: Taylor & Francis Group.

Park, C. L. (2007). Religiousness/spirituality and health: A meaning systems perspective. *Journal of Behavioral Medicine, 30*(4), 319–328. https://doi.org/10.1007/s10865-007-9111-x.
Park, C. L. (2010). Making sense of the meaning literature: An integrative review of meaning making and its effects on adjustment to stressful life events. *Psychological Bulletin, 136*(2), 257–301. https://doi.org/10.1037/a0018301.
Park, C. L., & George, L. S. (2013). Assessing meaning and meaning making in the context of stressful life events: Measurement tools and approaches. *The Journal of Positive Psychology, 8*(6), 483–504. https://doi.org/10.1080/17439760.2013.830762.
Pedrotti, J. T., Edwards, J., & Lopez, S. J. (2008). Promoting hope: Suggestions for school counselors. *Professional School Counseling, 12*(2), 100–107. https://doi.org/10.5330/PSC.n.2010-12.100.
Peek, L. (2008). Children and disasters: Understanding vulnerability, developing capacities, and promoting resilience — An introduction. *Children Youth and Environments, 18*(1), 1–29. https://doi.org/10.7721/chilyoutenvi.18.1.0001.
Perkins, D. D., & Zimmerman, M. A. (1995). Empowerment theory, research, and application. *American Journal of Community Psychology, 23*(5), 569–579. https://doi.org/10.1007/BF02506982.
Pfefferbaum, B., Nitiéma, P., Tucker, P., & Newman, E. (2017). Early child DMH interventions: A review of the empirical evidence. *Child & Youth Care Forum, 46*(5), 621–642. https://doi.org/10.1007/s10566-017-9397-y.
Rabalais, A. E., Ruggerio, K. J., & Scotti, J. R. (2002). Multicultural issues in the response of children to disasters. In A. M. La Greca, W. K. Silverman, E. M. Vernberg, & M. C. Roberts (Eds.), *Helping children cope with disasters and terrorism* (pp. 73–99). Washington, DC: American Psychological Association.
Reyes, G. (2006). Psychological first aid: Principles of community-based psychosocial support. In G. Reyes & G. A. Jacobs (Eds.), *Handbook of international disaster psychology: Practices and programs* (Vol. 2, pp. 1–12). Westport: Praeger Publishers/Greenwood Publishing Group.
Rockenbach, A. B., Hudson, T. D., & Tuchmayer, J. B. (2014). Fostering meaning, purpose, and enduring commitments to community service in college: A multidimensional conceptual model. *The Journal of Higher Education, 85*(3), 312–338. https://doi.org/10.1080/00221546.2014.11777330.
Russo-Netzer, P., Schulenberg, S. E., & Batthyany, A. (2016). *Clinical perspectives on meaning: Positive and existential psychotherapy*. Cham: Springer International Publishing.
Samonei, R., Abedi, M. R., & Ferdosi, M. (2014). The absence of positive psychology in disasters. *International Journal of Health System and Disaster Management, 2*(4), 241–245. https://doi.org/10.4103/2347-9019.144413.
Schulenberg, S. E. (2016). Disaster mental health and positive psychology – Considering the context of natural and technological disasters: An introduction to the special issue. *Journal of Clinical Psychology, 72*(12), 1223–1233. https://doi.org/10.1002/jclp.22409.
Schulenberg, S. E., Drescher, C. F., & Baczwaski, B. J. (2014). Perceived meaning and disaster mental health: A role for logotherapy in clinical-disaster psychology. In A. Batthyany & P. Russo-Netzer (Eds.), *Meaning in positive and existential psychology* (pp. 251–267). New York: Springer. https://doi.org/10.1007/978-1-4939-0308-5_15.
Schulenberg, S. E., Hutzell, R. R., Nassif, C., & Rogina, J. M. (2008). Logotherapy for clinical practice. *Psychotherapy: Theory, Research, Practice, Training, 45*(4), 447–463. https://doi.org/10.1037/a0014331.
Seligman, M. E., & Csikszentmihalyi, M. (2000). Positive psychology: An introduction. *The American Psychologist, 55*(1), 5–14. https://doi.org/10.1037/0003-066X.55.1.5.
Shemesh, E., Newcorn, J. H., Rockmore, L., Shneider, B. L., Emre, S., Gelb, B. D., et al. (2005). Comparison of parent and child reports of emotional trauma symptoms in pediatric outpatient settings. *Pediatrics, 115*(5), e582–e589. https://doi.org/10.1542/peds.2004-2201.
Snyder, C. R. (1994). *The psychology of hope: You can get there from here*. New York: Free Press.
Snyder, C. R., Harris, C., Anderson, J. R., Holleran, S. A., Irving, L. M., Sigmon, S. T., et al. (1991). The will and the ways: Development and validation of an individual-differences

measure of hope. *Journal of Personality and Social Psychology, 60*(4), 570–585. https://doi.org/10.1037/0022-3514.60.4.570.

Snyder, C. R., Hoza, B., Pelham, W. E., Rapoff, M., Ware, L., Danovsky, M., et al. (1997). The development and validation of the Children's Hope Scale. *Journal of Pediatric Psychology, 22*(3), 399–421. https://doi.org/10.1093/jpepsy/22.3.399.

Snyder, C. R., Ilardi, S. S., Cheavens, J., Michael, S. T., Yamhure, L., & Sympson, S. (2000). The role of hope in cognitive-behavior therapies. *Cognitive Therapy and Research, 24*(6), 747–762. https://doi.org/10.1023/A:1005547730153.

Southwick, S. M., & Charney, D. S. (2018). *Resilience: The science of mastering life's greatest challenges* (2nd ed.). Cambridge: Cambridge University Press.

Speier, A. H. (2000). *Psychosocial issues for children and adolescents in disasters* (2nd ed.). (DHHS Publication No. ADM86-1070R). Retrieved from https://permanent.access.gpo.gov/lps72252/ADM86-1070R.pdf.

Steger, M. F. (2012). Making meaning in life. *Psychological Inquiry, 23*(4), 381–385. https://doi.org/10.1080/1047840X.2012.720832.

Steger, M. F., & Frazier, P. (2005). Meaning in life: One link in the chain from religion to wellbeing. *Journal of Counseling Psychology, 52*(4), 574–582. https://doi.org/10.1037/0022-0167.52.4.574.

Szente, J. (2016). Assisting children caught in disasters: Resources and suggestions for practitioners. *Early Childhood Education Journal, 44*(3), 201–207. https://doi.org/10.1007/s10643-015-0709-2.

Tedeschi, R. G., Shakespeare-Finch, J., Taku, K., & Calhoun, L. G. (2018). *Posttraumatic growth: Theory, research, and applications*. New York: Routledge.

Thompson, S. C., & Pitts, J. (1994). Factors relating to a person's ability to find meaning after a diagnosis of cancer. *Journal of Psychosocial Oncology, 11*(3), 1–22. https://doi.org/10.1300/J077V11N03_01.

Types of Emergencies. (2019). Retrieved May 12, 2019, from https://www.redcross.org/get-help/how-to-prepare-for-emergencies/types-of-emergencies.html.

U.S. Census Bureau. (2014). Current Population Survey, annual social and economic supplement. Retrieved from http://www.census.gov/cps/data/cpstablecreator.html

United Nations Children's Fund (UNICEF). (2000). *Helping children cope with the stresses of war: A manual for parents and teachers*. New York: M. Macksoud.

Vernberg, E. M. (2002). Intervention approaches following disasters. In A. M. La Greca, W. K. Silverman, E. M. Vernberg, & M. C. Roberts (Eds.), *Helping children cope with disasters and terrorism* (pp. 55–72). Washington, DC: American Psychological Association. https://doi.org/10.1037/10454-003.

Vernberg, E. M., Hambrick, E. P., Cho, B., & Hendrickson, M. L. (2016). Positive psychology and DMH: Strategies for working with children and adolescents. *Journal of Clinical Psychology, 72*(12), 1333–1347. https://doi.org/10.1002/jclp.22289.

Weber, M. C., Pavlacic, J. M., Gawlik, E. A., Schulenberg, S. E., & Buchanan, E. M. (2019). Modeling resilience, meaning in life, posttraumatic growth, and disaster preparedness with two samples of tornado survivors. *Traumatology*. Advance online publication. https://doi.org/10.1037/trm0000210

Winter, A. S., & Sampson, R. J. (2017). From lead exposure in early childhood to adolescent health: A Chicago birth cohort. *American Journal of Public Health, 107*(9), 1496–1501. https://doi.org/10.2105/AJPH.2017.303903.

World Health Organization (WHO). (2011). *Psychological first aid: Guide for field workers*. Geneva: World Health Organization. Retrieved from https://apps.who.int/iris/bitstream/handle/10665/44615/9789241548205_eng.pdf?sequence=1.

Chapter 9
Strengths and Application of Response Team vs. Community-Based Models of Psychological First Aid

Gerard A. Jacobs

There are two major models of Psychological First Aid (PFA): Response Team and Community-Based. Over the years, proponents of one or the other of these models have taken sides in a dichotomous debate about the merits of the two models. It may be much more profitable, however, to appreciate the appropriateness of each of the models in different situations. Furthermore, a discussion of the contrasting approach of Disaster Mental Health may provide some added perspective.

Disaster Mental Health

In the aftermath of responding to the crash of Flight 232 in Sioux City, IA in 1989, Randy Quevillon and this author proposed to both the American Red Cross (Red Cross) and the American Psychological Association (APA) that a collaborative national system be developed, including standardized policies, training, and prepared mental health professionals to provide psychological support to those impacted by disasters. Initially, APA attempted to develop a model without the Red Cross/APA collaboration. Concerns about that model led APA to revisit the original proposed collaborative model, and in November, 1991, the Red Cross and APA announced the beginning of Disaster Mental Health Services as part of Red Cross Disaster Services. Other mental health professional organizations also participated in the development of this strategy. In 1992 APA announced that Disaster Mental Health was APA's gift to the American people on the occasion of APA's 100th anniversary (Daw 2001).

G. A. Jacobs (✉)
Disaster Mental Health Institute, University of South Dakota, Vermillion, SD, USA
e-mail: gerard.jacobs@usd.edu

S. E. Schulenberg (ed.), *Positive Psychological Approaches to Disaster*,
https://doi.org/10.1007/978-3-030-32007-2_9

Disaster Mental Health involves licensed mental health professionals using their professional knowledge and skills (e.g., psychological support [psychological triage, crisis intervention, casualty family support], education, problem solving, advocacy and instrumental support, and monitoring organizational stress) to provide basic psychological support, and to refer those who need more formal clinical services to appropriate traditional mental health providers and systems. Different mental health professions bring different lenses to the analyses of individuals and/or situations. But all mental health professionals bring years of graduate level training to the table, as well as a more complex understanding of people and situations than that which a day or two of training can provide to even the most intelligent or insightful non-professional without those years of graduate training.

My mentor was the late Charles D. Spielberger, one of the founders of community psychology. Long before the beginning of disaster mental health, when we first met in 1975, Spielberger told me that there would never be a sufficient number of psychologists to provide all the psychological support needed by a community. He said the role of psychologists was to teach the residents in the community to support one another. This was his concept of "community psychology"; a preventative model, rather than simply placing treatment centers in communities, each serving a defined catchment area.

The disaster mental health model is limited in a number of ways. In the aftermath of the terrorist attacks of September 2001, the model was used to respond to every request for psychological support that came in to the Red Cross disaster relief operations. But in the after-action review, the "technical experts" from the Red Cross Disaster Mental Health Services recognized that if the event had been even slightly larger, the model would have failed. There are practical limitations to the model in terms of the number of licensed mental health professionals available to participate in a disaster response at a given time and in terms of the challenge of transporting mental health professionals to the affected area. This is particularly relevant in the event of a pandemic or bioterrorist attack, or in the case of a nuclear event. In these circumstances there are likely to be restrictions on entering the affected area. Moreover, disaster response is different from the daily work of the great majority of mental health professionals. Therefore, it is important to ensure that mental health professionals who want to provide disaster mental health be trained in traumatic stress, crisis intervention, the general standards and restrictions governing mental health services in disaster response, and the importance of adapting services to racial, ethnic, and cultural differences in individuals and communities. The Disaster Mental Health Institute at the University of South Dakota offers an online graduate curriculum to provide that training and more.

The Red Cross Disaster Mental Health Services technical experts agreed to recommend that the Red Cross assist the nation in developing a knowledge of basic psychological support, often referred to as "psychological first aid" or PFA. With a widespread understanding of basic psychological support, members of the public could be more resilient themselves and could provide psychological support to family, friends, neighbors, and colleagues. Furthermore, if the training included developing an understanding of the limitations of PFA, individuals could understand when and how to refer someone into the traditional mental health system.

The International Context

American Red Cross Disaster Mental Health Services includes practitioners from most mental health professions. Different professions can provide different perspectives of the same situations, and this can be valuable. In international settings, organizations may provide different contexts or frameworks for understanding a situation. For example, clinical psychologists from Iceland, Turkey, Kenya, and Japan may have similar professional perspectives. Those perspectives may be augmented by organizational frameworks. For instance, working within the Red Cross/ Red Crescent system provides a framework built around the seven Fundamental Principles of the Red Cross Movement (Humanity, Impartiality, Neutrality, Independence, Voluntary service, Unity, and Universality), and that can enhance how quickly the complexities of a situation may be communicated.

The first time I worked within a very different international setting, I was thoroughly exhausted after the first day. Trying to understand the sensory input so different from anything I had experienced in my life up to that point was difficult. But after years of doing such work I realized that, even when moving into a completely new culture, I brought a set of strategies that helped me quickly organize the variant stimuli into a structured understanding. But, as Saths Cooper has described, even those years of professional training, an organizational framework, and lived experiences in disasters in different countries cannot substitute for a lifetime of cultural inculcation by someone who has lived and breathed that culture.

Cooper has said that although he lived most of his life in South African townships, he would not be so arrogant as to try to provide direct clinical services in the township next to his, without at least trying to understand the prevailing sociocultural dynamics. Yet he regularly saw Western mental health professionals presuming to come into Asia or Africa and provide direct services, often through an interpreter (translators work with the written word, interpreters with the spoken word), which adds yet another layer of problems. Different lives spent in a different culture, or even a different part of the country can provide different filters that can provide a different perspective, and result in a misunderstanding of the needs of the people who need to be served, and negatively impact the appropriateness of interventions.

Recognizing the difficulty of providing culturally responsive and effective services, the Inter-Agency Standing Committee developed a set of "Guidelines on Mental Health and Psychosocial Support in Emergency Settings" (IASC 2007). These guidelines were developed over a number of years and with the input of hundreds of experienced international mental health providers. The document was endorsed by the United Nations and by nearly every international humanitarian Non-Governmental Organization (NGO; a term for what would typically be labeled 'non-profit organizations' in the United States). These international guidelines encourage the provision of direct services by local providers, and that mental health professionals working outside their own country provide consultation and/or training to local providers. This builds the capacity of the local community to provide psychological support, as well as increasing the likelihood of those in need receiving culturally responsive care. Even within one's own country, a mental health provider needs to consider the background, culture, religion, ethnicity, and world view of the client to be served and carefully decide whether the professional has the requisite skills to provide appropriate services, or whether additional steps need to be taken to ensure appropriate care for the client. This is important to keep in mind regarding bringing psychological support providers into an affected area from elsewhere, a practice in both disaster mental health and response team models of PFA.

I have been asked whether I have ever provided direct services while working in any of the dozens of countries in which I have served. It has only happened a couple of times. When I was in Sri Lanka after the 2004 Indian Ocean tsunami, the NGO that had asked me to come arranged for me to speak to a group of children who had survived the destruction. I did not learn of the plan until late the night before, and the NGO would have lost face if the event had been canceled without warning, so I proceeded with the presentation. Afterwards, a young boy approached me and asked to talk with me. He apologized for causing the tsunami! The tsunami had resulted in the deaths of roughly 80% of the population in that region, and the destruction of virtually everything in the area. Imagine as a young child thinking that, somehow, you had caused that! It is fairly common for children to think that they caused a terrible event or contributed to it, and guilt is a major feature of traumatic stress in children and adolescents. I have always supported the idea that foreign nationals serve best as trainers and consultants, rather than providing direct service. Nevertheless, I didn't feel that I could let the boy's statement stand without a response. It was a bit of an ethical conundrum. Through my interpreter I told the boy that I was very impressed, and asked him what other kinds of weather he could control. He cocked his head to one side and then the other, obviously thinking about what I had said. Then he responded in a hesitant voice that he couldn't control any kind of weather that he knew of. I asked him, then, why he thought he had caused the tsunami. After another few moments of thinking, he looked up at me and said, "Maybe I *didn't* cause the tsunami." This was one of the shortest and most successful interventions I've done, but I still strongly endorse the idea that foreign nationals need to work as consultants and trainers, not as direct service providers.

Basic Psychological Support

Hobfoll et al. (2007) proposed five necessary elements for an effective model of basic psychological support in the aftermath of a traumatic event: (1) Promote a sense of safety; (2) Promote calming; (3) Promote a sense of self– and collective efficacy; (4) Promote connectedness; and (5) Promote hope. Their article has been widely accepted as a yardstick for psychological support programs.

Response Team Models of Psychological First Aid

The response team models of psychological first aid are probably the most well-known in the United States. The primary model in response team PFA is the National Center for Post-Traumatic Stress Disorder (NCPTSD)/National Children's Traumatic Stress Network (NCTSN) model (Brymer et al. 2006). This is a model that makes use of both mental health professionals and non-professionals. While this model seems to be a useful tool for "civilians," there is a wide divide between the skills brought to basic psychological support by a mental health professional compared to a non-mental health professional. It seems to me that professionals would be better served by being trained in disaster mental health.

It also seems highly inappropriate to refer to the work of licensed mental health professionals in an emergency situation as "first aid." Such terminology denigrates the expertise of the professionals. Physicians working in an emergency room do not refer to their work as "first aid." Their practice is "emergency medicine." It would behoove the mental health professions to recognize the pitfalls of disparaging our own professional activities.

There is a place for response team models in responding to traumatic events. Spielberger was right that there will probably never be enough mental health professionals to serve everyone's needs for psychological support. That is true in disaster response as well as in general life. PFA response teams can be a useful part of the psychological support team in a disaster relief operation. This is especially true in supporting communities that have not been trained in community-based PFA, which is described below.

The drawbacks of the response team models are similar to the limitations of the disaster mental health model. The providers typically need to be brought into the area from outside the community. That is not always practical, as discussed above. Moreover, the providers in a response team model may, therefore, be unfamiliar with the culture/language/ethnicity/world view of the community in need.

Community-Based Models

While serving as a Red Cross psychosocial delegate in response to the 2001 Gujarat, India earthquake, and coordinating psychosocial support in that response on behalf of the World Health Organization, I came to understand that in India the term "community" more commonly referred to a group of people who share common interests than to a specific geographic gathering. That seemed to me to be a profitable way to think of the word when used in the term "community-based."

A community-based program is ideally: (1) Designed by community members; (2) Run by community members; and (3) Builds on the strengths of the people and culture the program serves (Jacobs 2016). One of the best strategies that has emerged in trying to meet these ideals has been to ask the community that wants to develop a Community-Based PFA (CBPFA) program to form a committee that is authentically representative of the community. A community committee for a small group, such as a church or workplace, can be fairly simple. Trying to be representative of larger communities can be more difficult. For example, a town trying to develop a CBPFA program for its population is likely to include people of different political perspectives, different socioeconomic groups, different religions, and different ethnicities. There don't need to be separate representatives of every single group in the town on the committee. Large committees tend to be unwieldy, and more subject to "groupthink," a social process that can lead to less than optimal decisions. Many of the committees with which I have worked have, for example, had one religious leader who could consult with other community religious leaders, if necessary. Sometimes there have been subcommittees representing components of the community, with one member of the subcommittee reporting to the full committee.

It isn't realistic to have a community-based program designed and operated by people from outside the community. Outsiders can be useful as consultants and trainers, but for a real sense of ownership of the program by the community, members of the community need to be the ones designing and operating the program.

Curriculum in CBPFA

When helping a community develop a CBPFA program, we usually begin with an outline of components that are typically included in a basic CBPFA training program. Generally, this introductory list includes: how to be a helper; traumatic stress; active listening skills; problem-solving strategies; grief and bereavement; when, where, and how to refer someone for more traditional mental health services; ethics in providing psychological support; and self-care. The community committee then decides what topics, if any, might be removed or added to the list, depending on their needs and interests. I generally have urged committees to consider traumatic stress and active listening as essential components. The first time that I taught a program on my own after I was trained in this model in Copenhagen, Denmark by the International Federation of the Red Cross and Red Crescent Societies, I discarded the segment on how to be a helper, thinking that it was superfluous. The training participants raised all of the questions and concerns in that training that had been covered in the "helper" segment, and I went back to the trainers who taught me and asked them to review the segment with me so that I could include it in my basic training package. One common topic that the community committee may want to add is children's reactions to traumatic events and providing psychological support to children. Discussions of additions and subtractions also take place in the context of how the training can best be delivered. If the training is to take place in a single day, it may be necessary to balance the addition of topics with subtractions of others.

Each community has its own strengths, and may have different world views and cultural/religious traditions for managing stress. Those that are effective can be incorporated into the CBPFA model for that community. Again, the addition of these local features can increase the sense of ownership of the program by the community.

Training Strategy

My personal preference has been to deliver the initial CBPFA training in a full-day session. This introduces the participants to the overall picture of the CBPFA strategy for providing psychological support. Some groups prefer to deliver training in briefer modules. While such a training strategy may be necessary in some circumstances, it concerns me to teach some of the intervention strategies without also covering ethical issues, referral signs and strategies, and self-care. Putting these latter topics first (before traumatic stress and active listening) in a modular approach, however, may leave the participants with a less than complete appreciation of the usefulness of the tools in CBPFA. This, in turn, may lead to participants dropping out of the training before they get to the heart of the program. Some of my Native American colleagues have taught me that in the Lakota culture people expect to be given the overall picture; to understand the whole strategy. One metaphor was that it may be possible to teach someone about nuts and bolts in isolation, but if you don't teach that person about using the nuts and bolts to connect things, and how washers can strengthen them, the knowledge isn't very useful.

Another issue is the question of the length of the training. One country's government was interested in how popular the CBPFA training had been in a number of communities in which an NGO had conducted the training. Since I had provided the Training of Trainers (ToT) for that NGO, the government approached me and asked if it might be possible to conduct a CBPFA training that could be conducted in an online or electronic format. I responded that such a format was possible, but probably not as effective as personally conducted training. They asked about how long the training would need to be, and I indicated that the basic training was usually about eight hours. They asked if it could be done in less time, and I responded that it *could* be done in less time, but that it would be done at the price of losing valuable content. However, the whole idea of the community-based model is to make the training work for the specific target community. As the government representatives continued, however, they kept reducing the number of hours they wanted the training to be. When they asked for a two-hour version I told them that I would refuse to do that, since the integrity of the intervention would be severely compromised. It takes time to talk about the topics and the tools, and about the significance of individual differences. It is very difficult to have a quick canned training and have it be effective. I have given two-hour lectures on CBPFA, and even one-hour lectures, but those lectures are not teaching CBPFA, but teaching *about* CBPFA and what a full training can provide participants.

One medical center with which I worked has divided the training into shorter components offered on a scheduled basis. But they have the advantage of being able to require participation on an ongoing basis as a condition of employment. Such a model does, however, still have the drawback of either teaching techniques without the ethical caveats and protections of understanding the limitations of PFA, or of providing the ethical discussions and limitations discussions without understanding why those would be necessary or how they fit within the CBPFA model.

One NGO in a Mediterranean country required participants to have a substantial package of the skills and caveats involved in CBPFA. They also strongly advised their participants that ongoing training would be necessary, with periodic continuing modules providing role plays of using CBPFA to provide support in various situations, and covering such topics as children's reactions to traumatic events and strategies for providing psychological support for children of various ages. The participants were eager to be seen as providing support within their communities and this strategy seemed to be effective for them. It is important to understand, however, that the greater the percentage of the community trained in CBPFA, the more effective the strategy is. If you have CBPFA-trained people around you in your family, neighborhood, school, or workplace, you never have to go far to get support. If you need to get someone from outside your daily life, the technique begins to suffer from the same drawbacks as response team models.

One overseas community had begun their program with outside consultation, trainers, and financial assistance. They asked me to return and see what they had done after three years. There were deep divisions in the city along both religious and ethnic lines. In the initial consultation, I encouraged them to serve all the elements of the population. There was definite resistance to working together or even simply being together. After three years, however, they were proud to show me that all of the components of the community were being served, albeit separately. Not everything can be accomplished overnight. When I visited, they told me that, unfortunately, they were going to have to close the program because an external funding source was going to end their support. Few of the staff were paid, and those who *were* paid were paid very little. I asked them what financial support they needed, and they said there were very few costs other than salaries. I asked if they had considered running the program as volunteers, and they replied that volunteerism really wasn't common in their culture. I asked them if their religious communities had activities to serve their community's families in need, and they replied, "Of course." I asked if they were paid for those activities, and they were incredulous and somewhat offended, insisting, "Of course not." I replied, "So you volunteer." They slowly began to nod their heads. I asked them how many hours they actually spent on the psychological support program each week and most of them said they only spent one or two hours a week on the program. I asked them if the program was important enough to spend between four or eight hours a month as volunteers. They decided not to close down the program.

Examples of Community-Based Adaptations

In my doctoral education, Spielberger preached the importance of considering individual differences, and, at a higher level, the need to consider community and cultural differences when dealing with their psychological needs. Much of his work focused on cross-cultural efforts, adapting psychological theories and tools into different settings around the world. For example, the adaptation of his State-Trait Anxiety Inventory (Spielberger and Diaz-Guerrero 1976, one of the most widely used psychological assessment tools in the world) for a Scandinavian country included changing the intensity metric used for the state scale in the United States (Not at all, Somewhat, Moderately so, and Very much so) to a temperature metric (hot being very much so), in consultation with local colleagues. Changing the instrument was not a mere matter of translation; the different world view of the new location needed to be included in the adaptation process, and the psychometrics needed to be completely restandardized.

When I began working with traumatic (or overwhelming) stress internationally, I was struck by how much alike the impact of traumatic events were on people all over the world. I hypothesized that traumatic events are so overwhelming that they affect our most basic human instincts. But I also became aware that, while traumatic reactions may be at a basic human level, the experience of them is culturally influenced and expressed. When humans experience something novel that doesn't fit with their previous experiences, they can either assimilate the new experience or accommodate to them. Assimilation basically involves a person trying to explain the new experience to themselves as being similar to something else the person has experienced, and basically trying to fit the new event into their usual way of interacting with the world. If a new experience is so different that it cannot be effectively assimilated, the individual basically creates a whole new way of understanding and responding to the experience, which is known as the process of accommodation.

I was recently struck by a metaphor used in a book I was reading. The author compared the character of various cities based on colors, referring to one city as consisting of pastels and another as made up of primary colors, and suggested that the residents of those cities tended to reflect the character of the cities. In this way she indicated that even modern cities, which have much in common, have their own unique world view.

Early Experiences

Shortly after I began as a professor at the University of South Dakota, I was asked by the late John Williams (a renowned pioneer in higher education for substance abuse counselors, and a Native American himself) to teach a workshop on psychological support for faculty at a residential school that served Native American students. I began the workshop for the faculty, all of whom were themselves Native, by admitting that I had little knowledge of Native culture, and asked the faculty to stop me if I said something that was not culturally appropriate, assuring them that it would not be out of a lack of respect for their culture, but out of my own ignorance. The faculty squirmed uncomfortably, looking at one another. Then one raised his hand and said, "We will make an exception this one time, but in our culture, it is disrespectful to correct the teacher. No matter your age, as the teacher you are the elder in the room." Then he sat down. I reflected for a moment, and then asked if there was a time when I could become the student and they could be the teachers. They again looked at one another, then literally gathered into a huddle and discussed. After a few minutes, their spokesperson said that they would accept that arrangement. And from time to time across the two days of training, one or more of the students would raise their hand and say it was time for me to become the student. We would literally exchange places, and I would learn more about their culture. All of the faculty completed the training. They seemed pleased and evaluated the training positively, and I came away with a better understanding of their Native culture.

In one of my earliest disaster responses, I was asked to go to a small community that had suffered a horrible fire and explosion, resulting in death or severe burns to a handful of the community's volunteer firefighters. Before going there, I contacted a colleague in the area who was familiar with the town, and asked him to tell me about the town's personality. When I got to the town, I went to the town's single café, and asked a number of people how information was best distributed in the town. Everyone agreed that the school district's weekly newsletter was the fastest way to get information distributed in the town, and said that everyone in town read it weekly, including those adults who didn't have children in the schools. I also asked a variety of the town's residents who was the most trusted person in the town, trying to decide who should be the recipient and distributor of official information (a strategy for reducing rumors, which can create serious problems). Every response was the same (a remarkable thing in itself), identifying the spouse of one of the town's ministers; not one of the ministers, or one of the local elected officials, but the wife of a minister. And respondents included members of both religions in the town. Every town is unique.

In another early disaster response, we were serving a Northern Plains Native community that had suffered serious flooding. We began using the standard Red Cross flood coloring book with the children, but quickly realized that the children found the coloring books very confusing. The books portrayed floods as beginning with snow melt in the high mountains, and had images of communities that were unlike the reservation communities where the children lived. For young dwellers of the vast grasslands of the Northern plains, mountains could be completely unknown. We hired a Lakota artist to draw a new coloring book that would fit with the children's experience of the world, including the use of Lakota and Dakota language in addition to English, and the new coloring books were warmly received. One of the community members also complained about the use of the word "disaster" in our work. He said there was no word for "disaster" in their language (which was true). He said that in their belief system, every day was a gift from God, and that some gifts were simply harder to accept than others. We changed the language in our discussions and training materials to talk about difficult days and difficult times.

Gujarat India Earthquake

2001 was a complicated year. In the Spring I was asked to serve as an international delegate by the American Red Cross, responding to a major earthquake in Gujarat India. A number of cultural issues were significant in my experiences there. One of my activities was to go to affected towns and villages and meet with community leaders about whether they would accept a CBPFA program in their town.

The group of leaders in one town told me that the town would accept the program, but that it was unacceptable for the program to serve the Dalit community, the lowest caste in their culture, sometimes referred to as "outcasts." In the religious beliefs of the leaders, people were born into the Dalit caste as a punishment by the gods for sins the individual had committed in a past life, so improving their lives was an offense against the will of the gods. The program I was developing was being conducted as part of the American Red Cross relief effort, and I needed to adhere to Red Cross policies as much as possible. American Red Cross programs are not discriminatory, and don't exclude particular groups. So, I responded to the group of leaders, asking if it would be acceptable to educate members of the Dalit caste. The group went into a huddle for a few minutes and then said that, yes, teaching the Dalit was acceptable. (I knew this was at least minimally acceptable because Dalit children were not allowed *in* schools, but they *WERE* allowed to listen at the windows from outside the building and learn what they could.) I then explained that the CBPFA program that we were promoting was one in which people within the community supported one another; that we would educate members of communities to care for one another, but that we would not be helping anyone directly. The group of leaders again went into a huddle, and when they finished, told me that we were welcome to teach our program to the Dalit, as well as to the other castes and socioeconomic groups in the town.

I had a local counterpart, a health professional, who guided me in terms of cultural issues and translation, and I taught him about managing a disaster mental health response and the CBPFA model. In another village we came across a gathering of men, and I asked our driver to stop so that I could speak with them. My local counterpart cautioned me that these men were Islamic, and that the great tension in the area between Hindus and Islamic people meant that it would not be safe for me to stop and talk to them. I persisted in my request, and approached the group of men, who looked at me suspiciously. I greeted them loudly, "Asalaam aleikum." They looked taken aback, but all responded, "Aleikum Salaam." This is the spiritual greeting and response for the Islamic community there. The men immediately made room for me in the middle of the group, brought me a chair, and asked me to sit with them. We had a very good discussion. Greeting them in their own culture's custom indicated that I was not a threat to them, and might be interesting, or even useful.

I emphasized to my local counterpart that it was important that people of all faiths receive the same care and services. I was able to design the program during my time there, and received approval from local government officials and the national Indian Red Cross, but never received permission from the American Red Cross to begin the program. The delegate who took over the leadership of the program from me also completed her time without receiving permission to begin. Finally, however, Joseph O. Prewitt Diaz was allowed to begin the program. Although he started with the basic program I had designed, he added significant improvements. Three years later I returned to India to consult on the disaster response to the Indian Ocean tsunami. I was asked to return to Gujarat to see the psychological support program that they had developed there. The local Red Cross workers were excited to show me that they had the same services for the Hindu,

Islamic, and Christian communities, although they were physically separated. But they had also implemented a number of very creative programs after assessing the needs of the local affected community.

Approximately 40,000 people died in that earthquake, and there were many women who became widows. In that culture at that time, it was unacceptable to hire a widow; widows were basically non-persons. Therefore, it was very difficult for widows to support their families. The Psychological Support Program (PSP, based on a CBPFA model) helped the women start their own company (so no one needed to hire them), creating traditional artwork and marketing it to tourists. The program was very successful, and the widowed women were able to effectively support their families.

Children at a local elementary school approached their teachers. They had seen the PSP develop in their community, and saw that when something difficult happened to a family, residents of the neighborhood responded to provide psychological support to the affected family. The children said that they had also noted that there wasn't a corresponding supportive response to serve the children. The students asked that the teachers help them train the community's children so that the children themselves could provide psychological support to children in the affected families. The teachers worked with the PSP program to develop training for the children, and they did form children-to-children psychological support teams.

When I had initially designed the PSP CBPFA program for Gujarat, I had included separate initial training for the general public, for paraprofessionals, and for supervisory mental health professionals. Prewitt took the training a significant step further by adding additional stepped training to continually increase the knowledge and skills of residents who wanted to be official participants in the PSP. This was true for staff and volunteers at all levels of the PSP (even the Director). In adding this component, Prewitt's program produced a cadre of highly skilled supervisors, the most senior of whom led the development of PSP programs in Sri Lanka, the Maldives, and Indonesia following the 2004 Indian Ocean tsunami.

The PSP program for children and adolescents also required ongoing training and prosocial activities to serve their communities. Youths were publicly recognized when they completed certain tiers of training and service, and the communities came together to celebrate the prosocial accomplishments of their youths. (Imagine that. Youth getting attention from the community for the *good* things they did!) The PSP also organized a youth theater group in at least one of the temple communities. It is very common in Gujarat for residents to identify with the community that worships at their Hindu temple. The adolescents wrote and performed their own plays, and presented them as part of one of the religious celebrations that was also used to recognize youths who had achieved a new level of training and service. I had the opportunity to attend one of these celebrations, and the youths' plays were well-received by the temple community. Three plays were performed. Two were dramatic and included very emotional and difficult content. These were followed by one that was humorous, making good-natured fun of the local leader of the PSP program, and lifted the spirits of the audience.

Indian Ocean Tsunami

The Indian Ocean tsunami, as referred to earlier, occurred in December 2004. It resulted in the deaths of at least 220,000 people, and probably more, and created extensive devastation, primarily affecting Indonesia, Thailand, India, Sri Lanka, and the Maldives, but even affected part of the East coast of Africa. Indonesia had the additional burden of the effects of the magnitude 9.1 earthquake that caused the tsunami. In response to this catastrophe, the American Red Cross supported the development of PSP programs in Sri Lanka, India, the Maldives, and Indonesia. In each of these countries, the national directors for the American Red Cross PSP programs were those who had been at the senior level of administration in the Indian Red Cross/American Red Cross PSP program begun following the 2001 Gujarat earthquake. The programs developed in those countries began with the same basic structure, philosophy, and materials developed in the India program. But there was an extensive process of adaptation and accommodation to the individual needs and cultures of the affected countries and even specific areas within countries. That process involved *much* more than translation of the materials. It included community focus groups, and consultation and collaboration with both local mental health professionals, and with government officials. The community committees involved representatives of as many parts of each specific community as possible, trying to ensure that the voices of both the empowered and the disenfranchised were heard.

During the assessment of psychological support needs for a village in Sri Lanka, the community said that the most helpful thing that could be done for the psychological support of the community was to rebuild their school. The PSP representatives responded that, with respect, they were PSP workers, and weren't authorized to perform construction. A community representative responded that, "You asked us what would help us most, and we told you." The PSP program responded to the committee's request and provided building materials, and the adults in the affected community rebuilt the school. The children attended the school during the day, freeing up their parents to perform recovery work in the village, and at night the school became a community center where the adults met and made plans on what to do for their community's recovery the following day.

Another request made to the Sri Lankan PSP program by representatives of several villages was to have flags for grieving. I didn't understand the request and asked for clarification. The local PSP staff explained that in Sri Lankan Buddhism it was traditional that when someone in a village died, a particular color flag was flown along the street(s) of the village, and a different color was flown in front of the house where the deceased person had lived. It was a community statement that a death had occurred in their community and a statement by the deceased's family that they were the ones who had suffered a death. For a few dollars per village the PSP program provided a set of flags. So many people in each village had died that families took turns flying the differently colored flag in front of their homes.

Following a training segment explaining the process of community adaptation in a ToT for CBPFA, one of the participants approached me during the break. He explained that he was a government official responsible for building new housing for the villages that had been, literally, washed off the face of the earth. He had completed several housing clusters, but none of the homeless survivors seemed to want to move into them, despite the fact that at that time the survivors were living in shelters. He said that after the training's discussion about community adaptation he wondered if he should talk with the homeless residents he was targeting and ask them what kind of homes they wanted! He explained that he had been building modest modern homes, trying to update the communities, but the houses were completely different from the traditional homes that existed before the tsunami had struck. After discussion with community committees, he began building homes that were more traditional in appearance, if updated in the features of the homes, and he reported that the new, but nevertheless familiar, neighborhoods filled quickly.

In one momentous sign that the CBPFA program was being successful, the Sri Lankan PSP team was approached by the Buddhist Monastery. The monks reported that they could see that the PSP had become a part of the culture in the part of the country devastated by the tsunami, and the monks felt that they needed to learn the techniques themselves in order to truly be integrated into their communities. The PSP program conducted a separate training for the monastery.

Aceh, the Indonesian province nearest to the epicenter of the earthquake that caused the tsunami, suffered an extremely powerful earthquake that caused tremendous damage. This was followed minutes later by the enormous tsunami wave that resulted from the earthquake. Officials said that evidence indicated that the wave was roughly 90 feet high and moving 150 miles per hour, and penetrated about a mile inland. The PSP program developed for that region included a "Sense of Place" component. This concept related to the idea that there are certain characteristics of a person's environment that make it seem like one's own home. For example, if you needed to move to a new house, what would be the one or two things you would take from your old home to the new residence to make it feel like your own home? What are the things that make your street feel like home? In Aceh, entire villages had disappeared as a result of the double catastrophe of the earthquake and tsunami. While NGO's helped rebuild the houses for the survivors, and the surviving residents were very grateful for that, there still seemed to the community committees to be something missing. Assessments by the PSP team inquired about what had made the streets of their destroyed village seem like home. An almost unanimous response was that flowers made the neighborhood seem like home. The rebuilt villages had virtually no plants, due to the scouring effects of the tsunami. The PSP provided truckloads of flower plants to the villages, and after the residents had planted them, they reported feeling much more at home and reported a greater sense of community.

Other Program Adaptations

In 2004 I was asked to organize a symposium for the International Congress of Psychology in Beijing, China. I was asked to choose presenters who could illustrate how CBPFA could differ in different cultures. I chose presenters representing four programs with which I had worked, which began with nearly identical models of CBPFA, but which had chosen their own direction and developed their own unique paths.

- Sirry Thormar (2004) from Iceland described a program which was probably the first in the world that combined Disaster Mental Health and CBPFA. Both aspects of psychological support had been broadly accepted in the country.
- Rose Kasina (2004) described their program developed to provide support to Kenyans affected by the 1998 terrorist bombing of the U.S. Embassy in Nairobi. They served those in need of psychological support as a result of that bombing, and when the program seemed to have completed serving those needs, they adapted the program to provide support to Kenyans who were HIV positive.
- Burcu Aydin (2004) described the program developed following the 1999 Izmit earthquake in Turkey. Consultation by Judi Fairholm of the Canadian Red Cross had helped them develop a self-funding model. The PSP program rebuilt community centers that had been destroyed in affected villages. The community centers had long been an important part of Turkish culture. The centers had offered courses in such topics as sewing, gardening, cooking, parenting, home repair, and tool use. The centers' rooms could be rented for marriage receptions, birthday parties, etc., funding the operations of the center. The PSP program added a mental health professional to the traditional staff of each community center, and included classes in CBPFA along with all the traditional classes.
- Jun Maeda (2004) described a PSP model adapted to the uniqueness of Japanese society. It is uncommon in Japan for people to talk about their stress or other psychological difficulties with anyone but a medical professional. There is a concern that such negative expressions can negatively affect the community, and the community is seen as having greater importance than the individual. The Japanese program trained medical staff and hospital mental health professionals in strategies for providing psychological support to their patients, as well as having the staff support one another.

These were four entirely different programs, sprung from the same initial concepts, but adapted and well-suited to their communities.

Japan Tōhoku Earthquake

Hitomi Gunsolley (2017) successfully conducted an extremely difficult dissertation. She focused on cultural issues involved in the 2011 Tōhoku earthquake and the resulting tsunami and nuclear crisis in Japan. She was very fortunate to have Jun Maeda from the Muroran Institute of Technology in Hokkaido Japan agree to serve as a consultant to her. He had been a leader of the Japan Red Cross PSP program response for the overall tsunami and for the nuclear incident at Fukushima. Even though Hitomi had lived in Japan until she began college, there were cultural aspects to conducting research there of which she was unaware. Maeda-san helped her to understand how to solicit participation, and helped her develop culturally responsive instruments. Without his cultural and professional consultation, the research would probably not have been able to be conducted. Hospital directors provided further consultation on unique aspects of collecting data with their personnel.

Comparison of the Models

Disaster Mental Health has been a successful model. If there are adequate numbers of mental health professionals who are trained in traumatic stress and crisis intervention, it can be very effective. It still has the limitations described earlier in this chapter. But it can be an important part of the psychosocial preparedness, response, and recovery from a disaster or other traumatic event. And mental health professionals have more professional skills in assessment and interventions than even highly trained paraprofessionals.

The response team PFA models (whether NCPTSD/NCTSN or RAPID PFA, or another model that meets the Hobfoll et al. 2007 criteria) can also be valuable components of the immediate and short-term psychosocial response. Many communities have not developed a CBPFA program for their residents, and the immediate post-disaster psychosocial support needs of the community may be met, in part, by the efforts of a PFA-trained response team. In the long-term, however an effective psychosocial program needs to adapt to the community if it is to be sustained and continue to be effective.

I believe, however, that the ideal model is for a community to develop CBPFA to fit into their unique lives. CBPFA can be effective in providing support through the daily hassles of life, but also can help the community prepare to cope with traumatic events that affect individuals in the community (e.g., vehicular accidents, severe illness, personal physical or sexual assault, sudden death) and community-wide events (e.g., disasters). With CBPFA, there is no need for people to be brought into the community to provide basic psychological support, and the providers are sensitive to ethnic, cultural, and religious aspects of psychological support. The providers are also there for the long haul, not merely during the emergency response phase of a disaster.

Finally, I would like to describe how powerful a supportive community can be for those in need of support. Two months after the terrorist attacks of September 11, 2001, a jet taking off from Kennedy International Airport in New York rolled over and plummeted vertically to the ground, crashing in a residential neighborhood in the Rockaways, killing everyone on board. This was a community where very many of New York's firefighters lived, and many of the resident firefighters had died in the collapse of the World Trade Center towers. The community was fairly tight-knit, and there had been funerals nearly every day for weeks as the bodies of the dead were recovered and identified. The psychological toll on the community was immense. Then, two months to the day after the attacks, a passenger jet fell from the sky in their midst, killing some of their neighbors and escalating the horror through which they had been living. I was assigned to meet with the community and discuss next steps. The emotion in the room was palpable. The community was nearly at the limits of their coping capacity. I told them that in the event of aviation disasters, survivors were generally allowed to visit the crash site and pay their respects to their deceased loved ones. The room immediately erupted in emotion, with people shouting that they just couldn't take any more, that enough was enough. I acknowledged the enormous grief that they had been processing in the past two months, but told them that, based on my experience with many aviation disasters, if a visit to the site wasn't done as one scheduled event, the families would still come, but they would come a few at a time across weeks or even months. The shoulders of nearly everyone in the room visibly drooped, silence descended, and one of the group said, "Bring it on, then."

The visit to the impact site was scheduled for immediately after the memorial service for the deceased, an event required under federal law. The surviving family members of the aircraft passengers were put on buses to travel to the crash site to minimize the impact on the community where the aviation incident had occurred (rather than having the families come in many cars). The families were dropped off at one of two sides of the impact site and could walk down a pathway to view the site, and then return on another pathway to the buses to be returned to their cars at the location of the earlier memorial service. I rode on the first of the buses, and had some concern that there could be demonstrations against the crash site visit, given the strong feelings against it that had been voiced at the community meeting. But I was overwhelmed to find when I exited the bus, that the residents, who had been so extremely opposed to the event, had set up folding tables all along the entrance to the pathways. They had made fresh baked goods of all kinds, which were arrayed on the tables, together with various kinds of hot drinks (it was a cold November night). The residents reached out to the families, offering them condolences, and praying with them, treating them as honored and welcome guests. It was one of the most powerful acts of community love and support that I have ever seen, and the families of those who died in the crash were deeply moved by the welcome.

My hope for CBPFA is that all of our communities might become that welcoming and supportive of those in need of a shoulder to lean on. CBPFA is for providing basic psychological support to friends and family. The Lakota people have an expression that is core in their culture and which I find very powerful. In Lakota it is "Mitakuye oyassin," which translates to "We are *all* family."

References

Aydin, B. (2004, August). *Psychosocial support program in Turkey.* Paper presented at the 28th International Congress of Psychology, Beijing.

Brymer, M., Jacobs, A., Layne, C., Pynoos, R., Ruzek, J., Steinberg, A., et al. (2006). *Psychological first aid: Field operations guide* (2nd ed.). Los Angeles: National Child Traumatic Stress Network and National Center for Post-Traumatic Stress Disorder. Retrieved from http://www.nctsnet.org/nctsn_assets/pdfs/pfa/2/PsyFirstAid.pdf.

Daw, J. (2001). APA's Disaster Response Network: Help on the scene. *Monitor on Psychology, 32*(10), 14–15.

Gunsolley, H. (2017). *Japanese people's reactions to the Great East Japan Earthquake and development of theory of secondary control* (Order No. 10599993). Available from Dissertations & Theses @ University of South Dakota; ProQuest.

Hobfoll, S. E., Watson, P., Bell, C. C., Bryant, R. A., Brymer, M. J., Friedman, M. J., & Ursano, R. J. (2007). Five essential elements of immediate and mid-term mass trauma intervention: Empirical evidence. *Psychiatry: Interpersonal & Biological Processes, 70*(4), 283–315. https://doi.org/10.1521/psyc.2007.70.4.283.

Inter-Agency Standing Committee. (2007). *IASC guidelines on mental health and psychosocial support in emergency settings*. Geneva: Author.

Jacobs, G. A. (2016). *Community-based psychological first aid: A practical guide to helping individuals and communities during difficult times*. Amsterdam: Butterworth-Heinemann.

Maeda, J. (2004, August). *Development of psychological support program in Japan.* Paper presented at the 28th International Congress of Psychology, Beijing.

Ndetei, D., & Kasina, R. (2004, August). *Community psychosocial response to traumatic experiences in Kenya.* Paper presented at the 28th International Congress of Psychology, Beijing.

Spielberger, C. D., & Diaz-Guerrero, R. (Eds.). (1976). *Cross-cultural research on anxiety.* Washington, DC: Hemisphere/Wiley.

Thormar, S. (2004, August). *Psychological support program in Iceland.* Paper presented at the 28th International Congress of Psychology, Beijing.

Chapter 10
Posttraumatic Growth After Disasters

Olivia M. Riffle, Paisley R. Lewis, and Richard G. Tedeschi

Disasters are frightening, devastating, and unfortunately commonplace occurrences. The aftermath of a natural or manmade disaster can wreak havoc for years, creating considerable psychological distress in survivors' lives as they attempt to cope with the loss of loved ones and property, physical injuries, scarcity of basic necessities, and even complete geographical displacement. Despite these immense challenges and resultant distress, however, many individuals and communities who weather disasters also report *posttraumatic growth* (PTG), positive psychological changes that result from struggling with a highly difficult life circumstance (Tedeschi and Calhoun 1996). As the world recovers from a recent wave of catastrophic disasters –Hurricanes Harvey, Irma, and Maria in North America, monsoons in South Asia, earthquakes in Mexico, and more–there has never been a more opportune time to consider the ways in which these many affected populations might find meaning and positive life change amidst their suffering. The purpose of this chapter is to briefly describe the PTG model, explore this model in the context of disaster trauma and review recent empirical evidence, and propose future directions and considerations for this area of study.

An Overview of Posttraumatic Growth Theory

While traumatic events can lead to distress and posttraumatic stress symptoms, many individuals have reported growing from the challenge of incorporating these events into their life story. Although the study and measurement of PTG developed only in recent decades (Tedeschi and Calhoun 1995, 1996, 2004), the concept of transformative growth after suffering is a common theme throughout human history,

O. M. Riffle (✉) · P. R. Lewis · R. G. Tedeschi
University of North Carolina at Charlotte, Charlotte, NC, USA
e-mail: oriffle@uncc.edu

S. E. Schulenberg (ed.), *Positive Psychological Approaches to Disaster*,
https://doi.org/10.1007/978-3-030-32007-2_10

appearing in the teachings of Hinduism, Buddhism, Christianity, and Islam, as well as countless philosophical, literary, and artistic works (Tedeschi and Calhoun 1995). Importantly, PTG is distinct from the related concept of resilience. While resilience is characterized by the ability to continue living a life of meaning following hardship, it lacks the aspect of transformation that is critical to PTG (Calhoun and Tedeschi 2006; Tedeschi and Calhoun 2004); an individual who has experienced PTG is not the same person he or she used to be, for the better.

Factor analyses have demonstrated that PTG manifests in five distinct domains (Tedeschi and Calhoun 1996). Growth in *personal strength* may involve a newfound appreciation for previously untapped stores of strength. *New possibilities* can unfold as one develops novel interests or chooses to venture down new paths in life. Individuals may also report changes in *relating to others*, as connections with loved ones deepen and a heightened sense of compassion and empathy for the suffering of others emerges. Greater *appreciation of life* may develop, as priorities shift dramatically and the "little things" in life are recognized for their value. *Spiritual change* can also occur, even for those who do not identify with a religious faith, as fundamental existential dilemmas are clarified or new meaning is injected into life (Tedeschi and Calhoun 2004; Tedeschi et al. 2017b).

The PTG Model

Core Beliefs

The most recently published model of PTG (Calhoun et al. 2010) illuminates the mechanisms by which PTG is presumed to develop. The process that may ultimately lead to growth does not begin directly with a traumatic event; rather, it is prompted only when an event disrupts one's assumptive world beliefs—the set of assumptions that inform our understanding of the world, explain why things happen the way they do, and help us create meaning out of life (Cann et al. 2010; Tedeschi and Calhoun 2004). An earthquake metaphor is used to describe trauma in this context: Events with greater "seismic" impact are more likely to shatter assumptive world beliefs and prompt cognitive work as individuals attempt to reconcile traumatic experiences with pre-existing expectations of how the world should work, or to construct new core beliefs that better account for events that have been experienced (Tedeschi et al. 1998). Ultimately, this cognitive work can help individuals to accommodate their disruptive experiences within a new understanding of the world (Calhoun and Tedeschi 2006).

Rumination

Events that disrupt one's assumptive world beliefs are more likely to lead to rumination—a term considered synonymous with repetitive thinking or cognitive engagement (Cann et al. 2011). *Intrusive rumination* describes the unwanted, automatic thoughts that may appear in the immediate aftermath of a highly disruptive event (Cann et al. 2011). These intrusive thoughts are closely associated with distress (Calhoun et al. 2010). Attempts to manage the distress and to make sense of the event and its implications for one's worldview may result in greater *deliberate rumination*, a type of voluntary cognitive engagement whose powers can be harnessed for the purposes of understanding and accommodating an event (Cann et al. 2011). While there is no guarantee that PTG will occur following this cognitive work, it is likely to occur if the conditions are appropriate (Calhoun et al. 2010). As discussed later, other factors may further increase the likelihood of growth.

Associated Factors

Researchers have identified individual characteristics and behaviors that influence the process and outcomes of PTG. For example, higher levels of extraversion and openness to experience have been associated with a greater likelihood for experiencing growth (Tedeschi and Calhoun 1996). Disclosing one's experience with trauma and receiving support from others can also aid in the process of distress management and deliberate rumination, as social support offers individuals the opportunity to develop and share new personal narratives and to incorporate alternative perspectives into their changing views of the world (Calhoun et al. 2010). Cultural factors both proximal (e.g., interpersonal interactions and the social rules and norms of close others) and distal (e.g., broad societal narratives and expectations) may shape the content and trajectory of the ruminative process (Calhoun et al. 2010).

Outcomes of PTG

The implications of PTG for emotional adjustment following a trauma, as measured by levels of distress and well-being, have long interested researchers. Data on the relationship between PTG and distress are inconsistent, which supports the notion that growth and distress should be seen as separate dimensions (Baker et al. 2008; Tedeschi and Calhoun 2004). Distress and PTG can co-occur, and the development of growth in the wake of a traumatic event does not erase the pain of loss (Tedeschi et al. 1998). Despite the ongoing pain associated with trauma, however, Calhoun and Tedeschi (2006) argue that individuals who experience PTG are "living life in ways that, at least from their point of view, are fuller, richer, and perhaps more meaningful" (p. 7). Accordingly, well-being and life satisfaction are included as outcomes in the model of PTG. Throughout the process of growth, one's personal narrative becomes more complex in order to accommodate the coexistence of pain and growth, and wisdom may increase—leading, in turn, to greater well-being (Calhoun et al. 2010). Furthermore, although some of the positive association between PTG and well-being is a direct effect, the primary effect of PTG on well-being seems to be its indirect influence through increased meaning in life (Triplett et al. 2012).

Mutual Influences

Tedeschi and Calhoun (2004) conceptualize PTG as both a process and an outcome. This is described as occurring through the ongoing, mutual influence between PTG and co-occurring processes, such as the development of wisdom and the reconceptualization of one's personal narrative (Tedeschi and Calhoun 2004). PTG has also been examined in the context of resolution—the process by which a traumatic event comes to "make sense" (Tedeschi and Calhoun 2008). In one study, participants who were actively searching for resolution reported the highest PTG, followed by those who had already achieved resolution, those who gave up their search before finding resolution, and those who felt no need for resolution in the first place (Triplett et al. 2012). These results indicate that the process of trying to resolve and make sense of a life-changing event may facilitate recognition of the positive changes that have been brought about by one's struggle (Triplett et al. 2012). Readers interested in further information regarding the history and current considerations of the PTG model are referred to Tedeschi et al. (2017a).

Posttraumatic Growth in Disaster Contexts

Whether natural (e.g., floods, hurricanes, tsunamis, wildfires, earthquakes) or man-made/technological (e.g., chemical exposures, spills, fires, crashes, structural collapse), disasters have the potential to drastically upend an individual's life like few other situations. They are often rapid, unpredictable, and tremendous in scope, leading to loss of possessions, homes, entire communities, and lives. Individuals' physical health, financial status, social networks, and lifestyles may be changed irrevocably. Disasters also may lead to secondary stressors, such as evacuation and displacement, that exacerbate recovery. As such, disasters can lead to significant psychological distress, including posttraumatic stress disorder (PTSD), depression, and anxiety (Cherry 2015; Usami et al. 2016; Zwiebach et al. 2010). The degree of such distress may be a function of exposure severity, injury and other decreases in physical health, loss and bereavement, and displacement status (Chao 2016; Johannesson et al. 2015; Siqveland et al. 2015).

Despite these challenges, research suggests that disasters are fruitful opportunities for PTG, beginning with core belief challenge. In a disaster, a survivor's assumptions about his/her vulnerability, the safety of the world, controllability, and predictability are threatened (Dursun et al. 2016; Park 2016). Feelings of senselessness and a lack of control are only augmented by the non-intentionality of disasters. Amid property damage and a dearth of basic resources, survivors often question their assumptions about whether they can survive without their possessions or homes; within a matter of moments, they might be given no choice but to learn how (Cherry 2015). Individuals may question their "just world belief," or the idea that good things happen to good people and bad things to bad people (Cann et al. 2010). The formidable scale of disasters often feels beyond human capacity to understand,

and thus individuals may grapple with questions about the spiritual and supernatural (Nalipay et al. 2017; Park 2016), potentially leading to spiritual discontent and disillusionment with the nature of God or a higher power ("Why would He allow this to happen?"). In these ways and more, survivors must reconstruct an assumptive world that accommodates the realities of their post-disaster lives.

In turn, this core belief reconstruction and consequent rumination present opportunities to experience change among all domains of PTG. Survivors may increase their self-efficacy and personal strength through recognizing their ability to survive without the luxuries of life before disaster, a feat that perhaps once seemed unimaginable. Additionally, they may demonstrate strength through relief efforts, whether helping rebuild structures, distribute supplies, or support others. In recognizing their safety was acutely threatened, and perhaps in witnessing others' loss of life and damage to structures, survivors increase their appreciation of life. With the literal reconstruction of their physical environments and lifestyles, individuals may find newfound interests, preferences, and life roles, increasing a sense of new possibilities. Spiritual and religious changes may arise in relating to a higher power in a new way. Many disaster survivors rely on religious coping (Chan and Rhodes 2013) and thus might arrive at new ways of relating to God or ideas of meaning and purpose. Finally, as with any traumatic event collectively experienced by a group, disasters may bring individuals, families, and communities together in previously unimagined ways, offering many opportunities for changes in relating to others. Relationships may take on new meaning with increased prosocial values, a drive to connect with others and serve that has been linked with PTG (Frazier et al. 2013; Staub and Vollhardt 2008).

Recent Research in PTG Post-Disaster

The devastating impact of natural and manmade disasters render them opportune contexts in which to study PTG, as is evident in this burgeoning literature. For decades, researchers have sought to understand how PTG unfolds across different disaster types, specific disaster incidents or cohorts (e.g., Hurricane Katrina), and special populations. Studies have demonstrated PTG in survivors of earthquakes (e.g., He et al., 2013; Xu and Liao 2011), tsunamis (e.g., Augustine 2014; Sattler et al. 2014a; Tang 2006), hurricanes (e.g., Chan and Rhodes 2013; Kilmer and Gil-Rivas 2010a; Lowe et al. 2013), floods (Dursun et al. 2016; Mordeno et al. 2016), oil spills (Holgersen et al. 2011), and wildfires (Felix et al. 2015). Discussed here are developments in PTG disaster research including longitudinal investigations, youth and first responder populations, and community-level growth.

Longitudinal studies of PTG post-disaster have contributed to the central issue of understanding causality in the growth process. Such studies have demonstrated that over the long-term post-disaster, PTG and posttraumatic stress (PTS) remain strongly and positively related (Holgersen et al. 2010; Lowe et al. 2013) and ultimately positively predict mental health (Holgersen et al. 2010), supporting the idea that growth and distress are distinct and can co-occur. In addition, PTG may have a buffering effect over time on the negative impact of PTS on such outcomes as quality of life and depression after disaster (Siqveland et al. 2015). Another recent study spoke to the roles of increased "lessons learned" in disaster preparedness, social support, and prosocial values in experiences of positive change and meaning making after disasters (Stanko et al. 2015). Studies that continue to address changes in PTG over time after disasters will support efforts to implement interventions that nurture positive changes in their aftermath.

Researchers are increasingly attending to the unique growth processes and outcomes of special populations after disaster, one of which is youth (Alisic et al. 2008; Meyerson et al. 2011). Children and adolescents exposed to natural disasters seem to possess the capacity to reflect on changes in themselves and their situation (Cryder et al. 2006; Hafstad et al. 2010; Kilmer and Gil-Rivas 2010a; Little et al. 2011), although it is unclear as to how much of reported growth can be attributed to normative maturation as opposed to these traumatic experiences (Meyerson et al. 2011). Keeping in mind the impact of cognitive and emotional development on how growth unfolds, correlates and predictors of PTG in youth seem to parallel those seen in adults, including social support, intrusive and deliberate rumination, and coping strategies (e.g., religious coping), and beliefs in one's competency to successfully cope (Cryder et al. 2006; Meyerson et al. 2011). An important consideration regarding the validity of youth PTG is the impact of parents' influence on children's coping strategies and explanations or interpretations of disasters; it may be that PTG in children reflects values encouraged by their nuclear families and local communities, and not strictly their own. For example, children living in New Orleans and coping with Hurricane Katrina were more likely to endorse religious/spiritual change than children in other parts of the country, likely reflecting this region's more spiritual culture (Kilmer et al. 2009). As research increasingly incorporates a family-systems perspective, it will be important to consider how youths' growth post-disaster is a function of such socioecological influence.

Another population receiving increased attention in PTG research in disaster contexts is first responders. Whether on a professional or volunteer basis, firefighters, police, paramedics, and others in this group are trained specifically to work in acute emergency situations, including disaster events; as such, they have increased likelihood, compared to civilians, of traumatic exposure to others' suffering and/or endangerment to their own lives (Skeffington et al. 2017). Volunteers may be particularly vulnerable to PTS as compared to professionals, but have also reported PTG across multiple disaster contexts (Anderson et al. 2016; Bhushan and Kumar 2012). Increased efforts are being made to understand first responders' psychological experiences in disasters, increase resilience to PTS, and increase PTG post-event through both individual self-care and coping strategies as well as organizational and institutional policies to support such efforts (Armstrong et al. 2014; Kehl et al. 2015; Sattler et al. 2014b).

Finally, there is evidence that PTG can also exist on a group system scale, whether couples, families, or entire communities or societies (Calhoun and Tedeschi 2006). As disasters inevitably influence several people at once, they offer unique opportunities to study collective growth processes in these interpersonal dynamics.

PTG has been researched in couples, with recent research demonstrating a contagious "spread" of growth from one partner to another post-disaster (e.g., Canevello et al. 2016); among families as they negotiate new roles and relationships (e.g., Godwin et al. 2013; Hafstad et al. 2010; Kilmer and Gil-Rivas 2010b); and larger communities, as they engage in meaning making with the potential for larger-scale social change efforts (Bloom 1998; Tedeschi 1999). Communities may share posttraumatic responses and communicate collectively through the development of a *collective narrative*, or a way for its members to interpret and give meaning to the event, akin to the core belief reconstruction and meaning-making processes within individuals (Calhoun and Tedeschi 2006). In light of these unique collective processes, recent efforts have been made to understand communal growth post-disaster as a distinct phenomenon from individual PTG (Wlodarczyk et al. 2017).

Future Directions

Research on PTG in disaster contexts has flourished in recent decades, but many areas warrant further exploration. Broadly, continued efforts are needed to investigate the conditions under which adults, youths, families, and communities are most likely to experience growth post-trauma. Within this general recommendation are some specific targeted areas for investigation, including cultural differences in the experience of disaster traumas and PTG, and potentially high-risk populations such as older adults, and intervention.

Evidence suggests that Western and Eastern cultures, as a result of differing worldviews, may experience the impact of disasters differently (e.g., Tang 2006). For example, with more collectivistic values and a preference for extended social networks over nuclear families, disaster survivors in Eastern cultures might have more opportunities to gain support and opportunities to co-process emotional distress (Augustine 2014; Bhushan and Kumar 2012). Calhoun et al. (2010) outlined three areas in which distal culture might shape the process of posttraumatic rumination, which can inform how communities cope with disaster. First, Westerners are more likely to interpret events through a lens of personal control, assuming greater personal responsibility both for a traumatic event and for the positive changes that may follow it. Those from Eastern cultures, on the other hand, may be more likely to ruminate on changes in their perceptions of the world, and not on themselves as individuals. Second, Westerners attempting to make sense of an event may be more likely to seek answers in their own personal qualities ("What is it about me that led to this trauma?" [p. 9]) while Easterners may be more likely to seek answers in the context of the event itself ("How can I avoid these situations?" [p. 9]). Third, the Western expectation of linearity in predicting future events may lead to greater disruption of assumptive world beliefs—and more cognitive work—when unexpected traumatic events occur. Easterners, who are more familiar with nonlinear cycles, may more easily accommodate contradictions (and therefore experience less cognitive disruption following a traumatic event). These cultural differences in posttraumatic ruminative processes, combined with cultural differences in the perceptions of disasters, demonstrate that the process of PTG following disaster may look different around the globe.

Efforts should also be made to continue understanding special populations as they experience PTG post-disaster. While some research has been devoted to PTG in youth, there is a relative dearth of work in older adults, despite their higher vulnerability to physical and mental health issues post-disaster (Massey 1997; Tuohy and Stephens 2012). Some evidence suggests that older adults may exhibit resilience and narrative meaning making after disasters (Cherry et al. 2011; Tuohy and Stephens 2012), and others have demonstrated that elders can experience PTG as a result of traumatic events (e.g., Lopez, Camilli, and Noriega 2015; Palgi 2015; Park et al. 2005). However, more research is needed to understand how this process unfolds specifically in disaster contexts, when the elderly may be at higher risk for negative effects of trauma, or, potentially, for PTG.

A continued area of interest is the development of interventions to facilitate PTG post-disaster. PTG-focused interventions are aimed at using cognitive-behavioral, narrative, constructivist, and narrative approaches to facilitate schema change, meaning making, and growth processes (Calhoun and Tedeschi 2013; Tedeschi et al. 2015; Tedeschi and Riffle 2016). Cognitive-behavioral and narrative techniques have also been utilized in trauma-focused resilience interventions for children (Little et al. 2011; Scannell et al. 2017). Recent intervention efforts specifically regarding disasters have included eye movement desensitization therapy to promote PTG in adults after a ferry disaster (Jeon et al. 2017); a resilience-based psychoeducational web intervention for adolescents and their families after tornadoes (Ruggiero et al. 2015); and an in-person clinical intervention to reduce adolescent substance abuse post-Hurricane Katrina (Rowe and Liddle, 2008). However, much room remains for intervention development and implementation, and to incorporate PTG into these interventions.

One avenue for exploration is incorporating the role of *expert companionship* in facilitating PTG post-disaster. Expert companions are defined as individuals who nurture naturally occurring processes of healing in trauma survivors by offering empathic support along with knowledge of the tasks involved in said healing (Calhoun and Tedeschi, 2013; Tedeschi et al. 2015). Fostering mental health professionals' expertise of disaster-specific psychological concerns and growth processes, and increasing their availability to communities after such incidents, may promote PTG. Expert companions may also be found in the mutual help that is common in communities in the aftermath of disaster.

Conclusion

Despite the often devastating and distressing impact of disasters, many survivors also undergo positive psychological and life changes as a result of their experiences. In this chapter, we have reviewed the theory and model of posttraumatic growth (PTG), explored evidence of PTG in natural and technological disasters, and discussed opportunities for continued research. With concerns about the increasing frequency and severity of disasters in light of climate change, it will be imperative to continue efforts to understand and promote growth in disaster survivors, and, in turn, how growth can instigate community-wide changes in approaches to coping with traumas. PTG is an increasingly rich and complex psychological phenomenon with promise for improving the well-being of individuals and communities in the aftermath of disasters.

References

Alisic, E., van der Schoot, T. A. W., van Ginkel, J. R., & Kleber, R. J. (2008). Looking beyond posttraumatic stress disorder in children: Posttraumatic stress reactions, posttraumatic growth, and quality of life in a general population sample. *Journal of Clinical Psychiatry, 69*, 1455–1461. https://doi.org/10.4088/JCP.v69n0913.

Anderson, D., Prioleau, P., Taku, K., Naruse, Y., Sekine, H., Maeda, M., et al. (2016). Posttraumatic stress and growth among medical student volunteers after the March 2011 disaster in Fukushima, Japan: Implications for student involvement with future disasters. *Psychiatric Quarterly, 87*(2), 241–251. https://doi.org/10.1007/s11126-015-9381-3.

Armstrong, D., Shakespeare-Finch, J., & Shochet, I. (2014). Predicting post-traumatic growth and post-traumatic stress in firefighters. *Australian Journal of Psychology, 66*(1), 38–46. https://doi.org/10.1111/ajpy.12032.

Augustine, J. (2014). Predictors of posttraumatic growth among adult tsunami survivors: The role of employment, religion, and family attributes. *Journal of Social Service Research, 40*, 491–507. https://doi.org/10.1080/01488376.2014.894368.

Baker, J. M., Kelly, C., Calhoun, L. G., Cann, A., & Tedeschi, R. G. (2008). An examination of posttraumatic growth and posttraumatic depreciation: Two exploratory studies. *Journal of Loss and Trauma, 13*(5), 450–465. https://doi.org/10.1080/15325020802171367.

Bhushan, B., & Kumar, J. S. (2012). A study of posttraumatic stress and growth in tsunami relief volunteers. *Journal of Loss and Trauma, 17*(2), 113–124. https://doi.org/10.1080/15325024.2011.635580.

Bloom, S. L. (1998). By the crowd they have been broken, by the crowd they shall be healed: The social transformation of trauma. In R. G. Tedeschi, C. L. Park, & L. G. Calhoun (Eds.), *Posttraumatic growth: Positive changes in the aftermath of crisis* (pp. 179–213). Mahwah, NJ: Lawrence Erlbaum Associates.

Calhoun, L. G., Cann, A., & Tedeschi, R. G. (2010). The posttraumatic growth model: Sociocultural considerations. In T. Weiss & R. Berger (Eds.), *Posttraumatic growth and culturally competent practice: Lessons learned from around the globe* (pp. 1–14). Hoboken: Wiley.

Calhoun, L. G., & Tedeschi, R. G. (2006). The foundations of posttraumatic growth: An expanded framework. In L. G. Calhoun & R. G. Tedeschi (Eds.), *Handbook of posttraumatic growth: Research and practice* (pp. 3–23). Mahwah, NJ: Lawrence Erlbaum Associates.

Calhoun, L. G., & Tedeschi, R. G. (2013). *Posttraumatic growth in clinical practice*. New York, NY: Routledge.

Canevello, A., Michels, V., & Hilaire, N. (2016). Supporting close others' growth after trauma: The role of responsiveness in romantic partners' mutual posttraumatic growth. *Psychological Trauma: Theory, Research, Practice, and Policy, 8*(3), 334–342. https://doi.org/10.1037/tra0000084.

Cann, A., Calhoun, L. G., Tedeschi, R. G., Kilmer, R. P., Gil-Rivas, V., Vishnevsky, T., & Danhauer, S. C. (2010). The Core Beliefs Inventory: A brief measure of disruption in the assumptive world. *Anxiety, Stress & Coping, 23*(1), 19–34. https://doi.org/10.1080/10615800802573013.

Cann, A., Calhoun, L. G., Tedeschi, R. G., Triplett, K. N., Vishnevsky, T., & Lindstrom, C. M. (2011). Assessing posttraumatic cognitive processes: The Event Related Rumination Inventory. *Anxiety, Stress & Coping, 24*(2), 137–156. https://doi.org/10.1080/10615806.2010.529901.

Chan, C. S., & Rhodes, J. E. (2013). Religious coping, posttraumatic stress, psychological distress, and posttraumatic growth among female survivors four years after Hurricane Katrina. *Journal of Traumatic Stress, 26*(2), 257–265. https://doi.org/10.1002/jts.21801.

Chao, S.-F. (2016). Outdoor activities and depressive symptoms in displaced older adults following natural disaster: Community cohesion as mediator and moderator. *Aging & Mental Health, 20*(9), 940–947. https://doi.org/10.1080/13607863.2015.1044940.

Cherry, K. E. (Ed.). (2015). *Traumatic stress and long-term recovery: Coping with disasters and other negative life events*. Cham: Springer.

Cherry, K. E., Brown, J. S., Marks, L. D., Galea, S., Volaufova, J., Lefante, C., et al. (2011). Longitudinal assessment of cognitive and psychosocial functioning after Hurricanes Katrina and Rita: Exploring disaster impact on middle-aged, older, and oldest-old adults. *Journal of Applied Biobehavioral Research, 16*(3/4), 187–211. https://doi.org/10.1111/j.1751-9861.2011.00073.x.

Cryder, C. H., Kilmer, R. P., Tedeschi, R. G., & Calhoun, L. G. (2006). An exploratory study of posttraumatic growth in children following a natural disaster. *American Journal of Orthopsychiatry, 76*(1), 65–69. https://doi.org/10.1037/0002-9432.76.1.65.

Dursun, P., Steger, M. F., Bentele, C., & Schulenberg, S. E. (2016). Meaning and posttraumatic growth among survivors of the September 2013 Colorado floods. *Journal of Clinical Psychology, 72*, 1247–1263. https://doi.org/10.1002/jclp.22344.

Felix, E., Afifi, T., Kia-Keating, M., Brown, L., Afifi, W., & Reyes, G. (2015). Family functioning and posttraumatic growth among parents and youth following wildfire disasters. *American Journal of Orthopsychiatry, 85*(2), 191–200. https://doi.org/10.1037/ort0000054.

Frazier, P., Greer, C., Gabrielsen, S., Tennen, H., Park, C., & Tomich, P. (2013). The relation between trauma exposure and prosocial behavior. *Psychological Trauma: Theory, Research, Practice, and Policy, 5*(3), 286–294. https://doi.org/10.1037/a0027255.

Godwin, E. E., Foster, V. A., & Keefe, E. P. (2013). Hurricane Katrina families: Social class and the family in trauma recovery. *The Family Journal, 21*(1), 15–27. https://doi.org/10.1177/1066480712458224.

Hafstad, G. S., Gil-Rivas, V., Kilmer, R. P., & Raeder, S. (2010). Parental adjustment, family functioning, and posttraumatic growth among Norwegian children and adolescents following a natural disaster. *American Journal of Orthopsychiatry, 80*(2), 248–257. https://doi.org/10.1111/j.1939-0025.2010.01028.x.

He, L., Xu, J., & Wu, Z. (2013). Coping strategies as a mediator of posttraumatic growth among adult survivors of the Wenchuan earthquake. *PLoS One, 8*(12), 841–864. https://doi.org/10.1371/journal.pone.0084164.

Holgersen, K. H., Boe, H. J., & Holen, A. (2010). Long-term perspectives on posttraumatic growth in disaster survivors. *Journal of Traumatic Stress, 23*(3), 413–416. https://doi.org/10.1002/jts.20530.

Holgersen, K. H., Klöckner, C. A., Jakob Boe, H., Weisæth, L., & Holen, A. (2011). Disaster survivors in their third decade: Trajectories of initial stress responses and long-term course of mental health. *Journal of Traumatic Stress, 24*(3), 334–341. https://doi.org/10.1002/jts.20636.

Jeon, S. W., Han, C., Choi, J., Ko, Y.-H., Yoon, H.-K., & Kim, Y.-K. (2017). Eye movement desensitization and reprocessing to facilitate posttraumatic growth: A prospective clinical pilot study on ferry disaster survivors. *Clinical Psychopharmacology and Neuroscience, 15*(4), 320–327. https://doi.org/10.9758/cpn.2017.15.4.320.

Johannesson, K. B., Arinell, H., & Arnberg, F. K. (2015). Six years after the wave: Trajectories of posttraumatic stress following a natural disaster. *Journal of Anxiety Disorders, 36*(Suppl C), 15–24. https://doi.org/10.1016/j.janxdis.2015.07.007.

Kehl, D., Knuth, D., Hulse, L., & Schmidt, S. (2015). Predictors of postevent distress and growth among firefighters after work-related emergencies—A cross-national study. *Psychological Trauma: Theory, Research, Practice, and Policy, 7*(3), 203–211. https://doi.org/10.1037/a0037954.

Kilmer, R. P., & Gil-Rivas, V. (2010a). Exploring posttraumatic growth in children impacted by Hurricane Katrina: Correlates of the phenomenon and developmental considerations. *Child Development, 81*(4), 1211–1227. https://doi.org/10.1111/j.1467-8624.2010.01463.x.

Kilmer, R. P., & Gil-Rivas, V. (2010b). Responding to the needs of children and families after a disaster: Linkages between unmet needs and caregiver functioning. *American Journal of Orthopsychiatry, 80*(1), 135–142. https://doi.org/10.1111/j.1939-0025.2010.01016.x.

Kilmer, R. P., Gil-Rivas, V., Tedeschi, R. G., Cann, A., Calhoun, L. G., Buchanan, T., & Taku, K. (2009). Use of the revised Posttraumatic Growth Inventory for Children. *Journal of Traumatic Stress, 22*(3), 248–253. https://doi.org/10.1002/jts.20410.

Little, S. G., Akin-Little, A., & Somerville, M. P. (2011). Response to trauma in children: An examination of effective intervention and post-traumatic growth. *School Psychology International, 32*(5), 448–463. https://doi.org/10.1177/0143034311402916.

Lopez, J., Camilli, C., & Noriega, C. (2015). Posttraumatic growth in widowed and non-widowed older adults: Religiosity and sense of coherence. *Journal of Religious Health, 54*, 1612–1628. https://doi.org/10.1007/s10943-014-9876-5.

Lowe, S. R., Manove, E. E., & Rhodes, J. E. (2013). Posttraumatic stress and posttraumatic growth among low-income mothers who survived Hurricane Katrina. *Journal of Consulting and Clinical Psychology, 81*(5), 877–889. https://doi.org/10.1037/a0033252.

Massey, B. A. (1997). Victims or survivors? A three-part approach to working with older adults in disaster. *Journal of Geriatric Psychiatry, 30*, 193–202.

Meyerson, D. A., Grant, K. E., Carter, J. S., & Kilmer, R. P. (2011). Posttraumatic growth among children and adolescents: A systematic review. *Clinical Psychology Review, 31*(6), 949–964. https://doi.org/10.1016/j.cpr.2011.06.003.

Mordeno, I. G., Nalipay, M. J. N., Alfonso, M. K. S., & Cue, M. P. (2016). Examining the latent structure of posttraumatic growth between male and female survivors in the immediate aftermath of a flash flood disaster. *Current Psychology, 35*(4), 587–594. https://doi.org/10.1007/s12144-015-9325-y.

Nalipay, M. J. N., Bernardo, A. B. I., & Mordeno, I. G. (2017). Posttraumatic growth in survivors of a natural disaster: The role of social axioms of religiosity, reward for application, and social cynicism. *The Journal of Positive Psychology, 12*(4), 342–353. https://doi.org/10.1080/17439760.2016.1187199.

Palgi, Y. (2015). Subjective age and perceived distance-to-death moderate the association between posttraumatic stress symptoms and posttraumatic growth among older adults. *Aging & Mental Health, 20*(9), 948–954.

Park, C. L. (2016). Meaning making in the context of disasters. *Journal of Clinical Psychology, 72*, 1234–1246. https://doi.org/10.1002/jclp.22270.

Park, C. L., Mills-Baxter, M. A., & Fenster, J. R. (2005). Posttraumatic growth from life's most traumatic event: Influences on elders' current coping and adjustment. *Traumatology, 11*, 297–306.

Rowe, C. L., & Liddle, H. A. (2008). When the levee breaks: Treating adolescents and families in the aftermath of Hurricane Katrina. *Journal of Marital and Family Therapy, 34*(2), 132–148. https://doi.org/10.1111/j.1752-0606.2008.00060.x.

Ruggiero, K. J., Davidson, T. M., McCauley, J., Gros, K. S., Welsh, K., Price, M., et al. (2015). *Bounce Back Now*! Protocol of a population-based randomized controlled trial to examine the efficacy of a web-based intervention with disaster-affected families. *Contemporary Clinical Trials, 40*(Suppl. C), 138–149. https://doi.org/10.1016/j.cct.2014.11.018.

Sattler, D. N., Assanangkornchai, S., Moller, A. M., Kestavana-Dohrs, W., & Graham, J. M. (2014a). Indian Ocean tsunami: Relationships among posttraumatic stress, posttraumatic growth, resource loss, and coping at 3 and 15 months. *Journal of Trauma & Dissociation, 15*(2), 219–239. https://doi.org/10.1080/15299732.2014.869144.

Sattler, D. N., Boyd, B., & Kirsch, J. (2014b). Trauma-exposed firefighters: Relationships among posttraumatic growth, posttraumatic stress, resource availability, coping and critical incident stress debriefing experience. *Stress and Health, 30*(5), 356–365. https://doi.org/10.1002/smi.2608.

Scannell, L., Cox, R. S., & Fletcher, S. (2017). Place-based loss and resilience among disaster-affected youth. *Journal of Community Psychology, 45*, 859–876. https://doi.org/10.1002/jcop.21897.

Siqveland, J., Nygaard, E., Hussain, A., Tedeschi, R. G., & Heir, T. (2015). Posttraumatic growth, depression and posttraumatic stress in relation to quality of life in tsunami survivors: A longitudinal study. *Health & Quality of Life Outcomes, 13*, 1–8. https://doi.org/10.1186/s12955-014-0202-4.

Skeffington, P. M., Rees, C. S., & Mazzucchelli, T. (2017). Trauma exposure and post-traumatic stress disorder within fire and emergency services in Western Australia. *Australian Journal of Psychology, 69*, 20–28. https://doi.org/10.1111/ajpy.12120.

Stanko, K. E., Cherry, K. E., Ryker, K. S., Mughal, F., Marks, L. D., Brown, J. S., et al. (2015). Looking for the silver lining: Benefit finding after Hurricanes Katrina and Rita in middle-aged, older, and oldest-old adults. *Current Psychology: Research & Reviews, 34*, 564–575. https://doi.org/10.1007/s12144-015-9366-2.

Staub, E., & Vollhardt, J. R. (2008). Altruism born of suffering: The roots of caring and helping after victimization and other trauma. *The American Journal of Orthopsychiatry, 78*(3), 267–280.

Tang, C. S. (2006). Positive and negative postdisaster psychological adjustment among adult survivors of the southeast Asian earthquake-tsunami. *Journal of Psychosomatic Research, 61*, 699–705. https://doi.org/10.1016/j.jpsychores.2006.07.014.

Tedeschi, R. G. (1999). Violence transformed: Posttraumatic growth in survivors and their societies. *Aggression and Violent Behavior, 4*(3), 319–341.

Tedeschi, R. G., Blevins, C. L., & Riffle, O. M. (2017a). Posttraumatic growth: A brief history and evaluation. In M. A. Warren & S. I. Donaldson (Eds.), *Scientific advances in positive psychology* (pp. 131–164). Santa Barbara: Praeger.

Tedeschi, R. G., & Calhoun, L. G. (1995). *Trauma & transformation: Growing in the aftermath of suffering*. Thousand Oaks: Sage Publications.

Tedeschi, R. G., & Calhoun, L. G. (1996). The Posttraumatic Growth Inventory: Measuring the positive legacy of trauma. *Journal of Traumatic Stress, 9*, 455–471. https://doi.org/10.1007/BF02103658.

Tedeschi, R. G., & Calhoun, L. G. (2004). Posttraumatic growth: Conceptual foundations and empirical evidence. *Psychological Inquiry, 15*(1), 1–18.

Tedeschi, R. G., & Calhoun, L. G. (2008). Beyond the concept of recovery: Growth and the experience of loss. *Death Studies, 32*, 27–39.

Tedeschi, R. G., Calhoun, L. G., & Groleau, J. M. (2015). Clinical applications of posttraumatic growth. In S. Joseph (Ed.), *Positive psychology in practice: Promoting human flourishing in work, health, education, and everyday life* (2nd ed., pp. 503–518). Hoboken: Wiley.

Tedeschi, R. G., Cann, A., Taku, K., Senol-Durak, E., & Calhoun, L. G. (2017b). The Posttraumatic Growth Inventory: A revision integrating existential and spiritual change. *Journal of Traumatic Stress, 30*, 11–18. https://doi.org/10.1002/jts.22155.

Tedeschi, R. G., Park, C. L., & Calhoun, L. G. (Eds.). (1998). *Posttraumatic growth: Positive changes in the aftermath of crisis*. Mahwah, NJ: Lawrence Erlbaum Associates.

Tedeschi, R. G., & Riffle, O. M. (2016). Posttraumatic growth and logotherapy: Finding meaning in trauma. *The International Forum for Logotherapy, 39*, 40–47.

Triplett, K. N., Tedeschi, R. G., Cann, A., Calhoun, L. G., & Reeve, C. L. (2012). Posttraumatic growth, meaning in life, and life satisfaction in response to trauma. *Psychological Trauma: Theory, Research, Practice, and Policy, 4*, 400–410. https://doi.org/10.1037/a0024204.

Tuohy, R., & Stephens, C. (2012). Older adults' narratives about a flood disaster: Resilience, coherence, and personal identity. *Journal of Aging Studies, 26*, 26–34. https://doi.org/10.1016/j.jaging.2011.06.002.

Usami, M., Iwadare, Y., Watanabe, K., Kodaira, M., Ushijima, H., Tanaka, T., & Saito, K. (2016). Long-term fluctuations in traumatic symptoms of high school girls who survived from the 2011 Japan tsunami: Series of questionnaire-based cross-sectional surveys. *Child Psychiatry & Human Development, 47*, 1002–1008. https://doi.org/10.1007/s10578-016-0631-x.

Wlodarczyk, A., Basabe, N., Páez, D., Villagrán, L., & Reyes, C. (2017). Individual and collective posttraumatic growth in victims of natural disasters: A multidimensional perspective. *Journal of Loss and Trauma, 22*, 371–384. https://doi.org/10.1080/15325024.2017.1297657.

Xu, J., & Liao, Q. (2011). Prevalence and predictors of posttraumatic growth among adult survivors one year following 2008 Sichuan earthquake. *Journal of Affective Disorders, 133*, 274–280. https://doi.org/10.1016/j.jad.2011.03.034.

Zwiebach, L., Rhodes, J., & Roemer, L. (2010). Resource loss, resource gain, and mental health among survivors of Hurricane Katrina. *Journal of Traumatic Stress, 23*, 751–758. https://doi.org/10.1002/jts.20579.

Chapter 11
Facilitating Posttraumatic Growth in the Wake of Natural Disasters: Considerations for Crisis Response

David N. Sattler and Aaron Smith

Introduction

This chapter discusses posttraumatic growth and resilience within the context of large-scale natural disasters. In the first section, we provide an overview of natural disaster characteristics and psychological distress. We then discuss factors associated with posttraumatic growth and research examining how posttraumatic growth is associated with perceptions of future threats, such as climate change. In the second section, we consider clinical considerations relevant to the management of crises and posttraumatic growth development by community-based crisis responders and mental health professionals. This discussion adds to the growing body of literature exploring how community volunteers and mental health professionals can foster conditions that may promote posttraumatic growth and resilience in trauma's aftermath.

Natural Disasters and Psychological Functioning

Natural disasters such as earthquakes, hurricanes, tsunamis, floods, wildfires, and volcanic eruptions can threaten life and property, devastate infrastructure, and affect psychological functioning.[1] Disasters can compromise the ability to meet basic survival needs (e.g., food, water, shelter, and clothing), create profound economic

[1] Hurricane, cyclone, and typhoon refer to the same weather phenomenon. Hurricane refers to storms in the Atlantic Ocean and Northeast Pacific Ocean, cyclone refers to storms in the South Pacific Ocean and Indian Ocean, and typhoon refers to storms in the Northwest Pacific Ocean.

D. N. Sattler (✉) · A. Smith
Department of Psychology, Western Washington University, Bellingham, WA, USA
e-mail: David.Sattler@wwu.edu; Aaron.Smith@wwu.edu

S. E. Schulenberg (ed.), *Positive Psychological Approaches to Disaster*,
https://doi.org/10.1007/978-3-030-32007-2_11

problems (e.g., loss of home, employment, financial resources, business closure), and damage community infrastructure on a massive scale (e.g., loss of electric power, water, and sanitation services for an extended time; inaccessible roads, condemned buildings). Survivors may have great difficulty providing and receiving social support and assistance. They may live with systemic stressors for years. Systemic stressors occur when there is a "loss or lack of essential community resources necessary for the effective functioning of citizens and the community and that creates enduring hardships. Systemic stressors occur when essential systems that help citizens navigate life's challenges are insufficient to meet fundamental needs for an extended period" (Sattler et al. 2014b, p. 220).

Distress

Natural disaster exposure increases the risk of experiencing psychological distress, especially when the disaster threatens one's life or the lives of loved ones and close others, when resources vital to survival are damaged or lost, and when the ability to access social support systems is compromised or people have a limited social support system (Norris 2008; Sattler 2017; Sattler et al. 2014b). Some survivors may experience posttraumatic stress, which involves "clinically significant distress or impairment in the individual's social interactions, capacity to work or other important areas of functioning" (American Psychiatric Association 2013). Individuals may be at higher risk of developing posttraumatic stress when they have had other life threatening experiences prior to the disaster, experienced childhood trauma, felt helpless, lacked social support, had difficulty coping with a prior traumatic event, and experienced prior mental health issues (National Institute of Mental Health 2018). Individuals may be more resilient, cope more effectively, and be less likely to develop posttraumatic stress disorder when they have a social support system, implement an effective coping strategy to deal with adversity and promote recovery, and have a higher level of education (Canevelo and Michels 2016; National Institute of Mental Health 2018; Norris 2008; Sattler et al. 2014b).

Conservation of Resources Stress Theory

Conservation of resources stress theory is useful for considering how resource loss contributes to psychological distress and how resource gains contribute to posttraumatic growth. It identifies four resource domains that individuals may possess in varying degrees: personal characteristic resources (e.g., sense of optimism), condition resources (e.g., employment), energy resources (e.g., finances and time), and object resources (e.g., home possessions; Hobfoll 2012). According to the theory, threat of resource loss and actual loss contribute to psychological distress, including posttraumatic stress. Resource caravans are central to the theory. Resource loss caravans occur when loss of resources in one domain results in loss of resources in another domain. For example, loss of employment (a condition resource) may result in loss of optimism and self-esteem (personal characteristic resources). As a result of condition, energy, and/or object resource loss, people may begin to question their life goals and sense of purpose (e.g., experience loss of personal characteristic resources; Park 2016; Sattler 2017).

Resource gain caravans, in contrast, may help alleviate distress and contribute to the development of posttraumatic growth. When gains occur in one domain, the positive experience can overlap with other domains. For example, as the ability to connect with one's social support network is reestablished during recovery or as new social support networks are created (a condition resource), people may report an increase in optimism (a personal characteristic resource; Huynh et al. 2013; Sattler et al. 2014b). As people have some successes negotiating the challenges of recovery (e.g., replacement of object resources, employment), they may also experience other positives, including gaining a stronger sense of self-efficacy and learning new ways of coping (Groleau et al. 2013; Linley and Joseph 2004; Sattler et al. 2014b). These positives can balance out some of the negatives and help promote the development of posttraumatic growth (Groleau et al. 2013; Sattler et al. 2018). Resource gain caravans are instrumental in promoting psychological adjustment and may contribute to the development of posttraumatic growth.

Posttraumatic Growth

Posttraumatic growth occurs in response to a traumatic event wherein people reflect on their life priorities, reappraise and reassess their values, reinterpret the event, and give it new meaning (Sattler et al. 2014b; Tedeschi and Calhoun 1996). A growing number of studies document posttraumatic growth in the wake of natural disasters and the variables associated with it. Social support plays a significant role in the development of posttraumatic growth. After an earthquake in China, Zhou and Wu (2016) found that social support was associated with posttraumatic growth. However, gratitude, or an appreciation for assistance provided or for other matters, was related to social support. They suggest that during recovery, participants reframed negative experiences by focusing on gratitude and other positive experiences. After floods in Colorado, Dursun et al. (2016) found that search for meaning and perceived social support predicted posttraumatic growth. They emphasize the importance of actively searching for meaning as opposed to the belief that one has a meaningful life. "Engaging with the world, trying to have a purpose or mission or finding meaning in suffering can be a path to an increased appreciation of existence because major life crises help us realize how human life is vulnerable" (Dursun et al. 2016, p. 1256). Social support was associated with posttraumatic growth in the Fiji Islands after Cyclone Winston created extensive devastation (Sattler et al. 2018). It was the largest storm in recorded history to make landfall on the island group.

Problem-focused coping—attempting to reduce or eliminate the stressor—may help people reestablish feelings of control and self-efficacy. This is so because people may see tangible evidence that their actions have been effective in improving their situation and decreasing the effects of the stressor. Problem-focused coping may be especially useful, given that systemic stressors can place excessive demands on individuals and communities, and negatively impact one's sense of control, feelings of self-efficacy, and the ability to respond effectively to the demands. When people reinterpret the situation in a positive light and accommodate the stressor, they may be more likely to engage in problem-focused coping strategies; these approaches may facilitate posttraumatic growth. As such, there has been discussion as to whether posttraumatic growth reflects a way of coping with the situation (cf. Hobfoll 2011; Sattler et al. 2014b; Updegraff and Taylor 2000). After the Indian Ocean tsunami devastated coastal areas of Thailand, Sattler et al. (2014b) found that both problem-focused coping and social support were associated with posttraumatic growth.

Sense of coherence and other individual difference variables may be associated with posttraumatic growth. Sense of coherence is an orientation wherein individuals view a challenging situation as predictable and understandable, believe that resources needed to meet demands are available, and believe that a positive outcome will result if the individual directs the resources to meet the demands (Antonovsky 1987). Sense of coherence is associated with optimism and hardiness (Kaiser et al. 1996; Sattler et al. 2014b). Ragger et al. (2017) report that sense of coherence is associated with the development of posttraumatic growth following exposure to critical incidents. Research is needed to examine in more detail how personality traits and individual difference variables are associated with posttraumatic growth in the wake of disasters (cf. Aiena et al. 2016).

Posttraumatic Growth and Climate Change Adaptation

Might the experience of reflecting on life priorities, reappraising and reassessing values, and reinterpreting a traumatic event and giving it new meaning raise awareness about situations that may threaten that which one values, and increase motivation to take action to mitigate these threats? Sattler and colleagues are among the first to examine in multiple countries how posttraumatic growth may influence attitudes and behavioral intentions concerning disaster threats associated with climate change.

Climate change can adversely affect weather systems around the globe. It can increase the magnitude of storms such as hurricanes and promote conditions for drought and wildfires. Hurricanes are fueled by warm ocean water, and climate change can increase ocean temperature; warmer waters provide additional fuel that can increase the size and strength of hurricanes. Sattler et al. (2014a) examined risk perceptions concerning climate change in the Philippines in the wake of Super Typhoon Haiyan, one of the most powerful storms to strike land in recorded history. There was significant discussion concerning the role of climate change in intensifying the size and strength of the storm (Schiermeire 2013). Participants completed anonymous measures about their experiences with the storm, resource loss, posttraumatic stress, posttraumatic growth, and climate change risk perceptions. Climate change risk perceptions involve heightened concern about the adverse consequences of climate change and the potential threats they pose to life and property. The structural equation model showed the variables that contributed to posttraumatic growth and the consequences of it. In general, resource loss led to posttraumatic distress, which activated coping and social support, which led to posttraumatic growth, and which led to climate change risk perceptions. Sattler et al. (2016) used the same measures as in the Super Typhoon Haiyan Philippines study in the wake of Cyclone Winston in Fiji. Cyclone Winston was the strongest storm in recorded history to make landfall in Fiji, and climate change likely contributed to its strength (Di Liberto 2016). The structural equation model was generally the same as the one developed with the Philippines sample after Super Typhoon Haiyan. When taking into account the differences such as socioeconomic status, population size, and culture between the Philippines and Fiji, replicating the model provides strong support for the model. Sattler et al. (2018) extended the model by examining behavioral intentions to take action regarding climate change months after the first study in Fiji was conducted. The structural equation model showed that posttraumatic growth predicted behavioral intentions to alter actions that contribute to climate change.

In a recent study in Mongolia, Sattler et al. (2019) examined behavioral intentions to alter actions that contribute to climate change among nomadic herders. Mongolia has experienced unusually extreme weather in recent years—more intense and prolonged droughts and wider variations in the amount of rain and snow. This weather has adversely affected the ability of grasslands and water supplies to replenish. As a result, nomadic herders who rely on grasslands and water to sustain themselves and their herds of goats, horses, and camels are experiencing hardships. Nomadic herders completed measures similar to those completed by people in the Philippines after Super Typhoon Haiyan and in Fiji after Cyclone Winston. The structural equation model in Mongolia has many parallels to the model in the Philippines and Fiji. Posttraumatic growth led to climate change risk perceptions, which then led to intention to alter behaviors that contribute to climate change. The findings across countries underscore the commonality of the posttraumatic growth experience across various types of disasters and cultures, and demonstrate how posttraumatic growth can influence related attitudes and behaviors. Additional research is needed to examine other consequences of posttraumatic growth.

Considerations for Crisis Response

In the next section, we discuss clinical considerations regarding the development of posttraumatic growth in the wake of a natural disaster. We explore how mental health professionals may help clients engage in the process of reflection and experience support.

Facilitation of Posttraumatic Growth in Community Based Crisis Response

Because of the large numbers of people affected by a disaster, it is not uncommon for mental health services to be overwhelmed. The number of available providers may be insufficient to meet demand, and providers themselves may have experienced the disaster. For example, in the weeks after Hurricane Katrina struck the Gulf Coast states and the Indian Ocean tsunami struck Thailand, the availability of mental health services was limited (Sattler et al. 2014b). Community Based Crisis Response attempts to facilitate availability of mental health services in the wake of a crisis. It involves having mental health professionals enlist the assistance of community members to triage and address the needs of affected communities in the aftermath of large-scale disasters. Information gathered can include perceptions of safety and community connectedness, emergent best practices in crisis care, ongoing needs assessments, and cultural and spiritual practices needed for healing within the affected communities. This information can help providers tailor crisis response to meet the needs of affected communities (Watson et al. 2011). Given the perpetually changing needs of communities and resource availability during recovery, mental health crisis response should be flexible with services and goals.

When mental health professionals work with communities and individuals after a disaster, they should be aware of disparities in relief resources and services provided across communities, social justice issues, diversity issues, and sociocultural issues (Gil-Rivas and Kilmer 2016). Harrell and Bond (2006) underscore the importance of being open, caring, and respectful of community members and clients; being familiar with socio-political issues and institutions present in a community; being self-aware as to how one's own beliefs, values, identity, and history influence their interactions with others.

Community Based Crisis Response can be designed to implement approaches that promote psychological care and posttraumatic growth. Mental health professionals and community members involved with disaster response should carefully address the assessment and management of immediate crises, provide psychoeducation with the intent of normalization, and strive to cultivate meaning making and social support. Each of these are discussed in detail below.

Assessment and Management of Immediate Crises

The Psychological First Aid model provides a useful framework in crisis assessment and intervention and offers a structured approach to help survivors re-establish feelings of safety, reduce distress symptoms, provide opportunities for rest and resource gathering, adapt to the situation, and connect with their social support systems (James and Gilliland 2016; National Institute of Mental Health 2002). As an evidence-based approach to crisis assessment and intervention, Psychological First Aid intends to reduce stress reactions to traumatic events like natural disasters by addressing extant issues pertaining to safety, stability, social connection, empowerment, and hope (World Health Organization 2019). Providers of Psychological First Aid may not need to be licensed as a mental health counselor and may not need an advanced degree, making it a useful tool for properly trained community members.

For survivors, re-establishing feelings of safety, stability, and control may be necessary prerequisites to exploring the effects of trauma on perceptions of meaning and purpose (Herman 1997; Jacobs et al. 2016). Crisis assessment and intervention can help cultivate feelings of relative safety, stability, and control prior to any attempts at deriving deeper insights via traditional counseling (e.g., trying to process grief or explore alterations to survivors' assumptive worldviews). To help survivors reestablish these feelings, Southwick et al. (2016) recommend "getting adequate nutrition, exercise, and rest; engaging in positive distracting activities; focusing on practical solutions to problems; practicing relaxation techniques such as diaphragmatic breathing; reaching out and spending time with others; trying to maintain a regular routine and schedule; and avoiding maladaptive coping such as risk taking, emotional and physical withdrawal, or excessive use of substances" (p. 1365). These recommendations are consistent with decades of research showing factors that contribute to and minimize distress during disaster recovery (e.g., Sattler et al. 2006). The management of immediate crises prior to traditional counseling is founded, in part, on Maslow's (1943) Hierarchy of Needs, which asserts that physiological (e.g., food, water, and medical) and safety-related (e.g., housing, protection from the elements) needs precede ostensibly less essential needs, such as meaning making or pursuit of self-actualization.

Psychoeducation and Normalization

Psychoeducation involves providing information about expected psychological responses, and it can help normalize survivors' expectations and reactions. For example, for military service personnel, psychoeducation about common psychological reactions may help promote resilience in people deploying to combat (Grossman 2009). Similar approaches have been used with survivors of large-scale natural disasters. For example, in the wake of Hurricane Iniki in Hawaii, the Iniki Ohana Project provided brochures detailing common mental health reactions and effective coping strategies. The Federal Emergency Management Agency provides pamphlets and information on its website to help parents, teachers, and adults responsible for a child learn how to help children cope with their responses to natural disasters.

Psychoeducation can help inform survivors which reactions are normal and expected, and include information about stress management and coping strategies. It can provide direction concerning how to contend with challenges to their assumptive worlds, which may result in feelings of emptiness or meaninglessness (Janoff-Bulman 2002; Scott and Weems 2012). In addition, programs should encourage people to help and support one another. Community self-help activities can help people provide and receive social support, and replenish lost personal characteristic resources (e.g., feelings of control and self-worth). Programs also should consider cultural variables when developing programs and providing services (Sattler 2017).

In the aftermath of the Indian Ocean tsunami—the fourth deadliest disaster in recorded history—many survivors had limited access to information about the disaster or recovery. In Thailand, many were uncertain about future tsunami threats and help being provided. They reported that additional information about how tsunamis form, the warning signs of an impending tsunami, and aid being provided would help them understand what happened, what to do for future threats, and have a better sense of control, predictability, and safety. The uncertainties and lack of information created significant stress (Sattler et al. 2014b). To address these issues, the first author created the International Tsunami Museum in a community in Thailand that experienced loss of life and extensive devastation (Sattler 2008). The museum was designed to educate and inform survivors and others about the causes of a tsunami, the warning signs, aid and support provided by countries around the world, and the new tsunami warning system being developed. Exhibits were in Thai and English, and tens of thousands visited the museum. An evaluation of the museum showed that this information helped survivors reestablish feelings of control, safety, predictability, and trust, all of which are challenged by natural disasters (Baum 1991). To extend the reach of this information, the first author also produced an educational video that incorporated much of the information in the museum and distributed the DVD at no cost to local village schools. An assessment of the video showed that it, like the museum, increased knowledge but did not increase stress (Sattler 2010). Additional research is needed to examine how this type of information may facilitate posttraumatic growth.

Meaning Making

Existential philosophers have long asserted that humans are motivated by the search for a meaningful existence (e.g., Camus 1955; Kierkegaard 1980; Sartre 1948). A meaningful existence is characterized by the belief that one's life has a purpose. This purpose may be related to a greater goal, such as one's life-legacy, being a member of and assisting with the needs of a social group, or to living according to the guidance of a spiritual text, among other potential sources.

Viktor Frankl, Holocaust survivor and founder of Western existential psychotherapy, posited that challenging life experiences can negatively affect perceptions of meaningfulness. Frankl (1959) believed that people search for meaning in trauma's aftermath, in part, because of a philosophic presumption that the basic human motivation is the search for meaning, as opposed to seeking power, pleasure, or avoidance of pain that are more characteristic of non-existential paradigms of mental health. Thus, Frankl believed that at their core, human beings are psychologically driven to seek meaning for their existence, so blockages or disruptions to perceptions of meaning in life are often immediately replaced with a renewed search for purpose. This process of seeking meaning in the aftermath of experiences like trauma was referred to as noo-dynamics (Frankl 1959).

Recent work supports the hypothesis that the presence of meaning and the search for meaning are associated with posttraumatic growth and positive mental well-being (Triplett et al. 2012; Tsai et al. 2016; Zeligman et al. 2018). Triplett and colleagues (2012) found that the presence of meaning predicted posttraumatic growth in undergraduates, and that the presence of meaning helped to explain the relationship between posttraumatic growth and life satisfaction. This finding supports the idea that meaning making is an important process involved in posttraumatic resilience (i.e., responses to trauma that may eventuate in posttraumatic growth and life satisfaction). Tsai and colleagues found that purpose in life/presence of meaning predicted posttraumatic growth in a nationally representative sample of U.S. Veterans who reported at least one traumatic experience. Most recently, Zeligman et al. (2018) found that the presence of meaning predicted posttraumatic growth, and moderated relationships between social support and posttraumatic growth in survivors of chronic illnesses (Zeligman et al. 2018).

Zeligman et al. (2018) believe that the presence of meaning in life predicts posttraumatic growth and moderates the relationship between social support and posttraumatic growth by developing "common (and sometimes private) interpretations of meaning [that] can be constructively used to solve problems" (p. 60). They note that their findings may provide support for Adler's Individual Psychology, which posits that social support is both imperative for survival and meaning making. According to Adler (1927), one of Frankl's (1959) mentors, humans cultivate social interest and utilize social support, in part, to make meaning of their experiences. This position aligns with Tedeschi and Calhoun's (2004) Transformational Model of posttraumatic growth that posits that social support provides opportunities for intentional rumination (e.g., grappling, meaning making). Sattler et al. (2014c) found that social support and posttraumatic growth were negatively associated with posttraumatic stress symptoms among firefighters frequently exposed to critical incidents. These findings suggest that crisis workers seeking to promote meaning reconstruction during crises may benefit by working collaboratively with affected communities to identify and remove barriers to social support as this may influence the development of meaning making and posttraumatic growth (Tsai et al. 2016; Zeligman et al. 2018).

Facilitating Posttraumatic Growth during Individual Counseling

This section discusses clinical considerations that may be valuable for professionals working with persons who experience natural disasters. Here, we focus on ways the treatment process can help protect people from re-traumatization (National Center for Trauma Informed Care, 2018) and promote psychological growth in trauma's aftermath. These considerations are derived from posttraumatic growth research findings, the principles of Trauma Informed Care, and existential psychotherapy techniques that attempt to enhance meaning reconstruction and posttraumatic growth (Bugental 1965; Frankl 1959; May 1975; Yalom 1980). Clinical considerations include the development of safe therapeutic relationships, development of noetic (i.e., noo-dynamic) tension, and enhancement of social support.

Development of Safe Therapeutic Relationships

The National Center for Trauma Informed Care presents a set of evidence-based principles that are intended to protect trauma survivors receiving mental health services from re-traumatization via the treatment process (National Center for Trauma Informed Care 2018). One fundamental principle is the promotion of perceptions of safety in clients throughout therapy (Berliner and Kolko 2016). In general, clients are more willing to approach and process how trauma exposure has changed their lives when they feel safe doing so. Perceptions of safety are fostered when clients work with counselors in a warm, supportive, and unconditionally accepting collaborative therapeutic relationship (Adler 1927; Frankl 1959; Herman 1997; Rogers 1957; Yalom 1980). The American Psychological Association Task Force on Evidence-Based Therapy Relationships states that the perceived quality of the therapeutic relationship by clients in treatment (e.g., safety, trust) is one of the best predictors of a positive treatment outcome. It can account for at least as much variance in positive outcomes as the type of intervention being used (Norcross et al. 2011). Thus, a necessary condition for the facilitation of posttraumatic growth in survivors is a therapeutic relationship that establishes perceptions of safety that is sedulously protected throughout the treatment process.

Positive Reinterpretation and Meaning Making

Given that people who experience disasters are likely to experience resource loss and distress, it may be efficacious to include meaning-based techniques in clinical work with people who experienced a natural disaster. Clinical assessments should consider how the experience may have affected the presence or search for a meaningful existence (Frankl 1959; Scott and Weems 2012). Assessments should also examine whether clients' assumptive worlds have been altered (Herman 1997; Janoff-Bulman 2002), such as a belief that the world is a safe place or that people have interminable control over their well-being. Once the assessment has been completed, counselors can begin the process of selecting trauma-informed interventions and techniques they will use to empower survivors to safely begin approaching treatment goals.

The techniques used by existential therapists and counselors to help their clients begin the process of reconstructing a sense of meaning have largely emerged from the literature on Existential and Humanistic psychotherapies in counseling and psychology. Frankl (1959), for example, used Socratic Dialogue to create noetic tension in clients' lives by helping them explore–from their own phenomenological perspective–what they believe is being asked of them to ensure that they can continue leading a meaningful existence. Waytz et al. (2015) found that asking people to engage in counter-factual thinking (i.e., reflecting on how key people or events in their lives might not have come into their lives had the event not occurred) may increase perceptions of life meaning. Lantz (1992), in working with veterans who are survivors of combat trauma, used a community service approach (i.e., veterans using their experiences to help other veterans) to facilitate meaning making. Clinicians should critically weigh the clinical and cultural appropriateness of any clinical approach to ensure it aligns with the clients' goals and that it is multiculturally sensitive. Clinicians should consider existential approaches to therapy with survivors as a means of addressing existential anxiety (Tillich 1952) resultant from boundary experiences (Yalom 1980).

Existential Psychotherapy and Boundary Experiences

Existential psychotherapy was developed with the intention of addressing boundary experiences–circumstances where people must contend with each of four existential givens that are theorized to be shared by all of humanity: death, meaninglessness (i.e., the search for meaning), isolation (i.e., no one can ever understand us like we understand ourselves), and freedom (i.e., responsibility for one's choices or attitudes towards their circumstances; Yalom 1980). Natural disasters force people to confront and navigate these boundary experiences. They create physical threats to themselves and loved ones, force people to contend with losses to their sources of meaning (e.g., loss of homes, loss of cultural lifestyles due to climate change), and hamper their ability to connect with others (Sattler 2017). Survivors of natural disasters may also grapple with the consequences of their choices prior to, during, and in the aftermath of crises, including degree of preparedness and evacuating to a safe location to reduce physical harm. These types of experiences can result in existential anxiety or psychological distress related to three sub-categories of existential concerns: fate and death; emptiness and meaninglessness; guilt and condemnation (Tillich 1952).

Scott and Weems (2012) examined the presence of existential anxiety and its associations with symptoms of psychological distress among survivors of Hurricane Katrina. Participants reported manifestations of existential anxiety relating to perceptions of emptiness (74%), fate (71%), guilt (62%), perceptions of condemnation (60%), death (50%), and meaninglessness (25%). Anxieties related to guilt and emptiness were positively associated with the presence of posttraumatic stress symptoms, while meaninglessness and guilt were positively associated with suicidal ideation. This study appears to support theories and research behind existential psychotherapy: that an active search for meaning has positive implications for psychological well-being (Frankl 1959; Steger et al. 2011; Zeligman et al. 2018). The findings underscore the need for mental health professionals to remain vigilant of existential anxiety and its associations with symptoms of psychological distress (Scott and Weems 2012). Clinicians can use assessments like the Existential Anxiety Questionnaire to add an objective element to their assessment of existential anxiety (Weems et al. 2004). However, they should also take time to explore the survivor's own phenomenological (i.e., subjective) perceptions of these experiences, in accordance with the tenets of existential psychotherapy (Bugental 1965; Frankl 1959; May 1975; Yalom 1980).

Enhancement of Social Support

Social support is an important mediator between trauma and posttraumatic growth (Tedeschi and Calhoun 2004; Zeligman et al. 2018), and meaning making often occurs within the context of relationships (e.g., friends, family, community members; Canevelo and Michels 2016; Frankl 1959; Norcross et al. 2011; Yalom 1980). Assessing the perceived quality of social support may be an effective means to help promote meaning reconstruction and posttraumatic growth outside of the therapy office. These efforts should include an assessment of any perceived barriers to social support that might be addressed via therapy (e.g., working to minimize the deleterious effects of posttraumatic stress symptoms on relationships, exploring new beliefs about the world that may negatively affect attempts to seek and achieve social support). Because traumas like natural disasters are inherently disempowering, clinicians should seek to adopt interventions and techniques that promote empowerment (Herman 1997), such as those developed with the principles of trauma-informed care (National Center for Trauma-Informed Care 2018).

A Fictional Case Study in Posttraumatic Growth Development

The following fictional case study is presented to illustrate the concepts concerning considerations for clinical care and posttraumatic growth development. This account is loosely based on survivors of multiple forms of trauma treated by the second author while serving as a clinical mental health counselor. The case study is emblematic of the multitude of ways in which large-scale disasters might affect survivors' assumptive worlds and sources of meaning in life. This section highlights clinical considerations discussed in this chapter in an applied clinical setting. We note that treatment can vary across clients and approaches may be adapted based on the specific needs of each client (e.g., needs identified during the assessment process, cultural considerations).

Johanna is a 31-year-old survivor of Hurricane Katrina from New Orleans, Louisiana, which struck 9 months prior. Before Hurricane Katrina, Johanna owned and ran a small, successful construction company and had built her dream home for her and her partner Maria. Johanna was known throughout the country as an excellent runner and for her record-breaking marathon times. After the levees failed and resulted in the flooding of most of New Orleans, she lost her business and her dream home, and sustained as a direct result of the flood a debilitating spinal injury that left her in a wheelchair. While her partner was unharmed, the stresses of the trauma experience they both endured has caused substantial stress to their relationship. As Johanna was never very close to her biological family, the strains to her relationship with her partner have left her feeling isolated. Further, the loss of her prior sources of meaning (e.g., her job, her home, her business, her life and reputation as a runner) has resulted in perceptions of meaninglessness, a prime risk factor for suicide (Juhnke et al. 2007). After nine months of unsuccessful attempts at processing her losses after Hurricane Katrina and increasing social isolation, she decides to seek professional mental health services, "to regain a sense of control."

During the intake assessment, Johanna noted that she had recently considered taking her own life due to depression, grief, and hopelessness about the future–experiences she reported being the direct result of the physical and psychological traumas she experienced during and after the storm. Although her goals for counseling revolve mainly around her past traumas, the counselor put these goals on hold to minimize suspected potential for self-harm by engaging in crisis assessment and intervention. Johanna noted that while she does not have a plan to end her life, she felt, "desperate to be connected to others again." The counselor informs Johanna that according to the research on mental health outcomes, strong therapeutic relationships are the best predictor of a positive treatment outcome (Wampold 2015) and that if she permitted, she could begin the process of reconnecting to others by building a safe relationship with her counselor. After determining that Johanna's potential for self-harm was sufficiently managed via crisis intervention and safety planning, they turned their attention to treatment planning. Collaboratively-developed treatment goals included processing how her experiences during the hurricane have impacted her sense of safety, trust, and control in the disaster's aftermath, helping her reconstruct a sense of meaning, and removing barriers to social support networks. Johanna also received a referral for couples counseling with a different clinician so that she and her partner could work to heal their relationship, helping to enhance social support early on and throughout her individual counseling.

She was encouraged throughout the counseling process to frequently check-in with her counselor regarding how safe she perceived their therapeutic relationship to be, making adjustments where necessary. Towards these ends, her counselor also chose to only use techniques and interventions that are consistent with the principles of Trauma-Informed Care (National Center for Trauma-Informed Care 2018) to process her traumas, to minimize the likelihood of re-traumatization via the treatment process. Socratic Dialogue, a commonly used existential technique, was the primary tool used to help empower Johanna to explore how she believed her life might again experience meaning. Johanna's counselor asked Johanna to consider what kind of life-legacy she wished to leave the world when she eventually passes away many years from now, to which she noted, "I want to be remembered as someone that never gave up, someone that helped others, and someone that developed deep relationships with her community." Using a process of Socratic questioning,

Johanna believed she might be able to do this by using her knowledge of construction to assist people in her community construct homes that can survive future disasters. She also noted that since her traumatic spinal injury, she has considered volunteering to help others who were injured in similar ways to cope with being differently-abled.

With these new opportunities for meaning making afoot and the enhancement of social support created via her adjunctive couples counseling and reconnection to her community, she began to consider the ways in which her life has changed in positive ways as a direct result of the traumas that occurred during and in the aftermath of Hurricane Katrina (i.e., posttraumatic growth). She begins to re-appreciate how strong and resilient she is. She identifies new opportunities (i.e., focusing her knowledge of construction to serving and protecting the communities she wished to reconnect with) that would not have occurred otherwise and now that her relationship with Maria has begun to heal, she has a new-found appreciation for the importance of relationships in her life.

References

Adler, A. (1927). *Understanding human nature: The psychology of personality*. London: Oneworld.

Aiena, B. J., Buchanan, E. M., Smith, C. V., & Schulenberg, S. E. (2016). Meaning, resilience, and traumatic stress after the Deepwater Horizon oil spill: A study of Mississippi coastal residents seeking mental health services. *Journal of Clinical Psychology, 72*, 1264–1278. https://doi.org/10.1002/jclp.22232.

American Psychiatric Association. (2013). *Posttraumatic stress disorder*. Retrieved from http://www.dsm5.org/Documents/PTSD%20Fact%20Sheet.pdf on December 18, 2018.

Antonovsky, A. (1987). *Unraveling the mystery of health: How people manage stress and stay well*. San Francisco: Jossey-Bass.

Baum, A. (1991). Toxins, technology, and natural disasters. In A. Monat & R. S. Lazarus (Eds.), *Stress and coping: An anthology* (3rd ed., pp. 97–139). New York: Columbia University Press.

Berliner, L., & Kolko, D. J. (2016). Trauma informed care: A commentary and critique. *Child Maltreatment, 21*, 168–172. https://doi.org/10.1177/1077559516643785.

Bugental, J. (1965). The search for authenticity: An existential-analytic approach to psychotherapy. *American Journal of Orthopsychiatry, 36*, 571–576. https://doi.org/10.1111/j.1939-0025.1966.tb02400.x.

Camus, A. (1955). *The myth of Sisyphus and other essays*. New York: Vintage Books.

Canevelo, A., & Michels, V. (2016). Supporting close others' growth after trauma: The role of responsiveness in romantic partners' mutual posttraumatic growth. *Psychological Trauma: Theory, Research, Practice, and Policy, 8*, 334–342.

Di Liberto, T. (2016, February 23). *Tropical Cyclone Winston causes devastation in Fiji, a tropical paradise*. Climate.gov. Accessed from https://www.climate.gov/news-features/event-tracker/tropical-cyclone-winston-causes-devastation-fiji-tropical-paradise on 4 April 2016.

Dursun, P., Steger, M. F., Bentele, C., & Schulenberg, S. E. (2016). Meaning and posttraumatic growth among survivors of the September 2013 Colorado floods. *Journal of Clinical Psychology, 72*, 1247–1263. https://doi.org/10.1002/jclp.22344.

Frankl, V. (1959). *Man's search for meaning*. New York: Basic Books.

Gil-Rivas, V., & Kilmer, R. P. (2016). Building community capacity and fostering disaster resilience. *Journal of Clinical Psychology, 72*, 1318–1332. https://doi.org/10.1002/jclp.22281.

Groleau, J. M., Calhoun, L. G., Cann, A., & Tedeschi, R. G. (2013). The role of centrality of events in posttraumatic distress and posttraumatic growth. *Psychological Trauma: Theory, Research, Practice, and Policy, 5*, 477–483. https://doi.org/10.1037/a0028809.

Grossman, D. (2009). *On killing: The psychological cost of learning to kill in war and society*. New York: Back Bay Books.

Harrell, S. P., & Bond, M. A. (2006). Listening to diversity stories: Principles for practice in community research and action. *American Journal of Community Psychology, 37*, 365–376.

Herman, J. (1997). *Trauma and recovery*. New York: Basic Books.

Hobfoll, S. E. (2011). Conservation of resources theory: Its implications for stress, health, and resilience. In S. Folkman (Ed.), *The Oxford handbook of stress, health, and coping* (pp. 127–147). New York: Oxford University Press.

Hobfoll, S. E. (2012). Conservation of resources and disaster in cultural context: The caravans and passageways for resources. *Psychiatry, 73*, 227–233.

Huynh, J. Y., Xanthopoulou, D., & Winefield, A. H. (2013). Social support moderates the impact of demands on burnout and organizational connectedness: A two-wave study of volunteer firefighters. *Journal of Occupational Health Psychology, 18*, 9–15. https://doi.org/10.1037/a0030804.

Jacobs, G., Gray, B. L., Erickson, S. E., Gonzalez, E. D., & Quevillon, R. P. (2016). Disaster mental health and community-based psychological first aid: Concepts and education/training. *Journal of Clinical Psychology, 72*, 1307–1317. https://doi.org/10.1002/jclp.22316.

James, R., & Gilliland, B. (2016). *Crisis intervention strategies* (8th ed.). Boston: Cengage.

Janoff-Bulman, R. (2002). *Shattered assumptions: Towards a new psychology of trauma*. New York: The Free Press.

Juhnke, G., Granello, P., & Lebrón-Striker, M. (2007). *Is path warm? A suicide assessment mnemonic for counselors (ACAPCD-03)*. Alexandria: American Counseling Association.

Kaiser, C. F., Sattler, D. N., Bellack, D. R., & Dersin, J. (1996). A conservation of resources approach to a natural disaster: Sense of coherence and psychological distress. *Journal of Social Behavior and Personality, 11*, 459–476.

Kierkegaard, S. (1980). *The concept of anxiety: A simple psychologically oriented deliberation on the dogmatic issue of hereditary sin*. Princeton: Princeton University Press.

Lantz, J. (1992). Using Frankl's concepts with PTSD clients. *Journal of Traumatic Stress, 5*, 485–490. https://doi.org/10.1002/jts.2490050311.

Linley, P. A., & Joseph, S. (2004). Positive change following trauma and adversity: A review. *Journal of Traumatic Stress, 17*, 11–21.

Maslow, A. H. (1943). A theory of human motivation. *Psychological Review, 50*(4), 370–396. https://doi.org/10.1037/h0054346.

May, R. (1975). *The courage to create*. New York: Norton.

National Center for Trauma-Informed Care. (2018). *Trauma informed approaches and trauma specific interventions*. Retrieved from www.samha.gov/nctic/trauma-interventions on December 5, 2018.

National Institute of Mental Health. (2002). *Mental health and mass violence: Evidence-based early psychological intervention for victims/survivors of mass violence* (NIH Publication No. 02–5138). Washington, DC: U.S. Government Printing Office.

National Institute of Mental Health. (2018). *Posttraumatic stress disorder*. Retrieved from https://www.nimh.nih.gov/health/topics/post-traumatic-stress-disorder-ptsd/index.shtml on December 17, 2018.

Norcross, J., Wampold, B., & Hilsenroth, M. (2011). Evidence-based therapy relationships: Research conclusions and clinical practices. *Psychotherapy, 48*, 98–102. https://doi.org/10.1037/a0022161.

Norris, F. (2008). Longitudinal linkages between perceived social support and psychological distress: A test of sequential model of social causation and social selection. *Journal of Traumatic Stress, 21*, 274–281.

Park, C. L. (2016). Meaning making in the context of disasters. *Journal of Clinical Psychology, 72*(12), 1234–1246. https://doi.org/10.1002/jclp.22270.

Ragger, K., Hiebler-Ragger, M., Herzog, G., Kapfhammer, H.-P., & Unterrainer, F. (2017). Does sense of coherence promote posttraumatic growth after critical incidents in Austrian ambulance personnel? *Paper presented at the Neuropsychoanalysis Congress*. https://doi.org/10.13140/RG.2.2.16502.91200.

Rogers, C. (1957). The necessary and sufficient conditions of therapeutic personality change. *Journal of Consulting Psychology, 21*, 240–248. https://doi.org/10.1080/17439760.2011.569171.

Sartre, J. (1948). *Existentialism is a humanism*. Brooklyn: Haskell House.

Sattler, D. N. (2008). The International Tsunami Museum: Researchers make a difference in Thailand. *Natural Hazards Observer, 32*, 1–3.

Sattler, D. N. (2010). *International Tsunami Museum in Thailand*. Invited talk presented at the International Forum on Telling Live Lessons From Disasters Symposium. Kobe.

Sattler, D. N. (2017). Climate change and extreme weather events: The mental health impact. In W. Leal Filho (Ed.), *Climate change adaptation in Pacific countries: Fostering resilience and upkeeping life quality* (pp. 73–87). Berlin: Springer. https://doi.org/10.1007/978-3-319-50094-2_4.

Sattler, D. N., Glower de Alvarado, A. M., Blandon de Castro, N., Van Male, R., Zetino, A. M., & Vega, R. (2006). El Salvador earthquakes: Relationships among acute stress disorder symptoms, traumatic event exposure, and resource loss. *Journal of Traumatic Stress, 19*, 879–893.

Sattler, D. N., Atienza, R., & Graham, J. M. (2014a, June). Super typhoon Haiyan: Global warming concerns, resource loss, and psychological distress among survivors in the Philippines. *Paper presented at the Sixth International Conference on Climate Change: Impacts and Responses*, Reykavik.

Sattler, D., Assanangkornchai, S., Moller, A., Kesavatana-Dohrs, W., & Graham, J. (2014b). Indian Ocean tsunami: Relationships among posttraumatic stress, posttraumatic growth, resource loss, and coping at 3 and 15 months. *Journal of Trauma & Dissociation, 15*, 219–239. https://doi.org/10.1080/15299732.2014.869144.

Sattler, D., Boyd, B., & Kirsch, J. (2014c). Trauma-exposed firefighters: Relationships among posttraumatic growth, posttraumatic stress, resource availability, coping and critical incident stress debriefing experience. *Stress and Health, 30*, 356–365. https://doi.org/10.1002/smi.2608.

Sattler, D. N., Whippy, A., Johnson, J., Vucago, N., & Graham, J. (2016, July). Cyclone Winston in Fiji: Climate change risk perceptions, posttraumatic stress, coping, and resilience among survivors. *Paper presented at the Symposium on Climate Change Adaptation in the Pacific Region*, Lautoka.

Sattler, D. N., Whippy, A., Graham, J. M., & Johnson, J. (2018). A psychological model of climate change adaptation: Influence of resource loss, posttraumatic growth, norms, and risk perception following Cyclone Winston in Fiji. In W. Leal Filho (Ed.), *Climate change impacts and adaptation strategies in coastal communities* (pp. 427–443). Berlin: Springer. https://doi.org/10.1007/978-3-319-70703-7_22.

Sattler, D. N., Bishkhorloo, B., Graham, J., & Muskavage, B. (2019, February). Nomadic herders in Mongolia: Climate change risk perceptions and behavioral adaptation. *Paper presented at the conference on climate change and natural hazards: Coping with and managing hazards in the context of a changing climate*, Padova.

Schiermeire, Q. (2013, November 11). Did climate change cause Typhoon Haiyan? *Nature*. Retrieved from http://www.nature.com/news/did-climate-change-cause-typhoon-haiyan-1.14139 on April 25, 2014.

Scott, B., & Weems, C. (2012). Natural disasters and existential concerns: A test of Tillich's theory of existential anxiety. *Journal of Humanistic Psychology, 53*, 114–128. https://doi.org/10.1177/0022167812449190.

Southwick, S. M., Satodiya, R., & Pietrzak, R. H. (2016). Disaster mental health and positive psychology: An afterward to the special issue. *Journal of Clinical Psychology, 72*, 1364–1368.

Steger, M., Oishi, S., & Kesebir, S. (2011). Is a life without meaning satisfying? The moderating role of the search for meaning in satisfaction with life judgments. *Journal of Positive Psychology, 6*, 1372–1384. https://doi.org/10.1177/0146167210382304 3.

Tedeschi, R., & Calhoun, L. G. (1996). The Posttraumatic Growth Inventory: Measuring the positive legacy of trauma. *Journal of Traumatic Stress, 9*, 455–471. https://doi.org/10.1002/jts.2490090305.

Tedeschi, R., & Calhoun, L. (2004). Posttraumatic growth: Conceptual foundations and empirical evidence. *Psychological Inquiry, 15*, 10–18. https://doi.org/10.1207/15327965pli1501_01.

Tillich, P. (1952). *The courage to be*. New Haven: Yale University Press.

Triplett, K. N., Tedeschi, R. G., Cann, A., Calhoun, L. G., & Reeve, C. L. (2012). Posttraumatic growth, meaning in life, and life satisfaction in response to trauma. *Psychological Trauma: Theory, Research, Practice, and Policy, 4*(4), 400–410. https://doi.org/10.1037/a0024204.

Tsai, J., Sippel, L., Mota, N., Southwick, S., & Pietrzak, R. (2016). Longitudinal course of posttraumatic growth among US military veterans: Results from the National Health and Resilience in Veterans Study. *Depression and Anxiety, 33*, 9–18. https://doi.org/10.1002/da.22371.

Updegraff, J. A., & Taylor, S. E. (2000). From vulnerability to growth: Positive and negative effects of stressful life events. In J. H. Harvey & E. D. Miller (Eds.), *Loss and trauma: General and relationship perspectives* (pp. 3–28). Philadelphia: Brunner-Routledge.

Wampold, B. (2015). How important are the common factors in psychotherapy? An update. *World Psychiatry, 14*, 270–277. https://doi.org/10.1002/wps.20238.

Watson, P., Brymer, M., & Bonanno, G. (2011). Postdisaster psychological intervention since 9/11. *American Psychologist, 66*, 482–494. https://doi.org/10.1037/a0024806.

Waytz, A., Hershfield, H., & Tamir, D. (2015). Mental simulation and meaning in life. *Journal of Personality Psychology, 108*, 336–355. https://doi.org/10.1037/a0038322.

Weems, C., Costa, N., Dehorn, C., & Berman, S. (2004). Paul Tillich's theory of existential anxiety: A conceptual and empirical analysis. *Anxiety Stress & Coping: An International Journal, 17*, 383–399. https://doi.org/10.1080/10615800412331318616.

World Health Organization. (2019). *Psychological first aid: Guide for field workers*. Retrieved from https://www.who.int/mental_health/publications/guide_field_workers/en/ on January 2, 2019.

Yalom, I. (1980). *Existential psychotherapy*. New York: Basic Books.

Zeligman, M., Varney, M., Grad, R., & Huffstead, M. (2018). Posttraumatic growth in individuals with chronic illness: The role of social support and meaning making. *Journal of Counseling and Development, 96*, 53–63. https://doi.org/10.1002/jcad.12177.

Zhou, X., & Wu, X. (2016). The relationship between rumination, posttraumatic stress disorder, and posttraumatic growth among Chinese adolescents after earthquake: A longitudinal study. *Journal of Affective Disorders, 193*, 242–248. https://doi.org/10.1016/j.jad.2015.12.07.

Chapter 12
The Disaster Sciences Interdisciplinary Minor at the University of Mississippi: Positive Psychology in Action

Mikaela J. Raley, Marcela C. Weber, Christopher E. Lemon, and Stefan E. Schulenberg

Natural Disasters As Global Dilemma

Natural disasters (for example, hurricanes, tornadoes, earthquakes, and floods) are of increasing concern and prevalence. In 2018, the United Nations Office for Disaster Risk Reduction (UNISDR) estimated that approximately 60 million individuals worldwide were impacted by extreme weather and approximately 10,373 individuals perished as a direct result of natural disasters. The natural disasters with the largest death tolls in 2018 were earthquakes, floods, and storms, which killed approximately 9,000 people worldwide (UNDRR 2019). Similarly, in 2017, the most death-laden events were floods (killing 3,331 individuals), storms (killing 2,510), and landslides (killing 2,312; Centre for Research on Disasters Annual Disaster Statistical Review 2018, February 07).

The Centre for Research on Disasters (CRED 2018b) noted that of the 281 natural hazardous events that occurred in 2018, 61.7 million people were affected. The top three countries that had the most people affected by natural disasters in 2018 were India (23,900,348 people), the Philippines (6,490,216 people), and China (6,415,024; CRED 2018b). To place this statistic into perspective, the United States ranked number eight on this list with 1,762,103 individuals affected. Likewise, the top three countries with the largest death tolls in 2018 were Indonesia (4,535

The authors would like to thank the University of Mississippi's Departments of Psychology, Criminal Justice, Sociology, and Social Work, as well as the College of Liberal Arts and the School of Applied Sciences, for their support of the efforts to establish the Disaster Sciences interdisciplinary minor. The authors would like to thank Calli F. Holland, Courtney E. Pomfrey, Phoebe A. Lavin, Sunny N. Patel, Emily A. Gawlik, Matt A. Tkachuck, and David H. McElreath for their support and assistance with drafts of this chapter.

M. J. Raley · M. C. Weber · C. E. Lemon · S. E. Schulenberg (✉)
Department of Psychology, Clinical-Disaster Research Center, University of Mississippi, Oxford, MS, USA
e-mail: sschulen@olemiss.edu

S. E. Schulenberg (ed.), *Positive Psychological Approaches to Disaster*,
https://doi.org/10.1007/978-3-030-32007-2_12

people), India (1,388 people), and Guatemala (427). The U.S. was ranked seventh in the total death toll with 298 individuals (CRED 2018a). Natural disasters have increased both in their frequency and magnitude of destruction in recent years. The CRED (2018a) estimates that 1,221,465 individuals have died as a direct result of natural disasters since 2000.

Natural Disasters As Dilemma for the U.S.

Each year on average, more natural disasters strike the United States than any other country except China (Guha-Sapir et al. 2013; Guha-Sapir et al. 2014). The National Weather Service (NWS 2016) estimated that in 2017 alone, natural disasters killed over 500 individuals and injured over 1,200 more. Sadly, this death toll is not unusual, for natural disasters such as tornadoes, hurricanes, and earthquakes result in 549 fatalities on average each year in the United States. Three of the top five costliest U.S. hurricanes struck in 2017 (Harvey, Maria, and Irma). Together, these deadly hurricanes claimed the lives of over 300 individuals (NOAA 2019; Swiss Re Institute 2018).

The National Centers for Environmental Information (NCEI), a division of the National Oceanic and Atmospheric Administration (NOAA), reports on the economic cost of disasters in the United States. Since 1980, there have been 241 disasters in the United States where overall costs have been higher than one billion dollars (NCEI 2019). Together these disasters have cost the United States 1.6 trillion dollars. The NCEI reports the average number of natural disasters (that have overall costs of greater than one billion dollars) is on the rise. Since 1980, the average number of disasters per year has been 6.2. However, statistics from 2014–2018 indicate that this number is growing to 12.6 events per year, with 2016, 2017, and 2018 being three of the most active years on record (NCEI 2019). In 2018, the 14 costliest extreme weather and climate disasters exceeded one billion dollars in damage across the United States alone. As noted above, in 2017, the United States suffered several major hurricanes including Harvey, Maria, and Irma. Each of these hurricane events rank in the top five costliest hurricanes on record at 2, 3, and 5, respectively. A report by the Florida Department of Agriculture and Consumer Services (FDACS 2017) estimated the amount of crop damage from Hurricane Irma was $2,558,598,303 in Florida alone.

Natural Disasters As Dilemma for Mississippi

Natural disasters constitute a global problem, a national U.S. problem, and they represent a particular dilemma for specific U.S. states, such as Mississippi. Hurricanes, tornadoes, floods and earthquakes are high risks for various regions of Mississippi. In the Gulf Coast area, hurricanes are common. For example, when Hurricane Katrina struck the Gulf Coast in 2005, at least 1,833 lives were lost and over one million survivors were displaced (Knabb et al. 2011). In addition to the fatalities, costs from damages in Mississippi as a result of Hurricane Katrina ranged from $53 million to $26 billion.

In the north and west areas of the state, Mississippi is at great risk for tornadoes. Trend analysis over the past 50 years shows that the Gulf Coast, Mississippi River Valley, and the Carolinas frequently encounter tornadoes at a similar prevalence to the "Tornado Alley" region of the Great Plains (Boruff et al. 2003; Sherman-Morris et al. 2012). Furthermore, more people are killed by tornadoes per square kilometer in the Arkansas-Mississippi-Alabama region than in any other region of the U.S. (Ashley 2007). Second to Oklahoma, Mississippi experiences the most high-force tornadoes (EF4 and EF5) of any state (Sherman-Morris et al. 2012).

Earthquakes and floods are likewise high risks for Mississippi and the surrounding region. Due to the New Madrid Fault along the central Mississippi River, the river region including Arkansas, Mississippi, Tennessee, and Missouri is at the same risk of earthquake occurrence as Hawai'i and the Pacific Coast (Frankel et al. 2009). South of the New Madrid Fault, this region is at increased risk for flooding. A levee system is in place on the Mississippi River so that major flood damage will not occur, but the larger tributaries to the Mississippi River do not have levee systems. For this reason, the tributaries flood often, with severe flood damage occurring every three years on average (Sherman-Morris et al. 2012). Clearly, Mississippi is severely impacted by a range of natural disasters. They are a part of the state's culture.

As an educational institution in a natural disaster-prone state, the University of Mississippi (where the authors are located) and the surrounding region is at increased risk for natural disasters. Research and education in the disaster sciences and the practice of emergency management has particular relevance for this institution and outlying communities. While the examples above focus on natural disasters, disasters may be technological in origin (e.g., the Deepwater Horizon oil spill, the Flint water crisis 2014-present), may relate to disease (i.e., pandemic), may implicate climate change/environmental degradation (e.g., extreme temperatures), may involve domestic and international terrorism, and so on. Disasters affect individuals (e.g., physical health, mental health, job stress/loss, relationship stress/loss), families, neighborhoods, and entire communities (e.g., hindering provision of health care and related services, limiting distribution of food/medicine, damaging community infrastructures). Because they affect so many levels and systems, it is essential that research, education, training, and service provision be multidisciplinary in nature.

No two disasters are alike (Dursun et al. 2016), for each disaster occurs in unique circumstances. Some disasters are predictable, with slow onset, while others are sudden and unexpected. Sometimes there is an entity to blame (e.g., Deepwater Horizon oil spill), while at other times an event may be considered an act of nature (e.g., tornadoes, hurricanes). Some events occur in urban areas, while others occur in rural areas. Each disaster occurs in a unique socio-political-cultural-economic context, with wide-ranging implications. In a disaster like Hurricane Katrina, the storm itself was particularly harmful, but in response to the event, disaster-relief agencies and government at the local, regional, and national levels made numerous mistakes that significantly undermined response efforts. Agencies and organizations were disorganized, late, and in some cases negligent (these kinds of characteristics are sometimes referred to as "the second disaster"). There were preparedness, response, and infrastructure failures, as well as the existence of structural racism that exacerbated the post-disaster context. It is these kinds of characteristics that make it essential to understand disasters within the multicultural context. As noted by Jacobs (2016):

> Culture affects every aspect of our existence. It defines the relationship between genders, how we view children and the elderly, how we expect respect to be shown, what concepts such as time, success, wellness and healing mean to us, patterns of coping, methods of resolving conflict, the cadence of oral language, the appropriate amount of personal space, etc.... Culture also frames how people experience disaster or tragedy, how we decide the meaning of the event, what is considered to be traumatic, how traumatic stress is manifested, what is seen as help, and how one will know they are whole again. (pp. 178, 179)

The University of Mississippi is in a unique position to address the cultural climate of disaster that affects the campus, state, region, and country, from a multidisciplinary socio-political-cultural-economic contextual perspective; from the perspective of research, teaching, and service; and from the perspective of disaster trajectory (what happens before, during, and after a disaster). Along these lines, in the fall of 2018, a new interdisciplinary minor in Disaster Sciences was introduced.

The Interdisciplinary Minor in Disaster Sciences at the University of Mississippi

The Clinical-Disaster Research Center at the University of Mississippi, with the support of the Departments of Psychology, Criminal Justice, Sociology, and Social Work, as well as the College of Liberal Arts and the School of Applied Sciences, has established a new interdisciplinary minor in Disaster Sciences (DSci). The minor places special emphasis on exposing students to science and practice in fields such as emergency management and disaster mental health. The disaster context considered encompasses natural and technological disasters, pandemic, domestic and international terrorism, and climate change/environmental degradation. Students receive training in research areas within the disaster sciences, and with respect to occupations in emergency management. The minor promotes an integrated understanding of human behavior before, during, and after disasters, and an enhanced ability to work effectively across disciplines with implications for diverse disaster-related socio-political-cultural-economic contexts.

The Disaster Sciences Minor requires students to complete 18 credit hours including two courses that provide a foundational experience (see Table 12.1). These courses are Emergency Management and Criminal Justice (CJ 325) and Disasters and Mental Health (PSY 417). The Emergency Management and Criminal Justice course provides an overview of the characteristics, functions, and resources of an integrated system and how various emergency management services (fire personnel, police, security, health care providers, etc.) work together in a system of resources and capabilities. Emphasis is placed on how this system is applied to all hazards for all government levels in the U.S., across the phases and functions of

Table 12.1 *Course requirements for the Disaster Science minor at The University of Mississippi*

Required core courses (2 courses, 6 credit hours)	
CJ 325. Emergency management and criminal justice	
Psy 417. Disasters and mental health	
Foundations of human behavior, applications, and contexts domain	
Criminal justice	*Psychology*
CJ 100. Introduction to criminal justice	Psy 311. Abnormal psychology
CJ 115. Introduction to homeland security	Psy 319. Brain and behavior
CJ 285. Foundations of terrorism	Psy 321. Social psychology
CJ 435. Terrorism in the twenty-first century	Psy 327. Psychology and law
	Psy 365. Environmental psychology
Geology	Psy 430. Positive psychology
Geol 104/114. Env'l. geol. hazards and lab	
	Social work
Health and exercise science	SW 315. Introduction to social work
HP 191. Personal and community health	
HP 203. First Aid/CPR	*Sociology*
	Soc 311. Social problems
Nutrition and hospitality management	Soc 313. Social movements
NHM 111. Servsafe	Soc 332. Sociology of peace and justice
NHM 311. Nutrition	Soc 333. Juvenile corrections
	Soc 355. Sociology of human rights
Political science	Soc 411. Env't., technology, and society
Pol 332. Ethnic conflict and Int'l. terror	Soc 431. Criminology
Working with diversity domain	
Nutrition and hospitality management	*Social work*
NHM 323. Human development across the lifespan	SW 321. Human behavior and the social environment I
NHM 328. Child development	SW 322. Human behavior and the social environment II
	SW 326. Gerontology: Social welfare aspects
Psychology	SW 400. Human diversity and social work practice
Psy 301. Developmental psychology	
Psy 340. Multicultural psychology	*Sociology*
Rel 363. Religious perspectives on aging and death	Soc 325. Sociology of gender
	Soc 327. Genocide and women
	Soc 336. Sociology of religion
	Soc 413. Race and ethnicity

Note: A total of 18 credits are required including the two required core courses; at least one course from the domain Foundations of Human Behavior, Applications, and Contexts; and at least one course from the Working with Diversity domain emergency management. It includes the role of national, regional, and local services in a variety of manmade and natural disasters.

In the Disasters and Mental Health course (PSY 417), students learn about the roles played by psychologists and related mental health professionals before, during, and after disasters. Topics include preparedness and mitigation from a mental health perspective; normal/expected stress reactions; psychopathology after disasters; vulnerability, resilience, and meaning making related to mass casualty events; special populations; and mental health interventions and services. This course also offers a unique experience for students to receive standardized American Red Cross (ARC) training in the areas of Disaster Cycle Services, Shelter Operations, and Psychological First Aid (PFA). Thus, they are exposed to the culture of the American Red Cross as an example of the kind of work that can be done when affiliating with a disaster-relief agency. Moreover, they receive additional exposure and training in Jacobs' model of Community-Based Psychological First Aid (CBPFA), developed over a 30-year period across various international contexts (Jacobs 2016).

The remaining 12 credit hours are selected from two categories of courses comprised of offerings from such areas as Psychology, Criminal Justice, Sociology, Social Work, Political Science, and Nutrition and Hospitality Management. The "Foundations of Human Behavior, Applications, and Contexts" category provides a comprehensive overview of key elements that are present during disaster situations and promotes an integrated understanding of human behavior, before, during, and after disasters. Courses in the "Working with Diversity" category provide an enhanced understanding of working effectively across disciplines with implications for diverse disaster-related socio-political-cultural-economic contexts. For more information the interested reader is referred to https://catalog.olemiss.edu/liberal-arts/ba-distr-sci and http://disastersciences.olemiss.edu/

Positive Psychology in Action Through Disaster Sciences

The Disaster Sciences interdisciplinary minor is positive psychology in action on the college campus (see Wade et al. 2015). Positive psychology is the science of optimal human functioning, flourishing, or aspects that make for a meaningful life (Bretherton 2015; Dekel and Taubman-Ben-Ari 2015; Magyar-Moe 2015; Schulenberg 2016). Key constructs associated with the term, *positive psychology*, include resilience, meaning in life, purpose, posttraumatic growth, and self-efficacy, among many others (Schulenberg 2016). Thus, to enhance human flourishing in disaster-prone regions, the Disaster Sciences minor aims to (1) build community resilience towards disasters, (2) be a source of meaning, purpose, and posttraumatic growth, and (3) harness self-efficacy to aid in disaster preparedness and response.

Building Community Resilience Through Disaster Sciences

Disaster preparedness is an integral part of community resilience. Community resilience is "the ability of community members to take meaningful, deliberate, collective action to remedy the effect of a problem, including the ability to interpret the environment, intervene, and move on" (Pfefferbaum et al. 2008, p. 349). Because disasters are dilemmas that, by definition, impact whole communities, a critical component of community resilience is engagement in meaningful, collective action to combat them. Preparedness for disasters has been closely linked to community resilience (Gil-Rivas and Kilmer 2016). Models of community resilience incorporate action against disasters as a key factor. Preparedness for Emergencies is one of five factors of community resilience in one model (Cohen et al. 2013), while Disaster Management is one of four factors of community resilience in another model (Pfefferbaum et al. 2013). Thus, interventions to enhance disaster preparedness and management are community resilience interventions. In this way, the Disaster Sciences interdisciplinary minor is an intervention to build a more resilient community of college students. Supporting this link between disaster-prepared college students and community resilience, data from the Clinical-Disaster Research Center at the University of Mississippi has demonstrated that disaster-prepared college students have greater perceived psychological resilience and less posttraumatic stress from natural disasters, specifically tornadoes (Weber et al. 2019). By educating students in methods of addressing their community's disaster dilemma, the Disaster Sciences interdisciplinary minor is community resilience (i.e., positive psychology) in action.

Enhancing Meaning, Purpose, and Posttraumatic Growth Through Disaster Sciences

As Pfefferbaum et al. (2008) noted, community resilience involves meaningful action against community problems such as disasters. Indeed, when a disaster strikes it is critical for those affected to find meaning and purpose, through or in spite of the disaster (Schulenberg 2016; Schulenberg et al. 2014; see also Park 2010 and Park and Blake, this volume). Students, faculty, and staff at the University of Mississippi who have a greater sense of meaning or purpose are more resilient and more disaster prepared (Weber et al. 2019). It is our goal with the Disaster Sciences interdisciplinary minor to help students discover meaning and purpose in disaster preparedness, mitigation, response, and recovery. For example, when asked about Disaster Sciences in preparation for its proposed addition to the university's curriculum, one student remarked,

> The multidisciplinary minor seems like a good idea. I would like to learn to handle bad situations well. I would like to know how to be truly useful in bad situations and help other people out. (Schulenberg et al. 2017)

Another expressed,

> I think that the well-being of others is of great importance and … if [students] decided they were called to help others … they could adequately do that. (Schulenberg et al. 2017)

For these college students, minoring in Disaster Sciences would be a purposeful, intentional way to aid their community and to put community resilience into action.

Likewise, those who have experienced disasters may find meaning and posttraumatic growth through their education in Disaster Sciences. For example, another student interested in the minor said,

> After Hurricane Katrina, we wouldn't have made it two days without these agencies providing us with food, water, shelter, etc. I find it would be extremely useful to train others in these types of areas for not only natural disasters, but also to responding to things like massacre and other stressful/unpredictable times or disaster. (Schulenberg et al. 2017)

In this way, students coping with their own disaster experiences may discover meaning and posttraumatic growth through their learning in Disaster Sciences. Participation in education and research in Disaster Sciences is, therefore, a promising avenue for facilitating meaning and cultivating posttraumatic growth among college students in such a disaster-prone region.

Harnessing Self-Efficacy to Aid in Disaster Preparedness and Response

A third way that the Disaster Sciences interdisciplinary minor exemplifies positive psychology is by enhancing self-efficacy for disasters. Self-efficacy is an individual's belief that they are personally effective or their confidence that they can cope with stressful situations (Bandura and Adams 1977; Schwarzer and Jerusalem 1995). The Extended Parallel Process Model (Witte 1992, 1998)—a theory as to how an individual responds to danger—posits that an effective response to threats, like disasters, requires accurate threat perception in conjunction with self-efficacy. Research with University of Mississippi students, faculty, and staff has supported this theory, finding that self-efficacy predicts student preparedness for disasters in general (Tkachuck et al. 2018), as well as faculty and staff's preparedness for natural hazards and incidents of mass violence on the college campus (Weber et al. 2018).

Student perspectives on the Disaster Sciences interdisciplinary minor reflect the importance they place on self-efficacy for disasters. Regarding Community-Based

Psychological First Aid training that is a part of one of the minor's core courses (PSY 417 Disasters and Mental Health), one student noted,

> it would help teach students and adults the proper things they need when it comes to real life situations.

Another expressed enthusiasm for the minor by observing,

> the university will be teaching the people not only skills for their career, but skills to deal with something that is really stressful.

As mentioned above, one student exclaimed,

> I would like to know how to be truly useful in bad situations and help other people out.

These comments by college students show their desire to be more effective in preventing and combating the effects of disasters. Indeed, their comments suggest their interest in the minor hinged on its role in bolstering their self-efficacy for disasters. The concept of self-efficacy has roots that pre-date the positive psychology of today, yet we continue to apply self-efficacy theories to a wide range of situations, disasters in Mississippi being one example. By providing students with training for disaster preparedness, mitigation, response, and recovery, the Disaster Sciences interdisciplinary minor is an emerging application of self-efficacy with respect to disaster management.

Conclusions

Disaster Sciences is timely, with potential for growth across disciplines and contexts. Initially, those specializing in Psychology, Criminal Justice (Emphasis on Homeland Security), Social Work, and Sociology were encouraged to consider the minor as it is highly relevant to these areas of study (see Appendix A for a sample course layout). Career outlooks for those interested in Disaster Sciences include first responders, emergency management and mental health professionals, and volunteers. At the time of the writing of this chapter, Disaster Sciences is in its second year, and is approaching 50 minors. It appears to be successful, generating interest among students and faculty alike. Disaster Sciences is an interdisciplinary, proactive stance to disaster preparedness, mitigation, response, and recovery. It serves as one example of positive psychology in action via its emphasis on building community resilience, fostering meaning and purpose for those involved, cultivating resilience and posttraumatic growth with students who have experienced disasters, and harnessing self-efficacy for disaster management.

Appendix A

Psychology Major with Disaster Sciences Minor
Sample Course Layout

Fall 1st year
WRIT 101 First Year Writing I
SPAN 111 Intensive Elementary Spanish
BISC 102 Inquiry into Life Human Biology
BISC 103 Inquiry into Life Laboratory I
HST 130 Intro to U.S. History to 1877

Spring 1st year
PSY 201 General Psychology
WRIT 102 First Year Writing II
HST 131 Intro to U.S. History since 1877
SPAN 211 Intensive Intermediate Spanish
SOC 101 Introductory Sociology I

Fall 2nd year
PSY 202 Statistics for Behavioral Sciences
BISC 104 Inquiry into Life: The Environment
BISC 105 Inquiry into Life Laboratory II
ENG 223 Survey Am. Lit to the Civil War
PSY 301 Developmental Psychology

Spring 2nd year
PSY 309 Learning
PSY 321 Social Psychology
MATH 115 Elementary Statistics
ENG 224 Survey Am. Lit since the Civil War
PHIL 101 Introduction to Philosophy

Summer
PSY 350 Ecopsychology and International Youth

Fall 3rd year
PSY 392 Lab in Psy: Experimental Social PSY
SOC 333 Juvenile Delinquency
PSY 311 Abnormal Psychology
SOC 355 Sociology of Human Rights
CJ 100 Introduction to Criminal Justice

Spring 3rd year
PSY 327 Psychology and Law
SOC 323 Occupations and Professions
CJ 325 Emergency Management
EDHE 301 Career and Life Planning
SOC 431 Criminology

Fall 4th year
PSY 340 Multicultural Psychology
PSY 320 Cognitive Psychology
GEOL 104 Environmental Geology Hazards
PSY 322 Drugs and Behavior
PSY 405 Minor Research Problems
THEA 201 Appreciation of the Theater

Spring 4th year
HP 203 First Aid and CPR
PSY 417 Disasters and Mental Health
PSY 365 Environmental Psychology
PSY 430 Positive Psychology
PSY 405 Minor Research Problems

References

Ashley, W. S. (2007). Spatial and temporal analysis of tornado fatalities in the United States. 1880-2005. *Weather and Forecasting, 22*, 1214–1228.

Bandura, A., & Adams, N. E. (1977). Analysis of self-efficacy theory of behavioral change. *Cognitive Therapy and Research, 1*(4), 287–310.

Boruff, B. J., Easoz, J. A., Jones, S. D., Landry, H. R., Mitchem, J. D., & Cutter, S. L. (2003). Tornado hazards in the United States. *Climate Research, 24*, 103–117.

Bretherton, R. (2015). Existential dimensions of positive psychology. In S. Joseph (Ed.), *Positive psychology in practice: Promoting human flourishing in work, health, education, and everyday life* (2nd ed., pp. 47–59). Hoboken: Wiley.

Centre for Research on the Epidemiology of Disasters (CRED). (2018a, February 07). *Natural Disasters* 2017 (Rep.). Retrieved from https://cred.be/sites/default/files/adsr_2017.pdf.

Centre for Research on the Epidemiology of Disasters (CRED). (2018b). Annual Disaster Statistical Review, 2017. Retrieved from https://www.cred.be/annual-disaster-statistical-review-2017.

Cohen, O., Leykin, D., Lahad, M., Goldberg, A., & Aharonson-Daniel, L. (2013). The Conjoint Community Resiliency Assessment Measure as a baseline for profiling and predicting community resilience for emergencies. *Technological Forecasting and Social Change, 80*(9), 1732–1741. https://doi.org/10.1016/j.techfore.2012.12.009.

Dekel, R., & Taubman-Ben-Ari, O. (2015). The interface between positive psychology and social work in theory and practice. In S. Joseph (Ed.), *Positive psychology in practice: Promoting human flourishing in work, health, education, and everyday life* (2nd ed., pp. 681–694). Hoboken: Wiley.

Dursun, P., Steger, M. F., Bentele, C., & Schulenberg, S. E. (2016). Meaning and posttraumatic growth among survivors of the September 2013 Colorado floods. *Journal of Clinical Psychology, 72*(12), 1247–1263.

Florida Department of Agriculture and Consumer Services (FDACS, 2017). *2017 Annual Report*. Retrieved from https://www.freshfromflorida.com/content/download/80670/2336343/2017_DeptAnnualReport_Web.pdf.

Frankel, A. D., Applegate, D., Tuttle, M. P., & Williams, R. A. (2009, August 3). *Earthquake hazard in the New Madrid Seismic Zone remains a concern:* U.S. Geological Survey Fact Sheet 2009-3071. Retrieved from http://pubs.usgs.gov/fs/2009/3071/.

Gil-Rivas, V., & Kilmer, R. P. (2016). Building community capacity and fostering disaster resilience. *Journal of Clinical Psychology, 72*(12), 1318–1332. https://doi.org/10.1002/jclp.22281.

Guha-Sapir, D., Hoyois, P., & Below, R. (2013). Annual disaster statistical review 2012. Centre for Research on the Epidemiology of Disasters (CRED). Retrieved June 29, 2015, from http://reliefweb.int/report/world/.

Guha-Sapir, D., Hoyois, P., & Below, R. (2014). Annual disaster statistical review 2013. Centre for Research on the Epidemiology of Disasters (CRED). Retrieved June 29, 2015, from http://reliefweb.int/report/world/.

Jacobs, G. A. (2016). *Community-based psychological first aid: A practical guide to helping individuals and communities during difficult times*. Oxford: Butterworth-Heinemann.

Knabb, R. D., Rhome, J. R., & Brown, D. P. (2011). Hurricane Katrina: August 23-30, 2005. (Tropical cyclone report). United States National Oceanic and Atmospheric Administration's National Weather Service. Retrieved from http://www.nhc.noaa.gov/data/tcr/AL122005_Katrina.pdf.

Magyar-Moe, J. L. (2015). Positive psychology 101. In J. C. Wade, L. I. Marks, & R. D. Hetzel (Eds.), *Positive psychology on the college campus* (pp. 57–79). Oxford: Oxford University Press.

National Weather Service. (2016). National hazard statistics: Weather fatalities. Retrieved March 16, 2016, from http://www.nws.noaa.gov/om/hazstats.shtml.

NOAA National Centers for Environmental Information. (NCEI, 2019). U.S. billion-dollar weather and climate disasters. Retrieved February 11, 2019 https://www.ncdc.noaa.gov/billions/.

Park, C. L. (2010). Making sense of the meaning literature: An integrative review of meaning making and its effects on adjustment to stressful life events. *Psychological Bulletin, 136*, 257–301.
Pfefferbaum, B. J., Reissman, D. B., Pfefferbaum, R. L., Klomp, R. W., & Gurwitch, R. H. (2008). Building resilience to mass trauma events. In L. S. Doll, S. E. Bonzo, D. A. Sleet, J. A. Mercy, & E. N. Haas (Eds.), *Handbook of injury and violence prevention* (pp. 347–358). Boston: Springer.
Pfefferbaum, R. L., Pfefferbaum, B., Van Horn, R. L., Klomp, R. W., Norris, F. H., & Reissman, D. B. (2013). The Communities Advancing Resilience Toolkit (CART): An intervention to build community resilience to disasters. *Journal of Public Health Management and Practice, 19*(3), 250–258. https://doi.org/10.1097/PHH.0b013e318268aed8.
Schulenberg, S. E. (2016). Disaster mental health and positive psychology – Considering the context of natural and technological disasters: An introduction to the special issue. *Journal of Clinical Psychology, 72*(12), 1223–1233.
Schulenberg, S. E., Drescher, C. F., & Baczwaski, B. J. (2014). Perceived meaning and disaster mental health: A role for logotherapy in clinical-disaster psychology. In A. Batthyany & P. Russo-Netzer (Eds.), *Meaning in positive and existential psychology* (pp. 251–267). New York: Springer. https://doi.org/10.1007/978-1-4939-0308-5_15.
Schulenberg, S. E., Russo, B., Lair, E., McElreath, D., Cain, D., Frezzo, M., & Holben, D. (2017). *Disaster Sciences (DSci) – Mitigation, preparedness, response, and recovery: A multidisciplinary minor proposal* [Unpublished manuscript]. Department of Psychology, University of Mississippi.
Schwarzer, R., & Jerusalem, M. (1995). Generalized Self-Efficacy scale. In J. Weinman, S. Wright, & M. Johnston (Eds.), *Measures in health psychology: A user's portfolio. Causal and control beliefs* (pp. 35–37). NFER-NELSON: Windsor.
Sherman-Morris, K., Wax, C. L., & Brown, M. E. (2012). *Mississippi weather and climate*. Jackson: University Press of Mississippi.
Swiss Re Institute. (2018, January 1). Natural catastrophes and man-made disasters in 2017: A year of record-breaking losses. *Sigma*. Retrieved from https://reliefweb.int/sites/reliefweb.int/files/resources/sigma1_2018_en.pdf.
Tkachuck, M. A., Schulenberg, S. E., & Lair, E. C. (2018). Natural disaster preparedness in college students: Implications for institutions of higher learning. *Journal of American College Health, 66*, 269–279. https://doi.org/10.1080/07448481.2018.1431897.
United Nations Office for Disaster Risk Reduction (UNDRR). (2019, January 24). *2018: Extreme weather events affected 60 million people* [Press release]. Retrieved from https://www.unisdr.org/archive/63267.
Wade, J. C., Marks, L. I., & Hetzel, R. D. (Eds.). (2015). *Positive psychology on the college campus*. New York: Oxford University Press.
Weber, M. C., Pavlacic, J. M., Gawlik, E. A., Schulenberg, S. E., & Buchanan, E. M. (in press, advance online 2019, June 20). Modeling resilience, meaning in life, posttraumatic growth, and disaster preparedness with two samples of tornado survivors. *Traumatology*. https://doi.org/10.1037/trm0000210
Weber, M. C., Schulenberg, S. E., & Lair, E. C. (2018). University employees' preparedness for natural hazards and incidents of mass violence: An application of the Extended Parallel Process Model. *International Journal of Disaster Risk Reduction, 31*, 1082–1091. https://doi.org/10.1016/j.ijdrr.2018.03.032.
Witte, K. (1992). Putting the fear back into fear appeals: The Extended Parallel Process Model. *Communications Monographs, 59*(4), 329–349.
Witte, K. (1998). Fear as motivator, inhibitor: Using the Extended Parallel Process Model to explain fear appeal successes and failures. In P. A. Anderson & L. K. Guerrero (Eds.), *Handbook of communication and emotion: Research, theory, applications, and contexts* (pp. 423–450). San Diego: Academic.

Afterword to Positive Psychological Approaches to Disaster: Meaning, Resilience, and Posttraumatic Growth

The Other Shore

> "Together they had overcome the daily incomprehension, the instantaneous hatred, the reciprocal nastiness, and fabulous flashes of glory in the conjugal conspiracy. It was a time when they both loved each other best, without hurry or excess, when both were most conscious of and grateful for their incredible victories over adversity. Life would still present them with other moral trials, of course, but that no longer mattered: they were on the other shore."
>
> -Gabriel García Márquez, *Love in the Time of Cholera*

In this book, we find serious scholars tackling the heavy lifting that needs to be done to help people in the aftermath of disaster. Among the unique offerings of this book, though, is an emphasis on meaning, resilience, and posttraumatic growth. These three fields are closely linked, yet developed fairly independently. They present the rest of the picture of how people fare after difficulty, trauma, stress, and disaster. The vast research on meaning, resilience, and posttraumatic growth reminds us that people indeed are equipped to cope with such challenges, and that there is a great deal of good that can be done by expanding what we know and what we share about how to make meaning, how to stay resilient, and how to grow in some areas even as we incur damage in others.

By all accounts, we are going to need it.

Disasters, whether natural, caused by human action, or caused by human neglect, appear to be increasing in intensity and frequency. Young people stare aghast at older generations and the way those in charge recklessly bury their heads in the sand, or perseverate on property values, horsepower, 4K and 5G, and their supposed right to material prosperity. It can be difficult to shake the feeling that collectively we have learned too little from our past mistakes, done too little to change our course, and that we have secured for ourselves, for the coming generations, and for life on Earth a much worse future than we should have created. In such a climate it

S. E. Schulenberg (ed.), *Positive Psychological Approaches to Disaster*,
https://doi.org/10.1007/978-3-030-32007-2

is vital to understand the full range of human response to disaster, and the possibilities for hope, growth, and meaning.

Looking at people's routes through disaster from a meaning perspective automatically evokes the stirring account of Viktor Frankl's survival of World War II Nazi concentration camps. Frankl's thesis—that meaning and purpose can sustain people and enable their survival under even the most horrific conditions—has inspired so many people, and captures a perspective on meaning that feels distinctly relevant today. The fact that Frankl went on to share a 40+ year career as an intellectual leader devoted to increasing people's access to meaning and purpose seemed to perfectly personify the lessons of his work.

At the same time, the validity of posttraumatic growth and questions regarding whether people actually grow or simply believe they have grown have dogged the field. One might equally look at Frankl's life for clues that he always believed that meaning and purpose were important and that he always had a sophisticated and persuasive view on human nature. From such clues, one might then conclude that Frankl had not grown, was not transformed at all, instead that he was able to preserve who he was. This perspective, which we might think of as resilience, is itself a victory, of course. So many people do not survive, and the bias of expectations among the fields that work with survivors of trauma and disaster long has been to anticipate damage, that getting through such experiences relatively whole is a great and desirable outcome.

Yet, the question persists. Is resilience, is posttraumatic growth, is meaning-making, tangibly influencing people's lives for the better after difficult trials, such as disasters? This question feels so critical, so pressing, because in this time of disaster facing our world, we don't need people telling themselves idle stories about their imperviousness to threat or their "incredible victories over adversity," we don't need people imagining they've grown into better versions of their former selves, we don't need people finding a purpose in life that leaves them indifferent to the suffering and destruction in the world around them. We need truly resilient spirits, true personifications of growth, true champions of the kinds of purpose that can bring the best of all of us to confront the trials and adversity that loom.

Those of us who haven't yet been beset by disaster need to achieve these qualities, as well. Disaster is, by its nature, capricious and unpredictable. Our species seems hell-bent on making disaster more predictable if only by making them more frequent, more widely distributed, more calamitous, and more common. Rather than carrying on in a state of suspended fantasy that it will never happen to us, we all need to do what we can to act as if we have survived disaster already; we each need to make meaning, disseminate resilience, and grow.

This book lays out the scholarship charting how these goals might be achieved. Mapping out a world of positive growth, new insights, impassioned commitments, collective response, empathic aid given to others – with research-driven specificity – shocks the system in a way with jolts of optimism and hope. When awful circumstances fall on our heads, we still have nobility, community and perseverance within us. What a better reminder of the good work each of us can do to help us all reach The Other Shore.

It is my fervent hope that in a few years down the road this afterword will seem like a chicken-brained, alarmist ball of panic. It is my fervent hope that when we look back on this time of disaster from the safety of the other shore we will be able to feel proud that we responded to the adversity and trials facing us with the resilience, meaning and purpose, growth, and actual changes to the way we live that we see described in the chapters of this book.

Michael F. Steger, Ph.D.
August 13, 2019

References

García Márquez, G. (1989). *Love in the time of cholera* (p. 244). New York: Penguin.

Index

A

Active listening skills, 142
Adolescents
  developmental time period/sensitive periods, 115
  disaster-related context, 116
  disaster-related interventions, 119
  disasters (*see* Disasters)
  empirically-supported treatments, 119
  encouraging and creating opportunities, 121
  self-identity post-disaster, 118
  shelter setting post-disaster, 119
  stress reactions, 121
Adverse life experiences, 35
Adversity-related anxiety, 39
Agency, 123, 125, 189
American Psychological Association (APA), 137
American Red Cross (ARC), 137, 146, 147, 149, 192
American Red Cross Disaster Mental Health Services, 139
American Red Cross PSP programs, 149
Anxiety disorder, 62
Atheism, 53
Automatic and deliberate processes, 126

B

Behavioral activation, 86, 87
Big Five, 88
Brief Resilience Scale, 82
Buddhism, 53, 156

C

Carol Ryff's model, 86
Center for Disease Control's (CDC), 117
Centre for Research on Disasters (CRED), 187
Childhood, 115
Children, 115
Christianity, 156
Climate change, 172, 173
Clinical assessments, 178
Cognitive-behavior therapies, 86
Cognitive-behavioral and narrative techniques, 162
Cognitive dissonance theory, 33
Cognitive processing therapy (CPT), 86
Cognitive reappraisal, 86, 87, 92
Collective narrative, 161
Community adaptation, 150
Community based crisis response
  crisis assessment and intervention, 174, 175
  meaning making, 176, 177
  mental health, 174
  normalization, 175, 176
  psychoeducation, 175, 176
  psychological care, 174
Community-based PFA (CBPFA), 122, 192
  adaptations, 144–145
  community committee, 142
  and community-wide events, 152
  components, 142
  curriculum, 142
  and DMH, 151
  early experiences, 145–146
  ethnicities, 142
  geographic gathering, 141

S. E. Schulenberg (ed.), *Positive Psychological Approaches to Disaster*,
https://doi.org/10.1007/978-3-030-32007-2

Community-based PFA (CBPFA) (*cont.*)
  Gujarat India earthquake, 146–148
  identical models, 151
  Indian Ocean Tsunami, 149–150
  Izmit earthquake in Turkey, 151
  Japan Tōhoku earthquake, 151, 152
  political perspectives, 142
  programs, 141
  religions, 142
  socioeconomic groups, 142
  terrorist bombing, 151
  ToT, 149
  training strategy, 143–144
Community committees, 149, 150
Community psychology, 138
Community resilience, 193
Connectedness, 69–71, 75
Conservation of resources stress theory, 170, 171
Continued service
  deployments, 67
  loneliness, 66
  membership application process, 67
  military service, 67
  mortality, 65
  national civic service program, 66
  non-volunteers, 65
  opportunities, 65
  selfless, 65
  social interaction, 65
  social isolation, 66
  social support, 67
  veteran organization, 67
  volunteer service, 65
Coping, 28, 46, 121, 122, 126–128

D
Dalit community, 147
Deliberate rumination, 157
Department of Defense (DoD), 73
Department of Veterans Affairs (VA), 73
Depression, 62, 64
Developmental time period, 115, 116
Direct clinical services, 139
Disaster-affected communities, 68
Disaster management, 193
Disaster mental health (DMH), 192
  adolescents, 120
  adult-to-adult, 116
  APA, 137
  caregivers, 121
  and CBPFA, 151
  community psychology, 138
  crisis intervention, 152
  families, 121
  individuals/situations, 138
  international settings, 139–140
  interventions (*see* Interventions)
  licensed professionals, 138
  multiple methods, 129
  PFA guidelines, 122
  and positive psychology, 127
  professionals, 121, 130
  Red Cross Disaster Mental Health Services, 138
  schools, 121
  terrorist attacks, 138
  traumatic stress, 152
  workers, 119, 130
Disaster-related studies, 124
Disaster relief operation, 141
Disaster response
  impact, 71–72
  organization, 70
  physically and emotionally, 71
  resilience, 72–75
  sharing, 71
Disasters
  adverse effects, 117
  to daily tasks, 121
  definition, 117
  forms/classes, 117
  interventions (*see* Interventions)
  natural and technological, 117
  psychological effects, 118, 119
Disaster sciences (DSci)
  interdisciplinary minor, 190, 192
  positive psychology, 192–195
  research and education, 189
Distress, 170

E
Earthquakes and floods, 189
Emergency Management and Criminal Justice, 190
Emergency medicine, 141
Empowerment theory, 129
Erikson's stage theory, 125
Evidence-informed psychosocial interventions, 122
Existential anxiety, 179, 180
Existential psychotherapy, 179
Extended Parallel Process Model, 194

F
The Federal Emergency Management Agency (FEMA), 117, 175
Financial assistance, 144
Financial support, 144
Firefighters
  challenges, 99
  disaster rescue workers, 99
  fire service, 100, 110
  line-of-duty injuries, 100
  personality variables, 110
  preparedness, 100
  protective psychological factors (*see* Protective psychological factors)
  psychopathology, 100
  rebirth and growth, 99
  WRI personnel, 100
Fire service, 100
First aid, 141
Florida Department of Agriculture and Consumer Services (FDACS), 188

G
Global meaning, 16, 49
Graduate training, 138
Guidelines on Mental Health and Psychosocial Support in Emergency Settings, 139
Gujarat India earthquake
  CBPFA, 147
  children, 148
  cultural issues, 146
  Dalit community, 147
  DMH, 147
  health professional, 147
  Hindu, Islamic and Christian communities, 148
  Indian Red Cross, 147
  Islamic community, 147
  PSPs, 148
  socioeconomic groups, 147

H
Happiology, 83
Health care skills training, 68
Health Resources and Services Administration (HRSA), 68
Healthy postdisaster coping, 38
Heart rate variability (HRV), 106, 107
Hero's journey, 89–95
Hinduism, 53, 156
Hope theory
  agency, 120, 123
  applicability, 124
  applications, 124
  and components, 123
  concepts, 123, 124
  depression and anxiety, 124
  goal-directed determination, 123
  human strengths, 124
  and interventions, 127
  negative trend, 124
  pathways, 120, 123
  and PFA (*see* Psychological First Aid (PFA))
  positive psychology, 124
  self-agency, 120
  and self-efficacy, 128
  successful agency, 123
Housing clusters, 150
Hurricane Mitch, 47
Hurricanes Katrina, 9, 13–18
  and Rita, 13, 15

I
IAFF Peer Support training program, 109
Icelandic earthquakes, 19
In-depth qualitative interviews, 19
Indian Ocean Tsunami
  PSPs, 149–150
Indian Red Cross, 147
Individual counseling
  boundary experiences, 179, 180
  clinical considerations, 178
  development, safe therapeutic relationships, 178
  existential psychotherapy, 179, 180
  meaning making, 178, 179
  positive reinterpretation, 178, 179
  social support, 180
Indonesia, 149
Indonesian Tsunami, 16
Inter-Agency Standing Committee, 139
Interdisciplinary minor
  disaster mental health, 190, 192
  emergency management, 190
  foundational experience, 190
  human behavior, 190
International Association for Fire Fighters (IAFF), 109
Interpretive phenomenological study, 50

Interventions
  accurate information, 120
  developmentally-appropriate education and activities, 120
  disaster response activities, 120
  family members, 120
  and hope theory
    adolescents, 127
    borrowing, 128
    coping skills, 128
    empowerment theory, 129
    goals, 127
    instilling and promoting, 129
    meaning making, 128
    mental health professionals, 127
    negative self-scripts, 128
    peer support post-disaster, 127
    reflection, 128
    self-efficacy, 128, 129
    social support, 127
    strengthening, 128
    thinking and skill development, 128
  in-depth review, 119
  language, 120
  media and social networking safety, 120
  mental health professionals, 121
  psychological impacts, 119
  relief efforts, 119
  social support, 120
  supportive, 121
Intrapsychic cognitive process, 49
Intrusive rumination, 156
Islam, 156
Islamic community, 147
Izmit earthquake in Turkey, 151

J
Japan Tōhoku earthquake, 151, 152
Japanese society, 151
Journal of Clinical Psychology, 84

L
Language, 120
Logotherapy, 2

M
Meaning making, 10, 12, 20, 46, 49, 50, 54, 69–72, 75, 103, 176, 177
  application, 11
  appraisal, 10
  attributions, 10
  cognitive and emotional processing, 11
  coping, 12
  extant meaning system, 11
  global beliefs, 12
  global meaning, 12
  PTSD, 13
  situational meaning, 10
Medical model, 47
Memorial service, 153
Mental health, 174
  adaptive help-seeking behaviors, 120
  developmental time period, 116
  disaster-related events, 116
  neural pathways, 116
  and physical, 116
  professionals, 46, 116, 118
  recommendations, 116
  response and recovery post-disaster, 116
  and school-based professionals, 116
Methodological diversity, 41
Military culture, 64
"The Mission Continues", 66
Mitakuye oyassin, 153
Moral injury, 63
Mount Saint Helens volcanic eruption, 14

N
Narrative Exposure Therapy (NET), 90, 94
National Center for Post-Traumatic Stress Disorder (NCPTSD), 141
National Centers for Environmental Information (NCEI), 188
National Children's Traumatic Stress Network (NCTSN), 141
National Institutes of Mental Health, 82
National Oceanic and Atmospheric Administration (NOAA), 188
National Vietnam Veterans Longitudinal Study (NVVLS), 62
National Vietnam Veterans Readjustment Study (NVVRS), 62
National Weather Service (NWS), 188
Native culture, 145
Natural disasters, 49
  conservation of resources stress theory, 170, 171
  dilemma
    Mississippi, 188–190
    U.S., 188
  global dilemma, 187, 188
  and manmade, 159
  posttraumatic growth, 171–173
  psychological distress, 170

systemic stressors, 170
and technological, 117
Negative emotionality (NEM), 105
Negative religious coping, 17, 52
Non-Governmental Organization (NGO), 139, 140, 143, 144, 150
Non-linear relationship, 72
Non-profit organizations, 139
Northern Plains Native community, 146

O
Online/electronic format, 143
Organizational framework, 139

P
Pakistani earthquake, 16
Personality, 105, 106
Phoenix, 99, 110
Physical ground, 45
Physician Assistant (PA), 68
Positive psychology, 2, 40, 48, 61, 64, 81–84, 86, 93, 100, 104, 110
adolescent population, 124
adversity, 126
community resilience, 193
in disasters, 124
and DMH, 127
features of human life, 38
and hope theory, 124, 129
interventions, 124
literature, 125, 128
meaning in life, 193, 194
self-efficacy, 194, 195
virtues, 40
Positive religious coping, 17, 85
Post-deployment blues, 73
Postdisaster coping efforts, 38
Posttraumatic growth (PTG), 41, 100, 104, 105, 110, 162
climate change adaptation, 172, 173
clinical care, 180
cognitive work, 157
community based crisis (*see* Community Based Crisis Response)
counseling process, 181
crisis assessment and intervention, 181
disruptive experiences, 156
distress, 155
domains, 156
earthquake metaphor, 156
formidable scale, 158
implications, 157
individual counseling, 177–180
intake assessment, 181
longitudinal studies, 159
mutual influence, 158
problem focused coping, 171
PTS, 160
resilience, 156
secondary stressors, 158
sense of coherence, 172
social support, 171, 182
spiritual and religious, 159
traumatic event, 171
wellbeing and life satisfaction, 157
Posttraumatic Growth Inventory (PTGI), 81, 83, 102
Posttraumatic ruminative processes, 161
Posttraumatic stress (PTS), 159, 170, 173, 177, 179, 180
Posttraumatic stress disorder (PTSD), 9, 62, 99, 119
2010 Chilean earthquake/tsunami, 17
climate change, 54
coping, 10
depression, 66
depressive symptoms, 18
development of, 71
disaster literature, 14
global community, 46
growth-oriented approaches, 55
hurricane-related, 9
incidence, 9
post-disaster situational appraisals, 15
prevalence, 62
psychology, 46, 54
rates of, 62
religious coping, 15
religiousness and spirituality, 18
resilience, 9
symptoms, 14, 45, 53
veterans, 66, 71
Posttraumatic stress symptoms, 155
Pre-packaged meaning-making systems, 51
Professional training, 139
Prolonged exposure (PE), 86
Protective psychological factors
adaptive facets, 109
resilience (*see* Resilience)
Psychoeducation, 175, 176
Psychological distress, 49
Psychological effects of disaster, 118, 119
Psychological First Aid (PFA), 174
adolescents, 122
age groups, 122

Psychological First Aid (PFA) (*cont.*)
  CBPFA (*see* Community-based PFA (CBPFA))
  DMH (*see* Disaster mental health (DMH))
  guidelines, 122
  hope theory, 123
  limitations, 138
  multiple organizations, 122
  opportunity to participate, 122
  post-disaster and hope theory
    adolescents, 125, 126
    adversity, 126
    agency, 125
    agentic thinking, 125
    automatic and deliberate processes, 126
    availability, 125
    concepts and adaptive functioning, 126
    Erikson's stage theory, 125
    meaning, 126
    pathways, 125
    purpose, 126
    religiousness and spirituality, 126
    research and applications, 125
    self-efficacy, 125
    short-term and long-term recovery, 126
    task-oriented coping, 126
  and post-disaster utility, 122
  practical steps, 122
  PSPs (*see* Psychological support programs (PSPs))
  response team (*see* Response team PFA)
  team models, 140
  tMHFA, 122
Psychological flexibility, 107
Psychological research, 28
Psychological support programs (PSPs)
  assessment, 149
  CBPFA (*see* Community-based PFA (CBPFA))
  Gujarat India earthquake, 148
  Indian Ocean Tsunami, 149–150
  Japan Tōhoku earthquake, 151, 152
  Japanese society, 151
  response team, 141
  traumatic events and strategies, 144
Psychological treatment, 46
Psychological well-being, 72
Psychotherapy, 54
PTSD Checklist – Civilian version (PCL-C), 106

R

Red Crescent Societies, 142
Red Cross Disaster Mental Health Services, 138
Red Cross Movement, 139
Red Cross/Red Crescent system, 139
Regarding Community-Based Psychological First Aid, 194–195
Relief efforts, 119
Religion/spirituality (R/S), 28
  adverse events, 32
  cognitive proficiency, 37
  coherence, 29, 37
  communities, 36
  conceptual ambiguity, 28
  congruence, 29
  content, 33
  death and meaning, 30
  disaster, 29, 33
  distress, 29
  effort and energy, 33
  fears, 36
  features, 35
  God's power and engagement, 29
  meaning, 28
  people, 31
  person-perception research, 34
  process, 33
  and prosociality, 33
  religious cognitions, 30, 34
  role, 32
  significance, 30, 32
  source of meaning, 31
  supernatural attributions, 38
  survivors, 33
  theoretical model, 33
Religious and nonreligious meaning, 40
Religious and spiritual belief systems, 46
Religiousness, 13, 102
Resilience, 175, 177
  definition, 101
  disaster healthcare rescuers, 101
  disaster response, 72–75
  individual factors
    HRV, 106, 107
    meaning-making, 103
    personality, 105, 106
    psychological flexibility, 107
    PTG, 104, 105
    religiousness and spirituality, 102
    self-forgiveness, 106
  organizational factors, 108
  pre-crisis levels, 101
  situational factors
    external stigma, 108
    social support, 107
    work group coherence, 108

thriving (*see* Thriving and resilience)
trauma-related psychopathology, 101
Resource gains, 171
Resource loss, 170, 173, 178
Resultant distress, 48
Rising air temperature, 45

S
Self-care, 72, 73, 142
Self-Description Questionnaire, 102
Self-efficacy, 66, 125, 128, 129, 194, 195
Self-forgiveness, 106
Self-identity post-disaster, 118
Selfless service, 65
Sense of coherence, 172
Sense of Place component, 150
Sensitive periods, 115
Serious mental illness (SMI), 62
2008 Sichuan Earthquake, 50
Situational meaning, 10, 49
Social support, 66, 67, 71, 75, 86, 107, 171, 180
Socio-cultural dynamics, 139
Spiritual enterprise, 39
Spiritual First Aid (SFA), 55
Spiritual fortitude, 39
Spirituality, 13, 51, 102
Sri Lankan PSP program, 149, 150
State-Trait Anxiety Inventory, 144
Stigma, 108
Strengths-based approach, 56
Stress reactions, 121
Stress-related growth, 81
Substance use disorder, 62
Suicidal ideation, 107
Supernatural attributions, 38, 41
Supportive intervention, 121
Systemic stressors, 170

T
Task-oriented coping, 126
Team environment, 68
Team Rubicon (TR), 69
Teen Mental Health First Aid (tMHFA), 122
Temperature metric, 145
Terrorist attacks, 138, 152
Thematic analysis, 69
Theodicy, 52, 53
Thriving and resilience
broad-minded developmental psychology, 91
coherent narratives, 92
context of disaster, 82–83
disaster strikes, 91
disasters response, 85–86
empirically-supported treatments, 92
functional neuroimaging postdoc, 82
growth-oriented narrative, 91
human stressors and traumas, 92
humanities, 91
mental health workers, 94
motivation/inspiration, 94
multiple regression analyses, 81
positive psychology, 81–84, 93
predictors, 95
psychosocial resources, 82
redemptive theme, 91
resources, 94
security-oriented narrative, 91
social network, 94
socially and community-oriented, 93
statistical analysis, 90
trauma experience, 86–87
traumatic events, 89–90
variables and techniques, 87–89
Traditional medical model, 48
Trainers, 144
Training of Trainers (ToT), 143
Training strategy, CBPFA, 143–144
Transformational model, 177
Traumatic brain injury (TBI), 66
Traumatic events, 141, 145
Traumatic stress, 140, 142, 145
Tsunami, 140
Typhoon Haiyan, 10

U
United Nations Office for Disaster Risk Reduction (UNISDR), 187
University of South Dakota (USD), 1

V
Veterans
civilian occupation, 65
civilian peers, 61
continued service (*see* Continued service)
disaster response (*see* Disaster response)
engagement in disaster work, 68–69
meaning-making and connectedness, 69–71
meaning-oriented interventions, 64
mental health condition, 62
military, 61
moral injury, 63
positive psychology, 61, 64
PTSD, 62
servicemembers, 64

Views of Suffering Scale (VOSS), 53
Virtues, 41

W
Warrior culture, 102
Warriors Research Institute (WRI), 99
The Water Crisis in Flint, 117
Western and Eastern cultures, 161
Western psychology, 85, 91
Work group coherence, 108
World Trade Center (WTC) attacks (9/11), 71
Written Exposure Therapy (WET), 89, 94

Y
Youth, 115

The manufacturer's authorised representative in the EU is Springer Nature Customer Service Centre GmbH, Europaplatz 3, 69115 Heidelberg, Germany. If you have any concerns regarding our products, please contact ProductSafety@springernature.com

Printed and bound by CPI Group (UK) Ltd, Croydon, CR0 4YY
30/09/2026
02225449-0006